M000313710

PROJECTIONS 9

by the same editors

PROJECTIONS 1–8

PROJECTIONS 9

French Film-makers on Film-making

in association with *Positif*
edited by Michel Ciment and Noël Herpe
translated by Pierre Hodgson

executive editors: John Boorman and Walter Donohue

faber and faber
LONDON·NEW YORK

First published in 1999
by Faber and Faber Limited
3 Queen Square London WC1N 3AU
Published in the United States by Faber and Faber, Inc.,
a division of Farrar, Straus and Giroux, Inc., New York

Typeset by Faber and Faber Ltd
Printed in England by Clays Ltd, St Ives plc

All rights reserved

This collection © Positif, 1999

Translation © Pierre Hodgson, 1999
Introduction © Michel Ciment, 1999
Foreword © John Boorman, 1999

Copyright in the individual articles lies with the contributors and *Positif*

Cover photograph courtesy of *Cahiers du cinéma*

The publication of this book is supported by the Cultural Service of the French Embassy in London.
The editors of *Projections* wish to express their gratitude for this assistance.

institut français

*This book is sold subject to the condition that it shall not, by way of trade or otherwise,
be lent, resold, hired out or otherwise circulated without the publisher's prior consent in any
form of binding or cover other than that in which it is published and without a similar
condition including this condition being imposed on the subsequent purchaser*

A CIP record for this book
is available from the British Library

ISBN 0–571–19356–0

10 9 8 7 6 5 4 3 2 1

Contents

Foreword

John Boorman

Walter and I have long admired *Positif* and *Cahiers du Cinéma,* film periodicals whose depth, passion and influence have no rival in the anglophone world. We have drawn on their work from time to time for *Projections.* This volume is a series of interviews, spanning the eighties and nineties, with film-makers whom *Positif* has espoused and supported during that time.

Contemporary French cinema is producing work of extraordinary force and variety, including young film-makers such as Erick Zonca, Gaspar Noe, Bruno Dumont, Francois Ozon and Xavier Beauvois. A sense of the lineage of this work – the robust tradition of 'personal' and socially engaged film-making in France – may be traced through the interviews that follow. To each of these we have provided our own introductions and film synopses, primarily for our English-language readership who might be unfamiliar with some of the work under discussion.

What I find fascinating is the picture that emerges of the working methods of French film directors, functioning within their national system. We witness the process – screenwriting, casting, shooting, editing – and get an insight into the subsidized financing arrangements. The wide range of individual styles and diverse visions speaks of a richness that is a tribute to a system that respects and honours film-makers.

Introduction

Michel Ciment

Two decades in another country:
French cinema in the 1980s and 1990s

Relations between critics and films produced in their own country have always been equivocal. On the one hand, they are often in keeping with the old saying, 'familiarity breeds contempt', so that critics tend to denigrate pictures that closely reflect the trends and mood of their own times. On the other hand, critics are often in close personal contact with the film-makers they write about, and this leads to culpable indulgence. Oddly enough, these two attitudes are not incompatible. In the French press it is not uncommon for articles to appear bemoaning the state of film production in general, written by those very same critics who publish regular and considered pieces in praise of the various individual films submitted to them.

Since its foundation in 1952, *Positif* has been open to films from all over the world (see *Projections 4½*) and ensured coverage of new foreign cinemas and new foreign auteurs. But it has also paid close attention to the development of French cinema. A very few of its contributors have tried their hand at directing: Robert Benayoun, Ado Kyrou, Bernard Cohn. A large number have, on the other hand, developed into novelists, essayists, poets or philosophers. The fact that *Positif* contributors feel comfortable in their role as critics – proud of this role in fact – gives them a peculiar serenity which is beneficial to their work. This is important because two dangers lie in wait for those critics who are frustrated creators: either they compensate for the films they never made by systematically vilifying the ones they write about, or they feel obliged to overpraise work by people they feel close to, members of their gang, in the hope that, by some kind of *esprit de corps*, this will earn them subsequent entry into the select club of film directors.

Out of the considerable body of film-writing to have appeared in *Positif*, we have chosen pieces from the last two decades only, and we have covered only films that have been made during that period. By this means, we can provide a more accurate and more concentrated picture of a wider range of films. At the same time, this anthology delves into a distant past and looks forward to a not too distant future. One of the characteristics of French cinema, and in this it is probably unique, is that it contains several generations working side by side. Three generations are present in this volume, under the guiding influence of Robert Bresson (born 1901, now retired), whose last film, *L'Argent*, was made in

1983, and thus belongs, by right, to the period under scrutiny (1979–1998).

The first of these generations is still very active. It contains film-makers born in the 1920s and early 1930s, whose careers therefore began in the 1950s and early 1960s. Alain Resnais is often mentioned in connection with the New Wave, though, rightfully, he should be set apart. It was the success of the young Turks of the New Wave which enabled Resnais to cross over from making shorts to making features, but the fact is that these two directors had already, during the 1950s, acquired considerable professional experience and a reputation for directing some remarkable films. Eric Rohmer was editor of *Cahiers du Cinéma* and as such exercised considerable influence, along side André Bazin, over the various contributors to that magazine. With Claude Chabrol (who was the first to direct a feature film – *Le Beau Serge*), he represents the New Wave in these pages.

Four other directors, loners, appear beside these initial four: Claude Sautet, Louis Malle, Alain Cavalier, Maurice Pialat. Except for Malle, their international reputations have always suffered from the fact that they belonged to no school, a fact which deprived the press of those convenient labels which enable journalists to avoid having to judge each film on its own merits. Sautet trained as an assistant director, and, over the last thirty-five years, has constructed a formidable body of work. Like his friend Alain Cavalier, who was thirty-one when he made his first film, Louis Malle (the only one of the directors discussed in these pages to have died) started very young, at the age of twenty-six. The conditions under which their early films were made were not dissimilar to those under which the first New Wave films were made. Maurice Pialat was probably the most solitary figure of them all. A former painter, he made his first film, *L'Enfance Nue*, at the age of forty-five, before going on to become one of the leading figures in French cinema today.

Four film-makers of the second generation are included in this volume. They are Bertrand Tavernier, Claude Miller, Patrice Leconte and Catherine Breillat. All were born in the 1940s. They do not fall neatly in either of the two categories of the preceding generation. Learning from their predecessors, they may be considered as free of any kind of allegiance. They have also proved more than willing to resurrect genre film-making. Leconte and Tavernier are remarkably eclectic, while Breillat, is more personal in her approach. But then the New Wave itself contained some film-makers devoted to a classic, literary tradition (Truffaut, Chabrol), and others to an experimental one (Rivette, Godard).

The third generation surfaced, really, in the 1990s. It provides evidence of French cinema's constant regeneration. Olivier Assayas has evolved a style of near improvisation that is faithful to an established, modernist approach. Jacques Audiard has adopted a more literary approach, which lays emphasis on the quality of screen-writing. Arnaud Desplechin, more interested in structural experiment, seems to have inherited Alain Resnais's concern with formal innovation. Robert Guédiguian and Manuel Poirier concentrate on the social content of their stories, and give their working-class characters a status they have rarely had in contemporary French film-making.

What all the film-makers, from all three generations, have in common is that they are *auteurs*. All of them, with the exception of Resnais, write their own screenplays.

We have also been keen to include documentary film-making, partly because it plays an increasingly important part in our society, and partly because people like Marcel Ophuls are major film-makers in their own right. Television reportage is so pervasive that some kind of new perspective on reality, some kind of personal account of it, has proved necessary.

Finally, we have felt the need to show how the French film industry has, like Hollywood, provided one of the major focal points for foreign film-makers, from Russians fleeing the Bolshevik revolution in the 1920s to the German refugees of the 1930s, to *auteurs* from many countries, who chose a land in which love and knowledge of cinema were perhaps greater than elsewhere. In this anthology, Otar Iosseliani, a Georgian, provides a shining example of the cosmopolitan tradition in French cinema, as Luis Buñuel and Marco Ferreri did before him.

The twenty-one film-makers included in this anthology are not representative of French cinema as a whole. They are a subjective choice. They have excited us, though *Positif* had never been blindly devoted to the *auteur* theory. We are proud to have followed these filmmakers over their entire careers, at least those from the first and second generations. This has not prevented us from expressing, on occasion, some reticence about individual works. There can be no doubt that one of the reasons French cinema is so lively is that the cultural ambiance – we are not ashamed to admit it – is so favourable. There are a large number of film periodicals; daily newspapers give extended coverage to film issues; there is an established tradition of film criticism; for many years film clubs played an important role, though sadly no longer; and artists and intellectuals have shown an interest in the youngest of the arts from the earliest days. The authorities had no choice but to take account of this phenomenon. Governments, of the left and of the right, have protected film-makers, a political fact worth emphasizing. All these reasons go some way towards explaining why French cinema has resisted Hollywood better than most. France, of all the countries in Europe, produces and distributes more films, because there are more screens, there is more of an audience and because local production accounts for a larger part of the market than elsewhere. If France took a strong stand on cultural matters at the GATT negotiations and the more recent International Markets' Agreement, it is because French people are convinced that cultural expression – be it a film, a book or a song – must be subject to a different set of rules than those governing trade in refrigerators, coal or shoes.

One last word on the governing principle behind this anthology. Rather than selecting general interviews on whole careers, which would of necessity have given only a superficial account of the way film-makers think, we have chosen a set of wide-ranging conversations about specific films, which may or may not include comparisons and references to other works by the same film-maker. The *auteurs* are, roughly speaking, presented in chronological order, by date of birth, but the films selected all belóng to the last twenty years. This gives rise to interesting leaps of time. For instance, *Conte d'eté* by Eric Rohmer, *On connaît la chanson* by Alain Resnais and *Un Coeur en hiver* by Claude Sautet are all by older film-makers, though they were made much more recently than, say, *Un Dimanche à la campagne* by Bertrand Tavernier or *Garde à vue* by Claude Miller, which both belong to a more recent generation. The fact is that the age of a film has nothing to do with the age of its creator.

1 Robert Bresson on *L'Argent*

interviewed by Michel Ciment

Robert Bresson (foreground) directs *Le Diable, Probablement* (1977)

Robert Bresson is France's greatest living film director. His films include *Les Anges du péché* (1943), *Les Dames du Bois de Boulogne* (1945), *Journal d'un curé de campagne* (1951), *Pickpocket* (1959), *Le Procès de Jeanne d'Arc* (1962), *Au hasard, Balthasar* (1966), *Mouchette* (1967), *Une Femme douce* (1969) and *L'Argent* (1983).

L'Argent – the film under discussion here – is adapted from a story by Tolstoy. It was made when Bresson eighty-two, and is almost certainly his last film. The director's austere style, his use of non-professional actors and the Bach score epitomize a cinematic practice developed over thirty years and summarized in theoretical form in his widely read *Notes on the Cinematograph*. Ill health and a shift towards more commercial film-making, even in the highly subsidized French system, prevented the director from completing another film.

L'Argent
Paris. A forged banknote is circulated as a schoolboy prank. A young man, unwitting recipient of the false note, exchanges it in a photographer's shop, and swiftly finds himself at the mercy of the law. From this catastrophe, his life begins to unravel, and he is set on an ineluctable path towards theft, murder and incarceration.

People always refer to asceticism in connection with your film-making. It's become a kind of cliché. But what strikes me is the vigour.

Vigour comes from precision. Precision is vigorous. When I am working poorly, I am imprecise. Precision is another form of poetry.

Vigour and speed. Your screenplay, directed by someone else, would have made a 135-minute film, not an 85-minute film.

That is a question of composition. I use the word 'composition' as opposed to the word 'construction'. I listen to my films as I make them, the way a pianist listens to the sonata he is performing, and I make the picture conform to sound rather than the other way round. Transitions from one picture to another, from one scene to the next, are like shifts in a musical scale. Our eyesight occupies a large proportion of our brain, perhaps as much as two thirds. Yet our eyes are not so powerful a means of imagination, not so varied and profound as our ears. And so, as imagination is a critical element in any creative process, how could one not give priority to the sound aspect? It used to be that in between films I stopped thinking. Then I started taking notes – I even published them.* I was interested in what made me work the way I do. The answer is that it is entirely a question of instinct. It is not a matter of choice. I made my first film, *Affaires publiques*, in the 1930s. You could call it a burlesque, although the description is not really accurate. 'Burlesque' is a term that was applied to certain American films at the time. Painters, me included, would rush to the movies precisely because they moved, the leaves moved. The last scene of *Affaires publiques* depicted a ship being launched. I'd obtained footage of the launch of the *Normandie* from the Compagnie Transatlantique. The boat slipped into the water, sank down and the bottle wouldn't break. Just a matter of chance. I trust in chance. There was a clown in this film called Baby who was unbelievable. He didn't act. I let him do as he pleased. Which is how I realized that a film is not a matter of acting, but of successive inventions.

When I came to make my first full-length feature, *Les Anges du péché*, right at the start of shooting, I was appalled. I had only female actresses, playing nuns. I said, 'If that's the way it is, I'm quitting, the movie is over.' Their delivery and gestures were all wrong. Every night, the producer sent me a telegram asking me to ensure they acted. Every night, there were tears and lamentation. They were delightful ladies and they did their best to comply with what I wanted. And even then, it was my ear, rather than my eye, which hated what they were doing. The intonation, the modulations were harder to alter than their way of moving.

Equally, I was very slow to notice that mysteriously invisible orchestral scores were contrary to the essence of film. I was slow to realize that sound defines space on film. A voice treated like a sound effect seems to give the screen an extra dimension. People who experimented with 3D cinema were barking up the wrong

* *Notes sur le cinématographe*, Gallimard, Paris, 1975.

2

tree. The third dimension is sound. It gives the screen depth, it makes characters seem tangible. It makes it appear that one might walk amongst them.

Is your interest in sound the reason why there is so little depth of field in your films?
Maybe. But also because I use only one lens. I like to stand the camera at the same distance as the eye in real life. Which is why, in my films, the background is sometimes out of focus. Which is unimportant, because once again it is the sound which gives a sense of distance and perspective.

To go back to my initial question, *L'Argent* is unfashionably short. Why are today's films so long?
Because film-making has grown slovenly. Soon films will be three hours long because they don't know, they've stopped looking. It is a form of rest, a holiday for directors who are really theatre directors. I don't understand why it is that those who can write – and many of them can – don't write their own screenplays. I have a hunch the reason they use screenwriters is that, if film-making is an art, if the film-maker is responsible for everything he does, then constantly he undermines himself, it is a desperate business, whereas having a mate write the screenplay removes every last scrap of uncertainty, leaving you free to work more lazily.

I'd like to have a studio full of young film-makers with something to say. You know what Degas said, 'When you know nothing, life is easy.' In other words, knowledge is important, but when you're actually making a film, then it helps to forget everything you know, empty your mind and open yourself to your will. Cézanne used to say, 'I paint, I work, I am free of thought.' Cinema has got some way to go. Let it! Maybe it will turn out to find what it needs among actors. I doubt it, though. The strength of an art is in its purity. I have noticed that some directors choose non-professional actors and then get them to act. But you saw that in *L'Argent* no one acts. That's why it seems so fast. What they say is not what matters. Sometimes, I have found it hard to get non-professional actors to speak in a way that the audience's ear might find satisfactory. This time, I think that the dialogue is spoken 'right', but with infinitesimal modulations. All the different elements of a film must have something in common if they are to match at each transition. That is true of pictures as well as of sound. Non-professional actors must speak in a way that is entirely their own but which at the same time must not differ significantly from the way in which the others speak. If you charted the way actors speak on a graph, there would be enormous variations in the intensity of their speech, whereas in my films speech-patterns are more even. So that it all fits together properly. The same is true of the picture. I once said, I flatten the image as though I was ironing it. I do not deprive pictures of meaning, but I minimize it so that each image loses its independence. The same is true of actors, who, in most films, spend their time trying to emphasize their difference, proclaiming their persona, even though that persona does not really exist, is pure invention, an artificial self, not a real one.

You also say that powerful pictures and a powerful soundtrack must not go hand-in-hand.

True, when sound and picture support each other, the sum is bland and weak. But things are not quite that simple. What enters our eyes during a film shoot emerges from two supposedly perfect copying-machines, which are in fact nowhere near perfect. One of them, the camera, gives us a misleading notion of the appearance of people and things. The other, the sound-recorder, gives us an exact transcription of sound. If a film was to be entirely coherent, the camera would have to steal a bit of reality off the sound-recorder, which is too realistic. The audience would then get so much more out of film. Instead of which, audiences are only interested in how good the actor is and in the modulations of the actor's voice. At the end of *L'Argent*, I tried to capture the force in the air just before a storm. It is not something you can describe in words. I get it by not thinking about anything. There may be some kind of calculation going on, but if so it is not conscious. You have to go with your sensibility. There is nothing else. I've been called an intellectual but of course I'm not. Writing is unbelievably difficult but I have to do it, because everything must originate with me. I've been called a Jansenist,* which is madness. I'm the opposite. I am interested in impressions. I'll give you an example, taken from *L'Argent*. When I'm on the Grands Boulevards,† the first thing I think is 'What impression do the people make on me?' And the answer is a mass of legs and the sound of feet on the pavements. I try to communicate this impression by picture and by sound. Then people complain about my focusing on the bottom half of people's trousers. Brilliant! They made the same complaint about horses' legs in *Lancelot du Lac*. I showed the horses' legs without showing the riders, in order to draw the audience's attention to their muscular power when they back up at the start of a tournament. There's no point in showing the rider then. It would confuse everything. It would bring something else into play. People would look at the rider and think 'I wonder what he's going to do next.' In everyday life, we often look down at the ground as we walk, or perhaps a bit higher, but we don't necessarily look everyone full in the face, unless it's a pretty woman and we want to see what she looks like. I know why people expect films to show everyone full in the face. It's part of a theatrical tradition because in theatre you can see everything.

You no longer choose your 'models' for their moral resemblance to your characters.

---

* In common parlance, a puritan. In the seventeenth century, Jansenists, such as Pascal and Racine, were condemned as heretics. They practised an austere form of Catholicism, and were the Jesuits' principle enemies.

† For over a hundred years, a part of Paris where working-class people go for a night on the town.

4

So long as there is nothing in their physical appearance, in their voice or their way of expressing themselves, the decision is quickly taken. People are so full of contradictions, of oddities, the kind Dostoyevsky almost turned into a system. I enjoy working with strangers, they surprise me. I am never disappointed by my models. They always give me something new, that I would not have been able to think up and which suits my purpose. In any case, I believe in accidents, happy accidents. Lucien, the photographer's employee, like Yvon, the protagonist, is a combination of happy accidents and intuition. My intuition.

You've never used a writer, except for your first two films which were written by Giraudoux and Cocteau, no less!
I owe them a great deal. Afterwards, I was in a position to be sole craftsman, from writing to screening. But at first, I had to find help. Giraudoux worked with me and I was overawed, like a schoolboy. I'd say, it ought to be something like this, short, or long, and so on, and he would obey – he worked terribly fast. I'd laboriously written three quarters of the dialogue for *Les Dames du Bois de Boulogne* when I asked Cocteau for help. I'd tried in vain to work with Paul Morand, Nimier, Supervielle . . . It never came to anything. In the meantime, I wrote the dialogue myself, because I knew that in the end one has to do everything oneself. Then Cocteau solved all my problems in an hour and a half, scribbling on the corner of a tablecloth in his apartment.

What is the difference between your adaptations – even if the adaptation is very loose – from Bernanos, Dostoyevsky, Tolstoy and your original writing like *Au hasard, Balthazar* or *Le Diable, probablement*?
There is very little difference, I think. For *L'Argent*, I started with a short story of Tolstoy's called 'False Coupon' and the idea it is based on, which is an account of how evil spreads. Then I let myself get carried away by my own daydreams until the end, where I slip in the notion that the protagonist is redeemed, that he can save himself, which does not come at the same point in the short story. There comes a point when I let everything go, like a horse with its reins loose, and I let my imagination lead wherever it wants. Tolstoy's story is quite different. 'False Coupon' is a magnificent short story, but right at the start Tolstoy refers to God, to the Gospels. I couldn't go down that route, because my film is about today's unconscious indifference when people think about only themselves and their families. I made *Le Diable, probablement* against the same indifference, except that in that case I was concerned with the world at large. Perhaps you recall that at that time quite a few young people were burning themselves alive. Not any more. The present generation is not remotely interested in that. Very odd. To them it's all normal. They belong to an era in which the fact that we are ruining this earth of ours is not shocking. At the time of *Le Diable, probablement*, someone told me about a boy who had burnt himself alive in his school playground, somewhere in the north of France. I wrote to his parents

asking them to let me see his diary. I didn't use it. I wanted to find out what had gone on inside the head of this boy who didn't express his thoughts very clearly but who had got into a panic about what we were doing to the world.

How do you decide that a story you are reading is worth making into a film?
Regarding 'False Coupon', I knew right away. I saw the film immediately because it related to my wanting to make a film about a chain reaction leading to a major disaster. A banknote that ends up murdering loads of people. Why did Julien Sorel kill Madame de Rénal? Did he know five minutes before doing the deed that he was going to do it? Of course not. What happens at that precise juncture? The forces of rebellion are suddenly unleashed within one, all the hidden hatred that builds up inside. I was more interested in Tolstoy's account of all that than in his religious ideas, fascinating though these are, because one cannot discuss religion in the same way today.

Tolstoy's story has a complex structure; you combined several characters into the one.
I simplified everything, first by elimination on paper and then, much more so, during shooting, so as not to overburden the pictures, so as not to render them opaque, which perhaps lends the film its consistency. The poetry, if there is any, comes from the tautness. It is not a 'poetic' poetry, but a cinematic poetry. It arises out of my simplification, which is only a more direct way of seeing people and things.

In your *Notes sur le cinématographe*, you write in big letters 'ORDER AND DISORDER AT A RESPECTFUL DISTANCE', which relates to your method in that you prepare everything very meticulously, and then leave room for accident.
Shake the tree, as Charlie Chaplin used to say. Not too much, in my opinion. You need a bit of disorder, because it is real. Oddly enough, some of my films look very meticulously preproduced but weren't at all in fact. Like *Pickpocket*, written in three months and shot in big crowds, in a very short time. I also shot *Le Procès de Jeanne d'Arc* very rapidly, though that was easier in that there was a unity of place and characters. Regarding *L'Argent*, I was wary of the large number of locations, the crowds, and I was worried I might lose my thread. But I managed to move from one scene to the next using sound connections – perhaps I should say musical connections. In the old days, I used to fade through from one scene to the next, but an aural transition is so much better. No one does it. People say I drag out the end of each scene because nowadays as soon as the speaking is over, either they bring the music in or another scene's dialogue begins. Otherwise, they say there is a gap!

It is difficult to work out from watching your films how much you have improvised.
In my previous films, as in *L'Argent*, I never tried to settle in advance what I

would do nor how I would achieve it. There has to be a shock at the moment of doing, there has to be a feeling that the humans and things to be filmed are new, you have to throw surprises on film. That's what happened in the scene on the Grands Boulevards which I mentioned earlier. I could feel the steps, I focused on the protagonist's legs, and that way I could propel him through the crowd to where he needed to be. That's the Grands Boulevards, as far as I am concerned, all the motion. Otherwise, I might as well have used a picture postcard. The thing that struck me when I used to go to the cinema was that everything had been *wanted* in advance, down to the last detail. The actors prepared their performances, and so on. Painters do not know in advance how their picture is going to turn out, a sculptor cannot tell what his sculpture will be, a poet does not plan a poem in advance . . .

How do you find your titles? *L'Argent*, for instance.
It seems obvious. Right away: *L'Argent*. I don't even think about it. If someone had said, 'You can't use that, it's taken,' I should have replied that I didn't care . . . All anyone cares about is money, whether private individuals or governments. The only thing that people consider about a fellow human being is, is he wealthy? is he worth a great deal? I was astonished to see a poster in the Metro which said 'France's best-selling electric cooker'. Best-seller . . . The film that grosses the most is the best. Do you see? Money is what counts. With *Au hasard, Balthazar* I was looking for a Biblical title. Balthazar is one of the Three Wise Men. I liked the rhyme of *hasard* and Balthazar. *Le Diable probablement* came to me, early on, as I was writing.

In *Le Diable, probablement* there is a similar relationship between predetermination and free-will.
I am more and more convinced, I have a feeling that, increasingly, what people expect of film stars is that they should explain the psychologically inexplicable. Non-professional actors must not explain anything because they don't know themselves. If they did, they'd be geniuses and they'd serve another purpose. Non-professional actors are a complete mystery, like everyone I meet. Wanting to get to know someone is of interest. What is contained behind that forehead, those cheeks, those eyes? The most fascinating thing in life is curiosity. I want people to want to know, I want them to want to explore the mystery that is life, a mystery not to be imitated, only imagined.

Your films respect fragments of reality, but those fragments are assembled in a certain order.
Fragments of the real. The expression is in the relationship between them, in how they are put together, not in mimicry, in the intonations of actors as in the theatre. In a film, sound and picture progress jointly, overtake each other, slip back, come together again, move forwards jointly again. What interests me, on a screen, is counterpoint.

You emphasize what differentiates your film-making and theatre. But you, who are a painter and were born to paint, do not believe that there is any kind of competition between cinema and fine art.

I love theatre. But I do not believe that cinema ought to be photographing theatre, nor is it a synthesis of all the other arts. I like to quote Stendhal, who said, 'The other arts taught me the art of writing.' That's what I tell young people. One must acquire an eye and an ear.

Your pictures have a strong plastic quality but they never put one in mind of painting. Are you not concerned that cinema might be contaminated by painting?

No. If I ever think of painting, it is as a means of escape. I mean escaping picture postcards. That is not the reason I forego my painterly eye when composing pictures for films. You will have noticed that in *L'Argent* there are a series of close-ups whose only function is to add sensation. When the father, a piano-player, drops a glass, his daughter is in the kitchen. Her dustpan and sponge are ready. I do not then enter the room, but cut immediately to a close shot which I like very much, the wet floor with the sound of the sponge. That is music, rhythm, sensation. I am going to show a man entering a room, like in the theatre, or in most films. Only a door handle turning. You will have noticed, too, that the protagonist is not immediately described. First his legs are seen, then his back, then a three-quarter profile, then suddenly, walking alone, he reveals himself.

Contrary to general opinion, your camera moves a great deal but always in an almost imperceptible way. There are no ostentatious tracking shots or pans.

Because they seem totally false. When do we see lamps and tables move? That's the effect sudden camera motion has. I seek not description but vision. A sense of motion comes from building a series of visions and fitting them together. It is not really sayable in words. Increasingly, what I am after – and with *L'Argent* it became almost a working method – is to communicate impressions I feel. It is the impression of a thing and not the thing itself that matters. The real is something we make for ourselves. Everyone has their own. There is the real and there is our version of it. When I started out, with *Les Dames du Bois de Boulogne*, I was after something different, a kind of coherence, that's all. Nowadays, I show a basketful of potatoes as an old lady picks them, not her face. There's no need, because immediately after we see her doing something much more significant, when she stands up and is about to leave. This is also the only time she receives the young man's assistance.

Of all the many doors in *L'Argent*, the last, through which the prisoner passes, remains open.

If I choose, why can I not have ten times more doors in my films? Doors opening

L'Argent: X (Christian Patey) confronts another open door

and closing are magnificent, the way they point to unsolved mysteries. What's wrong with doors? They have a music to them, a rhythm. But habit is lethal! Perhaps it is too symbolic, but I love passers-by who stare into nothingness. Once upon a time, we had everything. Now we have nothing.

You say you are a jolly pessimist, but your recent films are more sombre than *Pickpocket* or *Un Condamné . . .*, which culminated in a kind of jubilation.
I am sorry that in *L'Argent* I was unable to linger on Yvon's redemption, on the idea of redemption, but the rhythm of the film, at that stage, would not stand for it. Perhaps I do see the world more sombrely than I used to, unintentionally. There is something to that.

You rarely commission film music, preferring classical composers like Mozart, Lully, Monteverdi, Schubert or Bach.
That is of no importance now that I have completely done away with atmospheric music in my films. It took me a long time to see how nefarious it was, particularly if it is glorious music. Immediately, it makes the images seem flat. Whereas a sound effect will give them depth.

Which of your films are you most satisfied with?
I don't know. I never see them again, or almost never. I got joy from all of them, while they were being made. Some, like *Pickpocket*, were made fast and easily. I like the way it moves, and the way one scene moves into the next. *Au hasard,*

Pickpocket: a moment's grace for Michel (Martin Lasalle) and Jeanne (Marika Green)

Balthazar has got some providential moments in it, as well as some flaws. It takes a series of unplanned, mad coincidences to make the impossible come right. In *Quatre nuits d'un rêveur*, I like the theme: 'Love is illusion, so let's get on with it!' That's hardly pessimistic. But no film is perfect.

All your films are about a collision between predestination and free-will, between chance and necessity.
Which is how we are. Three times out of four, chance governs us. And our will is absorbed by predestination.

Your profession opposes your predetermined intention with the chance occurrences of a film shoot.
There have been times when my willpower failed me, which was bad, but now it's soaring. I feel that I have so much to do that I shan't be able to do it all. I am in a rush to get down to work. I'd like to write another book too.

One of the characters says, 'Money, a visible God.' A false idol then, since what matters to you is the invisible.
Money is an abominable idol. It is everywhere. The only things that matter are invisible. Why are we here? What are life and death? Where are we going? Who is responsible for the miracle of animal and vegetable life? The two are considered very similar nowadays.

Can you picture your film before you make it?

Yes, and I carry on picturing it and hearing it all the time I am shooting it, as it comes to life. I do not aim for purity, nor to reproduce the ascetic quality of the screenplay. That is not the point. The trouble is that one cannot conceive of things in disorder. One cannot see a single leaf on a tree. In order to gain an impression of something, one must let one's spirit strip away all that prevents one from grasping it. If an image is over-burdened, it will not follow on smoothly from the previous image. There must be a notion of simplicity. But you know, I've said it before: photography is a lie. Light someone two different ways and you see two different people. In *L'Argent*, my protagonist has three different faces. Sometimes he is very handsome, sometimes he looks like he is eighteen years old. I found Christian Patey by chance. My wife knew him from where she used to live. He was a neighbour of hers. He came by to ask a favour. She thought he would be right for the part. He is unique. He must be strong, violent, but not look it. He cannot be a Parisian.

You came to colour very late.
It was too expensive. As soon as I could afford to, I was delighted to use it. Colour is light, it is in itself light. All day long, my eyes paint, I watch shapes and form and colour. The switch to colour was easy, it made no difference to the way I composed or the way I looked at people. Whatever people say, a painter has a ready-made drawing, at least the principal lines, in black-and-white. Sometimes I need a bright colour to set off duller shades.

Do you still paint?
No. I haven't painted for a very long time. I believe that painting is over. There is nowhere to go. I don't mean after Picasso, but after Cézanne. He went to the brink of what could not be done. Others may paint because they are of a different generation, but I felt very early on that I must not continue. When I stopped, it was horrible. At first, cinema was only a stop-gap, to occupy my mind. It was the right choice, I think, because cinema can go beyond painting. Unfortunately, though, cinema implies waiting for finance. And I don't like the fact that it is not manual. But for those who have something to say, cinema, or rather the Cine-matograph, is tomorrow's writing or painting, with two kinds of ink – one for the eye, one for the ear.

Which stage do you like best? Writing? Shooting? Or cutting?
The hardest is writing on paper. You sit there between four walls filled with doubt – as I was saying earlier – and I find writing very hard. Now, I've changed my method. I write as I walk down the street, or swimming in the sea. Then I take notes. During a shoot the trouble is that you have to move fast. The crew is aston-ished that sometimes I may have to stop for ten or fifteen minutes to have a think. Years ago, in Italy, where oddly I never managed to make a film, there were some directors, I remember, who would say – and no one thought this was odd – 'I am not inspired today, I'm off.' Wonderful. But if I pace up and down, if I change

angles, everyone seems surprised. All because cinema lives off pre-production. Everything is settled in advance. Everyone knows what angle has got to be shot, in what corner of the studio, because it usually is in a studio. And the result is a mish-mash of realism and the lack of it.

The magic is in the cutting-room, when suddenly images and sounds align. Life comes to life. From start to finish, films are a series of births and resurrections. What lies dead on paper is reborn during the shoot, and dead images are reborn in the cutting-room. That is our reward.

In your book, you describe the eye as capable of ejaculation.
It can create. Eyes demolish what they see and reassemble it according to a pre-conceived idea – a painter's eye according to his taste or his ideal.

Are not your characters motivated by desire?
A desire to live. And a will too. A desire to have what one loves pass before one's eyes. My characters are taken to the brink of themselves. I cannot do otherwise, or they would seem dead. If I were to paint a flower, I should not paint a bud, but a mature bloom, at its most mysterious.

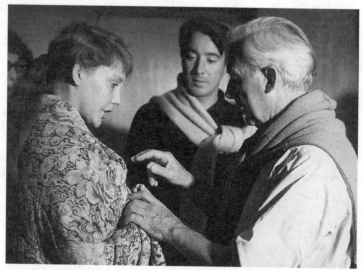

Au hasard, Balthazar: Bresson tends to Anna Wiazemsky's wardrobe

2 Eric Rohmer on *Conte d'été*

interviewed by Vincent Amiel and Noël Herpe

Eric Rohmer (facing) confers with Amanda Langlet (left) and Melvil Poupaud (right) on *Conte d'été*

From 1957 to 1963, Eric Rohmer edited the *Cahiers du cinéma*, the magazine which launched the New Wave. Contributors included François Truffaut, Jacques Rivette, Jean-Luc Godard and Claude Chabrol. His most famous films include *Ma nuit chez Maude* (1968) and *Le Genou de Claire* (1970). Many of his films have been gathered together in collections, such as 'Contes moraux' (1962–1972), 'Comédies et proverbes' (1981–1987) or 'Contes des quatre saisons' (since 1990).

Conte d'été is an exquisitely observed tale of infatuation which comprises the third part of the veteran director's 'The Four Seasons' collection. Regardless of subject matter, Rohmer's films have in common a characteristic style rooted in the use of small crews, naturalistic acting and lighting – a 16mm aesthetic which has developed as a conscious reaction against the more bombastic cinematic tone of our era. These are the elements which make a shot from a Rohmer film so instantly recognizable.

Conte d'été

Gaspard, a musically inclined maths graduate, comes to the seaside resort of Dinard to kill time, and meets Margot, a student who is waitressing for the summer. They become friends, but there's no romance – they're both waiting for their respective partners to show up. Gaspard has a plan – to visit the island of Ouessant. But who will accompany him? a) his elusive girlfriend Lena, b) Margot, c) Margot's frisky friend Solene, or d) none of the above?

In *Conte d'été*, the editing seems much faster and tighter than in your earlier work.

Yes, but that is not specifically an editing issue. I did not cut anything out. Everything is as planned during the shoot. In *Conte d'été*, the timeframe is disrupted: every new day is preceded by a title card, emphasizing the notion of a series of discrete moments. The presentation is quite dry.

The same punctuation is used in *Le Genou de Claire* and in *Le Rayon vert*. How does it affect rhythm?

My New Wave friends and I are silent film-makers, contrary to what is usually thought (especially in my films, where the characters talk a lot). We were brought up on silent movies, at a time when the Cinémathèque showed very few talkies. So we reckoned that instead of trying to work the date into dialogue, it was easier to use writing. At least, it's honest. What is nowadays called 'denotation' was then done literally in writing, not in the images, which had another job to do. Consequently, there are title cards in our first, amateur films, which were silent, and in Godard's films, where they are particularly significant. As for Rivette, he sometimes used datelines. I don't consider this an easy way out, rather a convenience which allows one to get straight to the point.

***Conte d'été* is an addition to something which is almost a private genre of yours, the holiday film. *La Collectionneuse, Le Genou de Claire, Pauline à la plage, Le Rayon vert* . . . Holidays are a moment when time seems to go at different speeds, which is one of the focal points of your work.**

It is true that the character in *Conte d'été* is defined in his own eyes in terms of a distant future: when he is thirty, he will find love, become a musician and so on. He throws himself into the future, and into the past a little, and fails to live in the present.

In the completed film, have you included any changes brought about by the actors – leaving aside obvious improvisation, like the sailor's.

The non-professional characters are the only ones to use improvisation. There is the sailor and also the accordionist. They had no lines. But there is one element that comes from the actor who plays the protagonist, and that is the music: if he had not been a guitarist, I don't think he would have been a songwriter in the story. I don't like to get people to fake that sort of thing, by using doubles and so on. In this instance, not only does he play the guitar, but he plays in a band in between acting jobs, a band which he started with his brother and which has just been on tour round France. So an important part of the character is based on him.

You mention the way extras on the beach occupy space, but the two protagonists' walks are also designed with a specific occupation of the screen in mind. One leaves the frame, accelerates, the other catches up . . . They literally come

Conte d'été: the laconic Gaspard (Melvil Poupaud) with the elusive Lena
(Aurélia Nolin)

full circle round one another, it really is like a dance movement.
That is because it suited the actors. I take them as they come. If an actor is static,
I'd rather he remained static, and not try to force him to move. In this instance, I
had actors who moved around a lot, and when that happens I am delighted to let
them do as they please. This is especially true of Melvil Poupaud and Amanda
Langlet who move very well – she mainly with her arms, him when he's walking.
They hardly needed directing. Anyway, as I've said a thousand times, I don't tell
actors what gestures to make. I don't like what are called 'expressive' gestures.
They are not spontaneous. They are theatrical. I prefer meaningless gestures.
They mean more, precisely because they are not intended to have meaning. So I
let them move around as much as they liked, and they did. The film was hard to
shoot because the camera was constantly moving. The relationship between camera and character had to be right. But then I don't think I've ever had actors quite
so conscious of how they were being framed.

**How much freedom, then, does the cameraman have in relation to you and in
relation to the actors?**
It's obviously a lot harder than when you say, 'And then you're here, and then
you're at this mark.' In this instance, my camerawoman, who also does the lighting, got on very well with them. Of course, I give the odd indication, suggestions
like, 'You can exit frame, then here you could get ahead of her', but nothing complicated; they get the hang of it immediately. As far as I remember, it felt quite natural to me. Similarly, during rehearsal, we'd say, 'We'll overtake them there, we'll
accelerate', and then it was settled. I don't really like the camera remaining at a

fixed distance from the characters, it seems unnatural to me, like when someone faces a camera moving back at an even pace; I prefer it when the actor is seen in three-quarter profile, then in profile, then is overtaken and so on. So the fact is that the relationship between actor and camera varied enormously.

Compared to your 'Contes moraux', which contrasted, if that is the right term, seduction and faithfulness, there is in this film a relatively new element, namely love .
Yes. In the end, yes. My intention is to cover related topics and, without ever changing genres, to keep varying my approach.

But the love involved is bitter. The end shows that fairly clearly.
Yes, but what I was interested in, with this film, was to show a moment when nothing very significant is taking place and which, in any case, ends without any kind of conclusion. There is something which bothers me about stories: if they have a definite ending, as tragedies do, it must be death. I've never wanted to write tragic stories, or even movies like Truffaut's, which I enjoy. *La Chambre verte*, for instance – which I like – or *La Femme d'à côté* – which I like less – both end in death. I don't want to mix genres. My films are comedies. But the difficulty is knowing what a happy end means in comedy. There is always a touch of bitterness. As Maupassant used to say, 'Happiness is no fun.' So, yes, there is always a touch of bitterness.

You give the impression of changing your way of seeing according to the character of the actress you are filming.
Yes. I was keen to show the male character altering according to the people he meets, according to the girls he is with. He is always the same, and always different. I also chose different locations for each girl; each girl has her own location.

Her own location, her own staging, in a very physical sense. Indeed, one could say that choosing to set a film in a seaside resort gives greater scope for abstraction. Compared to a film located in Paris, say, the set seems empty, a bit like a Greek theatre.
Maybe. There is definitely a relationship between character and location, but it is less strong than in *Conte d'hiver*, where the girl cannot bear the thought of moving into the apartment above a hairdresser's in Nevers. I could have set this film around a series of café conversations. The walks are not essential. But I enjoyed making them seem necessary. In the end, I was hoist on my own petard, since I can't now see how things could have been different.

Several times, Margot seems to capture the light in a significant manner. Is that something you are very specific about, according to the nature of the part?
No, it's not to do with the part. It's an approach which I developed a very long time ago, even before Nestor Almendros started lighting my films. It's a matter of

back-lighting. Almost everything is backlit and, at that particular moment, the light comes in very low. But I like using accident, and light is subject to this. When the sky is grey, that lends one kind of beauty and when the sky is bright, well, then there is the beauty that comes from going against the light. What I like about Brittany is that the light is so varied, and I didn't have that for *La Collectionneuse*.

Considering recent film-making, one has the impression that there are a number of people working in Rohmer's wake. Do you sense that you have had an influence on contemporary filmmaking, or is there another era which you feel closer to?
First of all, I don't see many films, especially not by young film-makers. And anyway, I'd rather not go into that, I'd rather remain apart.

Interviewed in Paris, 23 April 1996.

3 Claude Chabrol on *La Cérémonie*

interviewed by Pierre Berthomieu, Jean-Pierre Jeancolas and Claire Vassé

Claude Chabrol

Born in 1930, Claude Chabrol was the first of the New Wave directors to go into production, with *Le Beau Serge* (1958). Famous for a series of films starring his wife, Stéphane Audran, such as *Le Boucher* (1969) and *Les Noces rouges* (1973), he has now released fifty features. His latest films star Emmanuelle Béart (*L'Enfer*, 1993) and, in *La Cérémonie* (1995), Sandrine Bonnaire and Isabelle Huppert, with whom he has collaborated extensively.

La Cérémonie is adapted from Ruth Rendell's *Judgement in Stone* but, unlike many English or American directors, Chabrol's interest in thrillers is not primarily as a source of plot and suspense but as a means of describing the psychology of murder. He is motivated by what he calls the confrontation between character and story. The focus is on character and on how the camera can best describe the inner attitudes of his two leads. Chabrol is a woman's director and Isabelle Huppert, in recent years his most regular partner, is at her best in *La Cérémonie*.

La Cérémonie

Impeccably bourgeois Catherine Lelievre employs a young housekeeper, Sophie, who is secretly illiterate. Sophie strikes up a friendship with local postmistress Jeanne, based on their shared sense of dissatisfaction. But, both women harbour dark secrets – Sophie was implicated in the death of her father; Jeanne was accused of killing her child. The Lelievre family disapprove of this truculent friendship, and the women decide to enact their revenge.

Your starting-point was a novel by Ruth Rendell.

Yes. Her fifth or sixth. The first, I think, to depart from the normal process of police inquiry, with its recurrent detective figure – interesting though that process is. In this instance, the novel is a thriller only to the extent that she has chosen to maintain the formal appearance of a thriller. She might easily have chosen to make it a straight novel. I loved the book when it came out, fifteen or twenty years ago, but I hadn't thought of adapting it as it was written, with only two characters, the maid and the postwoman. The maid was called Eunice in the book. She was a wobbly, fat thing, unpleasant really. The postwoman was very different too. They were fairly typically British. So time passed. I read other novels of hers. I saw that she was developing, her work was changing. She was the one to suggest I modified the structure. The process of reading her more recent work told me how I should adapt this one.

What was Caroline Eliacheff's contribution?

She helped me in that, in one shake of a puppy dog's tale, she uncovered the underlying psychological and psychoanalytical structure. That enabled us to restructure it without altering Ruth Rendell's vision. She hasn't seen the film yet. I'd like to know what she thinks. I've tried to remain faithful to her way of thinking.

I asked Caroline to clean up the story for me, and she did a much more thorough job than I had expected. When I started working on the book, I had whole chunks of dialogue ready that would consolidate the psychiatric underpinning, so that the characters' reactions might remain consistent. Otherwise, we would have spun off into insanity. Very often, when films depict psychopaths, they allow one to forget, for the duration of one or two scenes, that the psychopaths are just that. And then the insanity returns. But in reality, insanity is a continuous phenomenon. Here, Sophie's illiteracy is always present, and Jeanne's craziness is always there too.

There's a sense in which the film marks a return to politics for you.

Yes. My last political film was *Poulet au vinaigre*. What I was interested in then was to show the provincial bourgeoisie as starkly as possible, not in too heavy a way, but so that that critique was definitely a feature of the film. Subsequently, I found no particularly stimulating social phenomena to observe. And it is only now, in the past two years, that I am beginning to reconsider. I had a conversation with a young hooligan which left me with a feeling that society was about to explode, or implode rather, because it's not just a marginal phenomenon. So I decided to make something of this feeling, but not in too precise a documentary way. Just as well, because Kassowitz's *La Haine* makes the point much better than I could have done. Our films are related, in that they reflect the beginnings of this explosion. He sees it as an explosion. I see it as an implosion. The young hooligan I mentioned thought things couldn't go on like this for long, no more than three or four years. Only two more years left!

La Cérémonie: devious duo Jeanne (Isabelle Huppert) and Sophie (Sandrine Bonnaire)

The film is a stylized account of class war.

Yes. I remember an article, I can't recall who by, it was after the fall of the Berlin Wall, which said that now the Wall was down, there could be no more class war. Only someone with money could ever say such a thing. Ask the lower orders if class war can ever end! *La Cérémonie* was an opportunity to deal with this area. Once a screenplay is ready to go, I always try and find a way of including a few personal preoccupations. In this case, it works. The film really does depict a schematic view of class war.

The film constantly draws on panes of glass and mirrors.

Especially the oval mirror in the hall, which is the entrance to another world, the world of the kitchen. I love mirrors. They let one pass through the surface of things. I have to be careful not to overdo it. I often tell the production designer not to put too many in. I love bells too and have to keep telling the editor, 'Not too many bells!' I know I can't turn them down once they are there. But that mirror was essential. A simple, straightforward indication of the separation between two worlds.

And the glass wall at the café, at the beginning?
The first shot? Yes, that's an interesting one. I hope you noticed Jacqueline Bisset's head, as the truck passes. I wanted the film to be perfectly constructed, in such a way that the construction didn't show. I decided that in the first shot the trickery must not show, so people didn't think, 'Lord, this is complicated.' The truck had to go past at just the right moment. Jacqueline could not be in shot at the turn, when Sandrine passes by on the pavement outside. And how was I going to get the right balance between indoor and outdoor lighting? The usual thing is to use translucent sheets, but that wasn't going to work in this case. There would have been too much of it, and it would have altered the light balance, as well as making it difficult to show Jacqueline's face. We decided that the outside should be slightly over-exposed. The result is disappointing. Because it gets even more over-exposed by a changing of the aperture as Sandrine enters. It was much too obvious. So we tried a new trick. We very slightly over-exposed the whole shot, which doesn't show.

It does at the start of the shot, which is very daring.
Yes. The shot is unsettling. We diminished the impact in the print. There was a margin for us to lighten or darken the shot. When the rushes came back, there was a phone call to say, 'It's over-exposed!' 'Yes, yes,' we said. 'We know.' I try, as far as possible, to shoot in chronological order. It helps the actors. In this case, I was determined to start with the first shot, so Sandrine would really feel she was arriving.

Is the camera hand-held?
No. It's a short track, about 50 cm in diameter. I'm not wild about hand-held shots. Laying tracks gives you freedom without being too obvious. I use some other tricks. When the two men are in the car and the child starts being insufferable, saying he hopes the maid won't be too disgusting, a tension develops. It was a tracking shot, pulling back on the car, and I used a very slight forward zoom. It's like a sauce beginning to thicken. At least, that's how it feels to me.

How did you cast the actresses?
Initially, I was looking to make another film with Isabelle [Huppert]. I thought, she's got plenty of choice. I wanted to cast her as Jeanne, but I wanted her to choose. She could easily have played the other part. I was thinking of Sandrine for the other character. But she could have played the postwoman. It would have been different, of course. I was delighted that Isabelle didn't hesitate. She said, 'I've played the other part already, twenty years ago.' But there is a real sense in which they are complementary.

Madame Bovary: Chabrol frames Huppert

They are different shapes. Sandrine is all lines and angles, Isabelle all curves, much more than in reality.

Ah, Isabelle's curves! For *Madame Bovary*, I told her she was too thin. The costume designer told me not to worry. She was right. Isabelle can go either way. It's the clothes which make the difference. Her shoulders are not round. Sandrine is thinner than usual in this film, after giving birth. She's perfect.

What about Jacqueline Bisset?

I wanted someone beautiful. I hadn't thought to make her English. With hindsight, I like the idea. It's interesting and fun. I had thought of casting Caroline Cellier, but she didn't feel up to it. Dominique Sanda was unavailable. My agent, who is also Jacqueline Bisset's agent, suggested her. We met and there it was. She's superb. The fact that she has a slight accent, that French is her second language, that the intonation is sometimes slightly off, makes her seem more fragile, more uncertain, which is good. It's one of the nice surprises I have had on finishing the film. The opaqueness is essential. Openness wouldn't have worked. They each have their little secrets, two of them keep those secrets – Jacqueline and her son.

The other two give more away, they are less mysterious. They are at home. There's no mystery about being at home. She's an immigrant, albeit perfectly integrated.

In your films, it's character which immediately grasps one. Do you start with plot situations, or with characters?

My starting-point is the relationship between the story and a character. In this film, the audience is not aware of the fact that there is no story. The characters gradually reveal themselves, their relationships evolve, but there is no real plot. Like Simenon, I'm a great believer in structures that arise out of the confrontation between different characters. I take an important characteristic that determines the character (e.g. sex, for Betty), and try to monitor its development in relation to others. It's chemistry, really. A chemistry of affinity. Although I make plenty of thrillers, I am not really interested in plot. What I am interested in is the mystery, the intrinsic mystery of the characters. The best Agatha Christie is *Pension Vanilos*. Poirot is investigating a student hostel. He discovers the killer, a young man who is on his tenth murder. No one had noticed the monster in him. The idea is magnificent. The last fifteen pages are a true accumulation of horror.

Are there any actresses you find particularly inspiring?

I am not like Ingmar Bergman. I don't need to sleep with my actresses. But I do need to feel there is some communication, some mutual respect. I also have to like what I've seen. Then I think, 'Hey, maybe we'd get on.' Sometimes someone I've worked with says, 'Look, you really should meet so-and-so.' Or my daughter, who sees practically everything that gets released. She was the one who recommended Virginie Ledoyen. She said she'd be right. And she was. I get on with both Isabelle and Sandrine, though they are very different.

Can one shoot with an actress one does not get on with?

I have done. I don't make a meal of it, I hate tense situations. Pialat only works in a crisis. There have been some people I've found tricky. Dear Romy, for example. She cheated me. She said, 'I warn you, I don't have an ounce of humour.' Amazing! A girl who can say such a thing. The trouble was, it was true. It went well. But she spent as much time acting in between takes as in front of the camera. We had a fight at the dub.

Do you write for specific actresses?

No. It's often wrong to write for specific actors because one ends up using what is least interesting about them, their mannerisms and habits. I prefer not to write for specific people.

There seem to be three distinct periods in your work: one during which your main characters are men; one during which Michel Bouquet and Stéphane Audran share the main parts equally; and now, when you are really a women's director.

Yes, probably. I've always enjoyed women's company. A woman is subject-matter enough. We speak of Hercules' labours, not Hercula's labours. A woman confronting men is a proper subject, it is inexhaustible. I am fascinated by homosexuals too. A very interesting subject. I even wrote a film about two men who wanted to have a baby. I must have been drunk one night and let the cat out of the bag. The real subject-matter was the emptiness of things, compared with human beings. Someone made the film, starring Souchon. They messed it up completely.

Without going into the story of how *L'Enfer* was written, what exactly were your relations with Clouzot?
Clouzot and Becker were the two people who were genuinely kind to me when I was starting out. We played bridge together while Clouzot was in pre-production on *L'Enfer*, and so I saw him again, and his then wife Vera, with whom I was great friends. Making *L'Enfer* was fun, it was pleasant. I tried to make something personal out of a screenplay which was not originally for me and which I had not originally chosen to do.

Which gives the writing its idiosyncratic style, deliberately stylized.
It would have been hard to do otherwise. There was one thing which I thought was tremendous fun, namely finding as many angles as possible within the confines of a single room. Almost half the film is in that one room. I was delighted with François Cluzet, who is great. I didn't want the actors to hate each other too soon. They got on very well. Emmanuelle Béart has lots of energy, she's very strong. Which meant François could let himself slide a little. Finally, we made it into that damn room, after doing the exteriors. They were in there for three weeks, tearing into each other. In the end, they couldn't stand each other. Which is logical! Neither would give in to the other. I expect they've patched it up since.

What about future projects?
A comedy called *Trompe l'oeil*, about appearances. I'd like to shoot it in an hotel, during a seaside health cure. People looking after their bodies is always fun. I've also got a long-standing project which I'd like to bring off. When I announce future projects, I always end up doing another film first. I am also thinking about a very free adaptation of an old book by Philip McDonald, *Murder Gone Mad*, which I think is translated as *Le Vampire*. It's a story about anarchic crime, people killed for no reason, illogically. A very difficult subject. Having said which, anything could happen. Perhaps I'll treat myself to a TV movie and show what can be done for television. There is a conspiracy in the TV magazines. I get worried when I see *Navarro*[*] has three stars and *Night of the Hunter* only two. I am

[*] A French TV thriller series.

not being paranoid. It can't be by accident. There must be a deliberate policy of boosting TV movies quite beyond what is reasonable. I don't care how many stars I get, two, three or four, so long as I get as many as *Navarro*.

Interviewed in Paris, 10 July 1995

4   Alain Resnais on *On connaît la chanson*

interviewed by François Thomas

Alain Resnais

Alain Resnais's best known films include *Hiroshima, mon amour* (1959), *L'Année dernière à Marienbad* (1961) and *Providence* (1977), with Dirk Bogarde. His most recent films include *Smoking* and *No Smoking*, adapted from Alan Ayckbourn's plays of the same name, and *On connaît la chanson*, a musical comedy that was the surprise hit of 1998.

Like Chabrol, Alain Resnais seems, in old age, to be turning to a peculiar Anglophilia. His previous films, *Smoking* and *No Smoking*, were based on Alan Ayckbourn's plays and preserved the English settings of the originals. In this interview, he explains how Dennis Potter's *The Singing Detective* provides the inspiration for the use of music in *On connaît la chanson*. But the setting, this time, is firmly French and the songs belong to the canon of French popular music. Resnais uses extracts from these songs as sung dialogue at significant plot points where the lyrics suit the characters' mood.

On connaît la chanson

Parisians Odile (Sabine Azema) and Nicolas (Jean-Pierre Bacri) are old flames now married to other people. Each is seeking a new apartment. The estate agency they consult produces a boyfriend Marc (Lambert Wilson) for Odile's sister, tour guide Camille (Agnes Jaoul) – though Marc's boss Simon (Andre Dussolier) is also besotted by Camille. For his part, Nicolas is still attracted to Odile, and he and Simon console one another, as Odile moves into what seems to be her dream home with anxious husband Claude (Pierre Arditi).

What was the starting-point for *On connaît la chanson*?

After *Smoking* and *No Smoking*, Bruno Pesery suggested making an opera specially commissioned for the cinema. But it takes a composer at least five years to fulfil a commission for an opera and that's supposing you find the right composer and that he is available. We might have managed with a libretto in English, but I didn't think my English was up to such an undertaking. So while I was waiting to meet a feasible French composer, I looked for another route.

The English dramatist and screenwriter, Dennis Potter, who died three years ago, was an inspiration. I never met Potter but I find his narrative experiments fascinating. He is such a meticulous writer that, regardless of who directs his work, it always seems as if it was him who supervised the cutting. In some of his writing, such as *Pennies from Heaven* (1978), *The Singing Detective* (1986) and *Lipstick on Your Collar* (1993),[*] Potter has the actors sing pop songs in playback, pushing the boundaries of this technique a little further with every production. I was also motivated by the fact that popular music plays such an important part in our imagination. The songs we like accompany us all our lives and provide us with a measure of the passage of time. I recall Nicole Vedrès, whose assistant I was in 1947 on *Paris 1900*, saying that pop songs are probably the most precise rendering of human emotion. Edith Piaf and Charles Trenet give a more accurate account of our emotions than a tasteful and sophisticated novel. There is another factor as well: my own experience. I sometimes quote from pop songs, in my everyday life, without realizing I am doing it. Which is interesting.

In the aftermath of *Smoking* and *No Smoking*, which had been adapted from Alan Ayckbourn's plays by Agnès Jaoui and Jean-Pierre Bacri, I decided that I wanted to work with them again. No one else working in theatre in France today produces such musical dialogue. And this was to be their first original screenplay. They accepted on condition that they could write in parts for themselves. They hadn't performed in our previous 'twin film' project, but I liked the idea. I stipulated that I wanted a part for André Dussolier, as I had not worked with him in *Smoking* and *No Smoking*. We spent three or four afternoons discussing character, structure, what film could and could not do. We rummaged through my story pile. I have a feeling that I even let them have a mad half-hour improvisation I'd recorded on tape. Some of these elements survive in *On connaît la chanson*: guided tours; a character who writes plays; another called von Choltitz; and – most importantly, I suppose – the idea of depicting someone with the mindset of a hermit-crab. We also decided that one of the main themes of our story would be how all of us live our lives in disguise. We abandon certain projects because of the way others would interpret them. We all attach a great deal of importance to ensuring that our self-image – usually, but not always, a positive image – is inter-

---

[*] Each of these series consists of about half a dozen episodes of one hour each, directed by Piers Haggard, Jon Amiel and Renny Rye, respectively. Dennis Potter himself directed *Blackeyes*, a series, in 1989 and *Secret Friends*, a movie, in 1992.

preted by others as we would like it to be, forgetting that we cannot control how others see us. We cannot control our appearance. From the start, we realized that, as our story developed, the various characters' self-images must be destroyed.

I played them Arletty's and Aquistapace's song, 'Et le Reste', which I had already listened to with Bruno Pesery. I wanted to make room for this song. I have a feeling that is what clinched it for them. I also showed Jaoui and Bacri extracts from Potter's TV movies, translating the dialogue. We borrowed Potter's use of playback, although our use is somewhat different to his. Out of respect, I could not just copy his ideas.

In *The Singing Detective* the way in which different timeframes and different levels of reality intermingle, and indeed the way the film is shot, are very reminiscent of your film *Providence*, and indeed of some the films you made in the 1960s.

It did not occur to me that Potter might have seen my films and, at the time, I had not seen his. The fact is that, in his work, I felt on familiar ground. I feel comfortable with intricate time games, with sound-slippage between scenes, with complicated editing and the whole abstraction of his world. I have always wondered why David Mercer, who wrote *Providence*, never told me about Potter. They must have known each other. I can picture the five main actors in *Providence* playing in a drama by Potter. Anyway, there is a connection between my discovering Potter and my working on Ayckbourn. I had enjoyed the movie version of *Pennies from Heaven*, directed by Herbert Ross, which in France never received the attention it deserved. But *The Singing Detective* captured my attention when I caught a few minutes of it on American television while staying in New York nearly ten years ago – because the actor was Michael Gambon, whom I've often seen on stage, including in Alan Ayckbourn plays. But I did not get to see the series in its entirety until many years later. The funny thing is that the bit I'd seen in New York had no songs in it. But it was written, acted and edited in such a way that I was instantly absorbed.

How did you depart from Dennis Potter's example in *On connaît la chanson*?

Almost always, with Potter, existing records are used to illustrate the characters' imagined worlds. Sometimes, they break into dance. We chose to incorporate songs in everyday life, as ordinary text. The film does comprise three or four 'imagined' scenes, like Dussolier dressed as a lifeguard, but these are not allowed to dominate. We weren't making a musical. Sometimes, on set, I'd shout, 'Careful, this isn't a musical.' That was my red flag, a signal that it was time to try out something different.

Presumably, the reason André Dussolier has to sing with his mouth full is to get across the point about songs cropping up in everyday life?

Yes. It is a question of realism. It's not like he breaks into song when the buffet is

On connaît la chanson: Old flames Nicolas (Jean-Pierre Bacri) and Odile (Sabine Azema)

over. Potter – and this is another big difference – uses whole songs, or nearly whole, complete with orchestral accompaniment. In that respect, too, we wanted something more realistic. Usually, when you recall a song, you remember the chorus. Nowadays, unlike in our parents' and grandparents' day, people don't really remember whole songs. I wanted very short extracts, sometimes cut off mid-line, like in real life. But then, some of the extracts are longer. There is no hard and fast rule.

Since we were going to chop the songs up, one of the main problems was going to be maintaining the harmonies. There would have to be a cadence, a harmonic solution, to avoid sounding like we'd just chopped a song in half. I assumed that we could find a composer who could extend the songs thematically, to avoid the extracts sounding too abrupt. I wanted the songs to appear and disappear harmoniously. I warned the producers that I could not sign a contract to do the film until I had met a musician who would undertake to do this harmonic work. Work on the script was continued, but the question of harmony remained unsolved till a couple of months before shooting began. Then one day Lambert Wilson introduced me to his accompanist, Bruno Fontaine, who is also Ute Lemper's and Hanna Schygulla's arranger. His work is unique. His arrangements, the transitions he writes from one song to another, are so daring that he should really be called a composer in his own right. When we met, I played him the truncated songs and I explained what the problem was. He told me that what I wanted was perfectly possible and that he would do it. So that meant we could green light the project.

Subsequently, I also asked Bruno Fontaine to write an original soundtrack. I was delighted to give him his first film music commission.

The soundtrack is at a very low level.
Yes. To avoid confusion with the songs. Otherwise, whenever the audience heard music, they'd immediately think one of the characters was about to break into song. I told Bruno Fontaine I didn't mind some of the themes from songs recurring elsewhere in the soundtrack, if that could provide an overall sense of unity. Consequently, he elaborated variations on 'Avoir un bon copain' and a couple of other tracks.

You say that you are wary of comparisons between *On connaît la chanson* and musicals.
Yes. If anything, I'd rather my film was called a vaudeville. I don't mean it's a French farce, in the tradition of Feydeau. At the end of the nineteenth century, vaudeville was a specific form, distinct from comic opera. It was a prose drama that included songs. The characters would break into song without necessarily interrupting the plot. In order for that to seem acceptable, the songs had to be hits. The playwright would rewrite the lyrics and use the tune. In a way, that's what we have done.

Dennis Potter is supposed to have loathed many of the songs he employed. Do you like the songs you use?
Potter had a love-hate relationship with his material. He can be scathing, true. There is something derisive about his choice of songs. I wouldn't say we went as far as that. A raised eyebrow, perhaps. Certainly, we never chose a song because we loved it, or because we loved the singer. We turned to a song because it seemed appropriate in terms of a particular character's emotional progress, in terms of a scene and in terms of narrative economy. In that respect, we are close to musicals. A song can communicate in a very short space of time feelings which words would take several minutes to render. Songs are faster and, I think, more profound.

Were there any other rules that governed your choice of songs?
Given the age difference between me and Jaoui/Bacri, it is possible that I promoted songs from the 1935–45 period, while they lobbied in favour of more recent songs. If we'd been told to use only recent hits, songs of 1996–7 that the audience would have known off by heart, I wouldn't have been able to do it. Most of the songs had to be hits, not least because it was important the audience didn't think they were written specially for the film, but you can tell a hit even if you've never heard it. I might never have heard of a particular song put forward by Jaoui and Bacri, but if, just by listening to it, I could tell it was a hit, I'd give it the OK. Because of this factor, mixing different periods was not a problem. Though we weren't out to produce a selection of greatest hits, nor a history of French pop music since the earliest days.

How did you set about matching the actors' performance with the singers'?
The actor had to refrain from being taken over by the singer's persona. You couldn't suddenly have a pastiche of Maurice Chevalier, Claude François or Charles Aznavour's gestures and expressions appearing on screen, or it would look like impersonation. The actor would have to stick to the rhythms of the song without imitating the singer's style. We had to be very careful about that.

The films opens with the sound of a cricket chirping over the distributor's logo, AMLF. You asked Richard Pezet, the managing director, to re-record the logo using the full name (Agence Méditerranéenne de Location de Films), then we see dolphins – which crop up in the dialogue – an octopus and so on. You've put your fondness for the animal kingdom into *On connaît la chanson.*
I was once told that in an anthill, 30 per cent of the ants just rush around pretending to be unbelievably busy, and ever since I've been convinced that human beings are full participants in the animal world. Dolphins are pure Jaoui/Bacri. Stick insects too. They told me, 'You're going to like this.' It was a joke. I must admit that, as we were dealing with the business of appearance, I did raise with them one of the great wonders of creation – namely, that certain animals should take on the outward appearance of other animals in order to stave off predators. For instance, there is a caterpillar that clings on to branches with its front paws, showing a tail that has the appearance of a poisonous snake. So it's hardly surprising we included a stick insect. But it is no more a symbol than the jellyfish in *L'Amour à mort.* When we were doing *L'Année dernière à Marienbad,* Robbe-Grillet and I had a rule that we would allow ourselves no symbols, even though our films were undoubtedly symbol-friendly. If the audience chooses to see something as symbolic, then what could we . . .? As a child, I remember a giant, dead jellyfish stranded on our beach, on the island in southern Brittany where I grew up. Me and my mates, we thought it was the last jellyfish on earth. There was no television then, no documentary films. How were we to know there were such things as jellyfish?

Characters often appear in front of or behind glass, glazing, brass doors, and so on. You play with focus, including even the reflections in characters' spectacles.
The characters in this story – in this they are like jellyfish – float indecisively. They are inconsistent. It is a kind of rhyme. I wanted a correspondence with the aquatic world.

You hold your shots for a long time. You shoot whole scenes in a single shot, only in such a way as this is not noticeable.
It seemed the most appropriate way of preserving a unity of acting styles, and emphasizing rhythms of speech. It seemed to fit the style of writing. Reverse angles would have seemed odd. But some scenes are shot more conventionally, like the scene with the three doctors. I'm not against reverses, but if I do use one,

I try to make sure I never use it twice or return to the same master shot – there are exceptions. I don't like to cut into a take in order to show the reverse, and then return to the same take. I do anything I can to make sure I don't come back to the same piece of film. In this film, I also made sure that I never cut back from one angle to the same angle – except for the last three shots when we come closer and closer to the father, shown alone in the main room of the apartment. A homage to Pudovkin, perhaps.

Les Statues meurent aussi, La Guerre est finie, Je t'aime, je t'aime, La Vie est un roman, I want to go home, On connaît la chanson . . . You seem to like set-phrase titles.

None of the titles originated with me. *Les Statues meurent* is Chris Marker's homage to Brecht. *I Want to Go Home* is Feiffer. It's a very popular phrase in America, which I've often come across in strips like Little Nemo or Gasoline Alley. I often brought Feiffer funnies to show him he was on to something. *La Vie n'est pas un roman* is something my father used to say at dinner and which I asked Jean Gruault to use. *Je t'aime, je t'aime* sounded to me like a signal, a beep-beep launched into outer space by astronauts in distress. As for *La Guerre est finie*, that's something a 24-year-old Spanish girl said to me when I was discussing a screenplay Semprun was writing with her. She said, 'But Mr Resnais, the war is over!' I jumped at it, particularly as the English translation, 'War is Over', was good. But neither in England nor in America was the title translated. They kept the French. And I realized I played a nasty trick on Semprun, because later, on tour, we kept having to explain that the title meant its opposite: the war is not over.

5

Louis Malle on *Au revoir les enfants*

interviewed by Françoise Audé and Jean-Pierre Jeancolas

Louis Malle directing Gaspard Manesse and Raphael Fejto on *Au revoir les enfants*

Louis Malle's first production was *Ascenseur pour l'échafaud* (1957), shot to a Miles Davis score. It was a considerable success, as was *Au revoir les enfants* (1987) – nearly his last production. He spent much of the time in between in the US, directing such films as *Pretty Baby* (1977), *Atlantic City* (1980) and *Uncle Vanya on 42nd Street*.

Such was the determination with which the French authorities of the post-war years enforced the idea that France had been a member of the victorious coalition which drove the Nazis from Europe that, for all the films about Resistance heroes, few writers or directors would tackle the thorny subject of French collaboration with the German occupying forces. Coming in the wake of Marcel Ophuls' *Le Chagrin et la pitié* and Jean Genet's stories about young right-wing militiamen, Louis Malle's controversial *Lacombe Lucien* (1974) was the first major film to do so. By the 1980s, after the election of the first post-war Socialist President, the political context had changed and with *Au revoir les enfants* Malle was able to return to the subject of how Jews were treated in France during the war years in a more personal and intimate vein. Along with Jacques Audiard's *A Self-Made Hero* and Marcel Ophuls' *Hôtel Terminus* – also the subject of interviews in this anthology – Malle's film testifies to the current, extraordinary revival of French interest in the moral paradoxes of the war years.

1944. Jean Bonnet, a diffident, intelligent youth, arrives at a Catholic boarding school in Fontainebleau, where he strikes up a friendship with a fellow
pupil, Julien Quintin. But Jean is often uneasy, and suffers the hostility of
other classmates. Finally Julien learns that Jean is one of three Jewish pupils
being sheltered by the headmaster, Father Jean. The ruse seems to be a success, until an informer's tip-off brings the Gestapo to the school gates.

**In your last interview with Gilles Jacob for *Positif*, in 1974, you describe the
story of *Au revoir les enfants* very precisely.**
Really?

**Absolutely. You say that you had thought to film it as a prologue to *Lacombe
Lucien* and that in the end you decided not to because you didn't feel ready.**
How odd. As it happens, I've told the story quite a few times. It must be my most
dramatic childhood memory. It appears in a five-volume *History of Resistance*
published by the Communist Party and written by someone called Guérin. I met
him when I was in pre-production on *Lacombe Lucien*, told him the story and he
included it in his book, where it occupies two pages. I also told it in a book published in 1979 called *Louis Malle by Louis Malle*, which did not have much impact
because the little publishing house that brought it out went bankrupt a week after
publication. Now that I've made the film, people say, 'You've told us about this
story before . . .' It's true that for years it kept resurfacing. Now that the film is finished, I know that the story I've told is not really all that close to what actually
happened. When I finished the first draft, I checked some scenes that I was sure
were based on real events and found that they did not relate to the reality of 1944
at all. For instance, my brother, who was in the same school as I was, remembered
things differently. In the end, I kept to what I thought was what I remembered,
even though I knew that it was somehow fictionalized. Let's just say, though this
is an over-simplification, that the film represents history as I would have liked it
to happen. Which is more interesting than what actually happened. My relationship with Bonnet in the film is more complex and more interesting than it was in
real life. One of the things we didn't have was time. And my memories include
the guilt which I felt, which I've kept, which has influenced me all my life, my way
of thinking and my work. That guilt is a sense that what happened was profoundly unjust, that it should not have happened and that, after all, we were all
responsible. In the film, Julien is somewhat blackened. Specifically, he feels that
he gave Bonnet away by turning round and looking at him in the classroom.
Well, that's probably something I've added. But it's how I remember things too.
My memory tells me I was partly responsible for Bonnet's death. Once – only
once, because I am not really given to reminiscing – I told a class reunion this

story and I realized that it had affected me much more than the others. They remembered it as a dramatic episode, but they had no clear memory of Bonnet, whereas I remembered him very clearly. Let's say I took it personally. Which is why I made the film. Inevitably, when a film is based on a true story that took place forty years earlier, the process of representation is tortured and complicated. I had no interest in making a film that was merely an accurate historical account. I think that what has happened is that I have injected my thinking about these events over the last forty years into the history. I could have made it my first film, but I would have been terrified. The memory was still alive, still developing. I am delighted to have been able to make the film now. I hope I have managed to go beyond myself.

Au revoir les enfants: Gaspard Manesse and Raphael Fejto

You have made this film in 1986/7. Is there any connection with current events?
Not only is there no connection, but what's quite strange is that the film was first shown during the Barbie trial. People said, 'Brilliant timing! Really! Fantastic!' As if I'd jumped at the chance. Now there's Le Pen. There is the increase in racism. There's *Shoah* on television. The fact is that when I started showing the screenplay, people – especially distributors – said, 'You've been away more than ten years, there's been a glut of films about the German occupation, no one wants them any more.' I wanted to make the film, anyway. I felt that the time was right for me, I'd waited long enough. I'd been telling myself for the previous few years that I ought to return to France, to make a film, go back to my roots. I'd always known that this would be the subject-matter. And then when I wrote it last summer, I felt that I was completely out of touch with what people wanted.

Of course, there's been a change subsequently. Last autumn, it looked like

Barbie would remain in jail for the rest of his life, people really felt he would never be put on trial, that too many interests were at stake. And then the film was already in pre-production when the student demonstrations happened in December, and they encouraged me. People say, 'There was 1968, and then there was a post-1968. There's been a move away from politics, both in the US and in France.' And then at the end of last year, we discovered that was totally untrue. Which I enjoyed. I found it encouraging that these people, the younger generation, might be interested in the film I was making.

I would have made it anyway. I've always made my films in the hope they'd capture people's interest, but you can't start out on a project just because it is in the spirit of the times.

When you made *Lacombe Lucien*, was that an indirect route into the same subject-matter?
The truth is that the very first draft of *Lacombe* – before my collaboration with Patrick Modiano – opened in a school and that the protagonist was the Joseph of *Au revoir les enfants*, a boy employed in a school kitchen who goes to the Gestapo out of revenge because he has been sacked. We cut that out very quickly. I reckoned it was part of a different film that I should make some day. The history of *Lacombe* was a complicated one. Initially, he was going to be a young Mexican. I also considered setting the story sometime around the end of the Algerian War. The character would have worked in any one of several different periods. When I realized it could be set under the German occupation, I remembered this incident from my childhood, and immediately afterwards I met a character who really had worked for the Gestapo and infiltrated the Resistance for them. This was in the Lot, where I shot the movie and where I live. Anyway, this man pointed me in the direction of a young farmer, ill-treated as a child, who saw his employment by the Gestapo as something of a social success. And that is how *Lacombe Lucien* came about.

In the case of *Au revoir les enfants*, things were much easier. The story was based on my own experience. It is truest in its re-creation of sociologically observed fact. The fact that the pupils all belong to the upper middle-class. And the fact that despite the cold and the lack of food – which were common to all – these children were very sheltered. There is the character of the mother, the conversation at lunch, the remark about Leon Blum. I remembered how much people hated Leon Blum in my family, it was monstrous. There is the character of Mr Meyer, the restaurant Jew, which is based on something a friend told me about his grandfather, a wealthy Jew who had been arrested in a restaurant. He couldn't believe anyone would dare to arrest or annoy him or that he could fall into the category of Yids. As far as he was concerned, he was a Frenchman through and through. I think Pétain in person had pinned a medal on his chest at Verdun. He died in the camps. The bits I invented dealt with the relationship between the two children.

The violence at the school is very striking.
Partly, that's a feature of the period, which was tough. And it is true that, compared to today, life was hard for children – even though, as I said earlier, these ones were sheltered. Right from the first draft, I wanted to show the game on stilts, which no longer exists or has been banned. It was unbelievably violent. But that was a statement of masculinity. As was the forest scouting. Actually, I toned that down a bit. The headmaster, Father Jean in the film, used to send us after curfew on a treasure-hunt in the Forest of Fontainebleau. It was mad. We were terrified. It was genuinely dangerous. Parents protested. It was supposed to be character-building. And the fact is, I think, that all boarding schools are violent. Children want to dominate each other. It's not really that unusual, the way Bonnet is treated: he is new, he is different. Apart from Julien, none of the boys are really interested in seeing beyond immediate differences. I feel that is fairly normal social practice. Outsiders are disliked.

Having said which, I am delighted the violence struck you. I was worried, on finishing the film, it might not be strong enough. What I remember is raw violence. There was an almost Darwinian sense in which the strong were allowed to dictate social behaviour, were allowed to rule. There were victims and torturers. But what I feel is most significant – other than the difference between bullies and those bullied – is the way in which adult violence intervenes. It is more abstract, artificially imposed from without. The children can't understand it. Their violence is natural, almost biological. But then the militia appear and throughout the rest of the film, nothing really makes sense. Not to Julien, certainly. When Julien asks his brother, 'What's a Jew?', it seems so awkward. Even the Vichy authorities had trouble defining Jewishness, before they sent the Jews into German concentration camps. It was easy at first. They sent off all those that weren't French, German or East European refugees. Then . . .

In the film, some of the Germans seem nice, or nearly so; for instance the Bavarian Catholics and the officers who intervene in the restaurant, even though they are only showing off to the mother.
To show all Germans as brutes would be a cliché. Most of the ones who came to France had been conscripted. The ones in the restaurant are pilots, with medals. The man who throws the French militiamen out is a career officer, obviously upper-class, and drunk to boot. He can't be doing with these Frenchmen who are obsessed with politics. They say that, in German. Which is ironic. I am sure that it is right to show that the majority of Germans in France were not much concerned with Nazi ideology. Which is why, in the end, the Barbie character appears – the Gestapo officer in Melun, who definitely was a Barbie-type, an efficient man called Kopf who had uncovered several Resistance networks. Because, believe it or not, those monks, Carmelites, were actually very active members of the Resistance. The Head of the Order, the Provincial head, was a member of the governing body of the Resistance, the Conseil National de la Résistance. The

headmaster thought hiding Jewish children was natural, that was his position.

It's a bit like *Lacombe Lucien*, in that it is another way of looking at the period, another way of looking at Frenchmen. There were people who behaved exceptionally well and some exceptionally badly, you know that. If you try and work things out in class terms, you can only get things badly wrong. People who say the bourgeoisie were all collaborators and the working-classes all Resistance heroes ... My family was upper-middle-class. One of my uncles was deported and went to Dachau; one of my cousins, older than me, escaped to Spain and thence to join up with De Gaulle. Maybe because we're from the North and in those parts Germans are the hereditary enemy. It wasn't a question of ideology. They were fiercely anti-Communist, like the rest of their class, but as far as they were concerned, the Germans had no business occupying France. They had to be fought. Oversimplification is always dangerous. People will say I'm at it again, like with Lucien Lacombe, who's a working-class boy turned German informer. And in a way, yes, Joseph is a kind of cousin of Lucien's, but his behaviour is understandable. The situations, the relationships are complex.

My parents were supporters of Pétain's too, until 1942. They thought Pétain was a good person. Then came Laval. As far as they were concerned, it was possible to support Pétain, yet fight the Germans. They realized gradually that Laval was a real collaborator. There was a falling-off. That's why the mother and brother have that exchange, 'Does he still like Pétain?' 'No one supports Pétain now.' It's not much, but it does reflect the reality of the time. Before going to that school, I'd been at the Jesuits' in Paris; we went around knocking on people's doors trying to sell pictures of the Marshal, as Pétain was called. 'I've made France a gift of my person.' That was in 1941/2. I was about nine. We were somewhat brainwashed. There was that whole business about National Revolution, a return to tradition. And people liked that where I came from. For instance, I like the idea that the children, when they get lost in the forest, start singing 'Maréchal nous voilà' to cheer themselves up. 'You've restored our hope,' the song goes. Even Bonnet sings along. We were all up to our necks in that stuff. I kept asking myself, 'What was it like to be eleven years old in those days, what did we know about the outside world?' I kept trying to use my own memories as a springboard. Hence all the ridiculous conversations about Pétain. After these events, I found myself in another school and I was there when the liberation came. And there's another memory, very specific and very shocking, which is of a procession of women with their heads shaved, perched on trucks, with their hands tied behind their backs.

The conversation between Julien and Bonnet on *The Three Musketeers* is a high point. Is that something that you actually remember?
I do remember one thing quite specifically. I'm not sure whether it happened then or later. I remember reading *The Three Musketeers* at night, by torchlight. I loved it. But I don't think I discussed *The Three Musketeers* with Bonnet – I mean the real Bonnet.

Books mean a lot to children. They steal reading time.

That's one of the bases of Julien's and Bonnet's friendship. The first time we come across Bonnet, when Father Jean brings him into the dorm, he brings out a stack of books. The other chap watches this and remarks on it. He's interested. I don't know why I came to choose that book, it just happened. One doesn't think about those things till later. Memories . . . The eroticism of the *Thousand and One Nights* in Dr Mardrus's decadent, symbolist and quite crazy translation, that's another thing I remember very clearly; it was a porn book that we passed from hand to hand.

And what about the bound volume, a prize perhaps, which reveals Bonnet's true identity to Julien? Is that really how you found out?

Not at all. I never discovered Bonnet's identity. We didn't know he was Jewish. And that's something which has tortured me ever since. If I had known, what would I have done? How would I have behaved? Julien discovers by chance that Bonnet is Jewish, but he hasn't the faintest idea what to do about it. I remember before I left Paris, before autumn 1943, we'd meet people wearing a yellow star and my parents would say, 'Be very nice to them.' That was it. The rest was theoretical. So Julien asks his brother, 'What's a Jew?' And the reply is not satisfactory. At the end of the day, the criteria by which people's group identity is defined don't amount to much. To someone aged eleven trying to make sense of the world, it really does seem very odd. Adults lead complicated lives.

There is another important element in Julien's life: his mother. Is there some kind of distant connection with the mother–son relationship in *Souffle au coeur*? A common source of inspiration?

They are variations on a theme – though the two mother characters are quite different. I expect the mother in *Au revoir les enfants* is closer to my real mother than the mother in *Souffle au coeur*. As it happens, *Souffle* was inspired by someone quite different. But to say that the mother in *Au revoir les enfants* is my mother is an oversimplification. During the shoot, I was put out by something Francette Racette told a journalist. She said, 'Louis Malle came and said, "Will you play my mother?" and I couldn't say no.' But she's nothing like my mother. She's Canadian. But the character, an upper-middle-class woman who is spontaneous and funny and tender, draws on my mother a great deal. Let us say that the strength of the relationship, which is found in both films, and also the violence of it, is a transposition. Again, I could say that I should have liked things to have been as passionate as they are in both films. In one respect, they are true to my own childhood. The person who matters, who is there, is the mother. My father was an absent figure. He had good reason, he was very busy. But, of course, his absence had a definite effect on me. The only time in my life I have had anything to do with a psychoanalyst, I didn't mention my mother. I discussed my father, even though my father had never really counted. I realized that my father's absence had mattered a great deal.

Le Souffle au coeur: Malle is charmed by his leading man, Benoit Ferreux

Le Souffle au coeur: Laurent (Benoit Ferreux) broaches a taboo subject with his mother (Lea Massari)

Three-quarters of the film, in terms of character, action, detail, is fictional. But at the same time I believe that every single minute of the film was written and shot for a reason. The main thing in the film, Julien's relationship with Bonnet, is infinitely more interesting than my relationship with the real-life Bonnet was. But that's how I was able to make something of it. When Bonnet appears, Julien has to cope with something which is outside his normal experience, a reflection of the particular historical circumstances of the time.

I am going to make a generalization, even though I loathe generalizations. My films are about people who suddenly find something in their way, that diverts them from their expected path, and makes them ask themselves questions that most people manage to avoid in the course of their everyday lives. That's the subject of this film, too. Julien does not know what to make of Bonnet. He is intrigued by him. Irritated by him. He has to change and observe. The dramatic energy of the film is driven by Julien's curiosity. When I tell people that it is this event, drawn from my childhood, which has driven me to become a film-maker, I know it sounds absurd. I did not particularly think about what had happened in the ensuing years. Nevertheless, I should like it to be true. I should like the fact of having encountered Bonnet to have altered the course of my existence. Otherwise, maybe I would have gone into sugar-refining.

Did the children understand the film they were making?
Very much so. I cast the two main parts very carefully. I chose remarkably intelligent boys. They had trouble identifying with boys of an earlier generation, but the main thing was that they were able, by using today's instincts, to react in a way appropriate to the period. I did not choose them for their outward aspect, nor for their ability to speak lines, but because I felt they would understand; I sensed that they were sensitive and clever. I screen-tested them, to see how they coped with a scene, how far they got the emotion of a scene. Which is how I realized that the passage of forty years had made no difference. Today's eleven-year-olds must ask themselves the same questions we did. I was encouraged to see that when the cops killed Malik Oussekine, people who weren't born in 1968 went into revolt. They did not see why one of them should be clubbed to death for no reason. People said, 'We're not having this.' It was a very important demonstration, very positive. And that's what I wanted Julien's feelings to be, even if in 1944, life was more violent and death a more common occurrence.

It was a secretive and opaque period.
True. People always say, 'Did people know?' Someone even asked me the other day, 'Did you know Bonnet would die in a concentration camp?' My belief is that people did know, but that they turned away from their own knowledge because it made them so uncomfortable. People say that the Germans didn't know there were camps, that the townspeople of Dachau didn't know. Well, people forget. When I was at the Institute of Political Science in Paris, I found some cuttings

from *Paris-Soir* which described the concentration camps. They were dated 1937. You can't let people get away with murder. In *Paris-Soir*, which was then the equivalent of *France-Soir*, there were articles about the camps. Having said which, that day, in the playground, we would never have been able to think that all four of them were on their way to their deaths. The priest, in particular. In his case, the Germans weren't particularly keen to make a martyr of him. The circumstances were rather unusual. He wanted to leave with the others. Which hardly affects the main point, namely that the man from the Gestapo says, 'The boy is not French. He is Jewish.' That is what is so shocking.

The only really nasty moment in the film is when the nun denounces the other two boys.
Maybe that's my old anti-clericalism coming out. Let us just say that I thought it would be a good idea if Joseph weren't the only bastard in the film. The nun is a coward. She gives Negus away out of cowardice. But during the shoot, I tried to make her less cut and dried. Some people don't notice. As I was making the film, I realized it was the first time in my life I was portraying priests as admirable. But that was my experience at school. They were great. Of course, another part of the Church collaborated with the Germans. The nun in the film treats Negus badly. She is afraid of the supervisor. I am not even sure that she knew Negus was Jewish. It's more, 'You'll get us all arrested . . .' I like the fact that there is this despicable nun.

You're not exactly lenient on the nun, nor on the cook. It's as though menials are more likely to behave vindictively.
The cook mistreats Joseph. But she is good to the students. That is drawn from my own recollection of a large woman who never stopped yelling at that poor boy. Yes, they are the two real workers at the school. That had not occurred to me. I'm asked so many questions. I'm learning about my own film.

I wrote the screenplay very fast, as with *Souffle au coeur*. I completed a first draft in ten days, then I fiddled with it. It mattered to me that the first part of the film should seem like a chronicle about what it was like to grow up and attend boarding school at that time. Then there is a shift and things get more dramatic. Getting this shift right, from period chronicle to tragedy, is what gave me the most work. I moved bits around, built in transition scenes. But the twenty crucial moments of the film came to me all at once. Then, later, I rewrote it so that Julien should become increasingly lonely. At the last minute I made another alteration: in the original screenplay, everyone was aware that it was Joseph who had given him away. But I decided it would be better if only Julien knew that. Just as only Julien knew that Bonnet was Jewish. So I set their encounter in a secluded part of the yard, away from the others, so that he alone should have the burden of knowledge. As if the knowledge was in itself almost a form of guilt. I have always felt guilty about Bonnet's death.

When I was eleven years old, I belonged to a world in which it was possible for someone to be arrested and sent to concentration camp. I did not learn till later that the three children had been taken to Auschwitz almost immediately and that they had been gassed as soon as they got off the train. The Germans kept lists and these were found. At the time, I obviously did not have this information. But over the years I developed two separate forms of guilt. The first was a general sense of guilt, at having belonged to a world where such things could happen, and the second was a kind of guilt that is rooted in my sense of curiosity, of knowledge. Curiosity implies some kind of commitment. During the shoot, I was able to make use of that intent look that the boy playing Julien gives, a look that says it is going to find something out. People who are more curious than most are implicated. Many of the friends I made during those years went on to lead normal lives. To them, all this was just a passing episode in their younger days. It did not affect them very profoundly. Maybe some of them are racist today. I couldn't be. That's the difference. When asked, I have a standard reply. I say, 'You know, curiosity is what drives me.' And that is the truth. I make documentaries. I hate repeating myself. And that's not just behavioural. It's a question of ethics.

La Poursuite du bonheur is also a product of your committed sense of curiosity.
Yes. *La Poursuite du bonheur* stems from the same attitude. In America, I was intrigued by new immigrants. And Americans would say to me, 'You've made a film about immigrants because you're an immigrant yourself.' But I wasn't really. A deluxe immigrant maybe. Obviously different to an illegal Pakistani fighting for survival. I was particularly interested in those who had just arrived, in finding out what it was that America did to them and what they ended up doing to America. Americans wanted to know whether 'those people' were going to change America – were they an invasion? But what America does to them is very interesting: there is the shock of coming out of well-established cultures and entering the world of American mass-communication; that's an enormous change. People travel three centuries in the space of a few months. Oddly enough, before *Pretty Baby*, I worked on a story about a young Mexican who entered the States illegally and went looking for work in Los Angeles. I worked with Jean-Pierre Gorin, who was in California, teaching college in San Diego. He's still there. We got together and shot the frontier scenes in *La Poursuite*.

In 1976, I had a two-film contract with Paramount and I was supposed to make this story about a young Mexican. I gave up because I decided I had not been in America long enough. There was a danger I'd end up with nothing but clichés and preconceived ideas. But the idea lived on. When I found myself with a moment to spare after making *Alamo Bay*, a TV company asked me to make a documentary. I dug out my old project. They liked the idea because it was the centenary of the Statue of Liberty. I told them I wasn't interested in nostalgia nor in souvenirs of Ellis Island. I wanted to show people coming to America now. With the exception of the Somozas – we know why they've come – in every single case, the audience has to ask itself, 'Why have these people come to America?' There are some standard replies, like 'In order to give my family a chance of a better life, in order to make money . . .' In the case of the Mexicans, the answer is obvious. Mexico is an economic disaster. And through sheer hard work and enthusiasm, they can adapt to American ways. In other cases, I am not sure I know why people want to come to America. Sometimes they seem to lose their own identity almost immediately. In other cases not. The American way of life seems unitary, but that is a façade. There are many different ways of life. Anyway, I am interested in all these themes. I made the film at a time when I was having trouble with America. Now I am not so sure, but at the time I thought my time there was over. It's a farewell movie of sorts. American audiences thought so. At the same time, it's a continuation of *Alamo Bay*. *Alamo Bay* could have been a documentary, except that the events had taken place four years earlier. I would have had to reconstruct things, which was not possible.

In *Alamo Bay* and in *Au revoir les enfants*, your style seems increasingly spare. Is this a conscious decision? Is it connected with the fact of making documentaries? In *Black Moon* and *Pretty Baby*, there was more prettiness.
That's a function of the subject-matter and the setting. I am not trying to impose a style of film-making in order to be able to say, artificially, that that is my style. It's almost a question of principle. When I appear on set at the start of a shoot, I arrive with a whole set of preconceived ideas about how to film that particular script. Within a week, all those ideas have been abandoned. When I was younger, I was more schematic. For instance, in *Les Amants*, each scene is shot as a single shot. Sometimes this is very artificial. When I see the film now, I sometimes long for a close-up of Jeanne Moreau's eyes, something a bit sharper. From *Le Feu follet* onwards, I loosened up. Script problems seemed to solve themselves according to the feel of the subject-matter. When *Le Voleur* came out, the critic Jean-Louis Bory was mad at me, and I took it to heart because I think he was right. He said something like, 'Louis Malle has stuck a top hat on his camera.' The fact is that the film was drowning in its set. But the subject of the film was someone being sucked back into the class from which he came. The opulence of the set was one of the poles of the story, it was part of the psychology of the character. With *Pretty Baby* it was the same: decadence, New Orleans turn-of-the-century brothels. Child prostitution was illegal, officially, but it was tolerated to such an extent that senators came to the brothel. And those brothels were unbelievably luxurious. Nykvist and I used the set, its luxury, as a metaphor for lust.

In the case of *Alamo Bay*, the subject-matter was quite different. It implied sunshine and offensive ugliness. And with *Au revoir les enfants*, I said to the cameraman, Renato Berta, 'I won't make this film in black-and-white because that would be facile, but I recall a world of blues and greys and blacks. Times were hard. I do not recall warm colours. The children wore navy blue, the priests dark brown.' I told Corinne Jory, the costume designer, that I didn't want any red whatsoever in the film. The coldness and hostile environment are significant. We were lucky in that the weather was abominable that winter. It snowed. When the children did the exteriors in the schoolyard in Provins, they were in shorts and the thermometer read minus 12. Steam comes out of their mouths as they speak.

As far as the actual style of film-making is concerned, perhaps *Au revoir les enfants* is more like John Ford. Oddly enough. In the sense that the screenplay is entirely about looks. Which is why the direction is perhaps more explicit. Critics never really notice – why should they, it's not their job – but I am often aware that the quality of direction is usually an indication as to whether the director is comfortable with his screenplay or not. Because if he isn't, he needs to protect himself; he goes off in several different directions, as if he is shooting several different versions. When I watch a movie, I can tell whether the director feels comfortable with his characters, whether he has doubts about the screenplay, sometimes even that he is having trouble with some of his actors. That can be beautiful. It can create a kind of open instability and sometimes the director can make the most of that. Not always. I had script problems with *Alamo Bay*. Whereas with *Au revoir les enfants*, the script worked well – other than that one scene I cut. Firstly, it was my script and I had spent time on it. I had rehearsed the children. So my direction was confident. I did not have to run for cover.

Have you ever worked on commission?
I've made a couple of films that were like commissions. *Vie privée* was one. But a commission can make a good film. Some people really go to town with them. In my case, it never works. The other one, *Crackers*, was never released in France. I spent two years refusing to shoot it, then I accepted by persuading myself I was going to make a brilliant job of it, then I messed it up. I felt uncomfortable with the project from start to finish, during the shoot and during the edit. Unless I am deeply committed to a project, a commission will make me cack-handed. I am not like some American directors who make very ordinary situations look brilliant, who know how to create magnificent variations on a theme.

It's another kind of film-making.
Yes, but as I work in America, it puts me in a ghastly, inferior position. Sometimes people make me interesting offers I have to refuse because I am on a slippery slope. David Puttnam, who is the greatest producer in the world today, offered me *The Killing Fields*. When Schanberg's original account was published in *The New York Times*, certain aspects had caught my eye. So there was a reason for me to make the film. Then Puttnam bought the rights and I thought, 'Pity.' Two years later, Puttnam sends me a voluminous screenplay written by a brilliant

English screenwriter. Reading it, I saw what Puttnam had in mind. He wanted to make an entertaining movie with what is called in English 'production values'. There were war scenes, masses of blood, bits of limb all over the place. Whereas what I was interested in was just one bit of Schanberg's tale. It's a bit set in the French Embassy in Phnom Penh, where all the foreigners have holed up with some Cambodians the Khmer Rouge are after. These Cambodians are handed over, one by one. In Joffé's film, it counts for just one scene. Some of the details have been cut out. For instance, in the article, there is a bit where the journalist wanders down a corridor in the Embassy, opens a door and catches four French policemen wolfing down huge steaks they've managed to stash away, though the others have practically nothing to eat. I was interested in making something which was not a huge film. Puttnam is a good producer. He knew that in order for the film to work, it would have to be spectacular. We did not reach agreement. And that was that.

Why did you an embark on an American career?
There is no simple answer. I can give five reasons. I've always been interested in America and American films. Since childhood. That and jazz were very important to me as a teenager. In the 1960s, when *Les Amants* turned into an international hit, the Americans found out I spoke good English and started sending me scripts. I waited a while because I knew that there is a long history of European directors coming to grief in the US. Then in the mid-70s I wanted a new start. I wanted to feel, somewhat self-indulgently, that I was starting over. Which is only half true, because I came to America as someone with an established reputation. At first, they were extremely hospitable and friendly. If you like, the real reason I went to America was to make *Pretty Baby*, which was a project I cared about a great deal. It was a way of paying a tribute to jazz, which I've always loved. Because I loved jazz, I was very familiar with the history of New Orleans at that period; with the story of Bellocq, the photographer, and the little girl. *Pretty Baby* was my first taste of America, and I have to say it was very hard. I had trouble with the script. I cared about the project so much and it turned out very differently to what I had hoped. I could even say it's a film I'd like to have another go at. I was lucky to happen on Brooke Shields, who was an extraordinary find, but there are lots of things in the film that do not correspond to what I had imagined. I paid my dues. I hung on in there. It took time, time to write the script, time to get acclimatized, to deal with studio production deadlines and with the fact that they couldn't make up their minds whether they really wanted to make the film or not. I thought, 'I can't leave it at that', at something which I considered a semi-failure. The film was well-received in the US, but I wasn't satisfied. I decided to stay on, though I never dreamed I would stay so long. Perhaps I stayed in America out of stubbornness. Time passed very fast. I shot *God's Country* in 1979, I think, and cut it years later. Then some Canadian producers

Atlantic City: Malle and his leading man, Burt Lancaster

came to me with tax-shelter money, desperate to shoot a movie. They said I could do whatever I wanted. I made *Atlantic City* with a brilliant American writer, John Guare, who worked on Forman's *Taking Off*. The film was totally ignored in France, but it was a success in America. Then I made *My Dinner with André* straight afterwards, which people liked too. And for a time, I felt I could do anything I wished in America. Those two had been low-budget movies, the second costing only $400,000, which, in American terms, is nothing. *Atlantic City*, of course, cost a bit more. But it was not an American film, in that it was a Franco-Canadian co-production. So I felt that I could make the films I wanted to make just as easily as in France. But now I am very clear as to what my problem with American film-making is. They regard cinema as an industry. They are obsessed with making money. The point of making films is to make money. There is no other purpose. I suppose you could say they are more honest than the French. French people feel the same, but dare not say so. In America, it's part of the deal. When a producer says, 'I am very interested in your script, but I don't think people will like it,' that is the kiss of death. Which is what happened to me before *Au revoir les enfants*.

I wanted to make a comedy, Moon over Miami, which all the studios said was too sophisticated. It must be said that however big the director's name, however important the actors interested in a script, it's the market research that counts. That's an industrial fact. The result is that an enormous amount of time is wasted. American directors, even the best known, have, say, five scripts on the go at once, knowing that only one of them will get made. Once again, I can't work like that. I can only work on one thing at a time.

Moon over Miami was fairly bold, about American political life, with John Belushi in the lead. And because Belushi was interested, I immediately signed up with a studio. It was a complex, expensive film. Very funny. Definitely a studio film. It was about to be made when Belushi died. Since my brother Vincent and I cared about the project a great deal, we tried to make it with other actors. Belushi's *alter ego*, Dan Aykroyd, was in the project too. He tried to help us. It took months. Which explains how I came to make *Crackers*. I realized it was two years since I had shot anything and it rattled me. If you live in Los Angeles, you are subject to this very unhealthy paranoia, which has ruined more than a few careers. Film-makers always need to think about just how many concessions they can make and in America that's an even tougher problem. You have to clear quite a few hurdles. The story of *Crackers* is unbelievable. Part One. A man at Universal convinces me to make the picture and offers very favourable conditions, including the use of the studio, because he is convinced the picture is going to be a big hit. I was interested in one particular aspect. The script of *Crackers* is an adaptation of a novel, but I had connected it to the economic crisis of the time. I had also discovered Hispanic neighbourhoods in San Francisco where unemployment was a major problem. I had been fascinated by these neighbourhoods and, once again, by the theme of immigrants who find themselves beleaguered in the land of opportunity with nothing to do. Half the film was shot on location in San Francisco. The rest was made on the Universal lot, which is kind of an enormous machine, comprising twenty different sets in activity at any one time. Eighteen were occupied by TV shoots. Brian De Palma and I were the only people making proper movies. I had huge crews, with faces that changed all the time because technicians were employed by the year and were shunted from one set to another. Then during the shoot, the head of production at Universal was replaced by someone else, who thought the whole project was terrible. The entire saga, culminating in a series of terrible previews and recuts, was a total nightmare. It illustrates the whole of American cinema: how the director never has the freedom of choice he has in Europe.

You didn't have the final cut?
I did. Absolutely. I had this producer, who was backed by Universal, the man who suggested I direct *Crackers* and he was a great guy. I said, 'I want the final cut.' He said that was impossible, which was true. In America, no one gets the final cut. Not even the greatest. But I got it. Because, otherwise, I wasn't shooting the movie. But then I realized, when we ran into trouble over the recuts, that he didn't have the final cut himself. He'd ripped me off. A delightful man, but a rip-off merchant. So I went to a lawyer. We could have wrangled for years. In France, creative people are protected by law, an author's rights are sacred. In America, they are definitely

not. Money always wins out. The law is biased in that direction. They didn't ask me to change or reshoot anything, there was just a kind of harassment and in the end I got fed up. We never lost our tempers. It was a gradual decline. You get to a stage when you're doing something and suddenly you think, 'What on earth am I doing here?' I could have done without the experience. The only thing I learnt was never to put myself in that position again. I don't think I'll ever make a studio picture again, a film within the industry. *Alamo Bay*, the next picture, is almost an underground film, financed by the distributor and made with a small crew. Overall, I was left feeling I'd wasted a lot of time in America. But on the positive side, America is such a fascinating and complicated country, that I am not sure I wouldn't be pleased to go back and work there again.

When I make a film like *Au revoir les enfants*, I am on totally familiar terrain because I am telling people about my childhood. If I were to make a contemporary film, I am not sure that I don't know America better than I know France. I have a feeling that because I've always been interested in America and studied it for years, I know America well. I've just spent quite a few months in France and – how can I put it? – I feel out of place. Of course, it's nice to feel out of place, an exile. I've always been a big Conrad fan. I like the literary tradition which depicts people transported from one place to another, whether they are writing about their own country from afar, or whether they are observing a society which is not their own, though they know it well. When I made *Au revoir les enfants*, we kept what we were doing secret. It was a low-budget film, financed by Karmitz[*] without difficulty. We worked in Provins, only 90 kilometres' drive from Paris, though it really is a provincial town. I felt as though I was re-inventing my past in a contemporary setting.

Should I go on making films in France that re-invent my own life, or should I alternate and combine this with films set today? Funnily enough, all the films I've made in France are set in the past. There is that distance. A historical perspective, even a slight one. Except *Ascenseur*. But even with *Les Amants*, absurdly, I considered that I had a three-year perspective on events. *Le Feu follet* was set in the present, but there was obviously a play on time, which worked much better than a period setting would have done. In America, apart from *Pretty Baby*, which was nearly a French film made in America, I've made only contemporary films. I have no roots there. What I have been after in America, whether in drama or in documentary, is to capture the essence of contemporary America, and what it is that strikes me about it that many Americans do not see.

I loved Otar Iosseliani's *Les Favoris de la lune*. He's caught the oddness of Parisians like no one else. When I saw it, I was living in America. I went with Candice, my wife. It made her laugh. She's American. She finds French people odd.

* Marin Karmitz, French producer/distributor – notably the producer of all Chabrol's recent films and Kieslowski's later work.

The distance Otar senses makes sense to her. And it was fun for me because I think that what Americans liked about *Atlantic City* was precisely that: I had a different perspective, which made me see their behaviour in a way they couldn't see it themselves.

Interviewed in Paris, 17 August 1987

6　Alain Cavalier on *Thérèse*

interviewed by François Ramasse

Alain Cavalier

Alain Cavalier's first feature was *L'Insoumis* (1962), starring Alain Delon. This established him as a director of the first order. He has a series of well-received productions to his name, culminating in *Thérèse* (1986). Since then, he has been experimenting with avant garde forms, including directing a documentary series in one hundred thumbnail parts, and a theatrically released video diary tribute to love, entitled *La Rencontre* (1996), which ran for one year.

Rarely has any experimental film reached such a wide audience as *Thérèse* which, despite its somewhat archaic subject-matter (how to become a Catholic saint), succeeded in touching a wide audience both in France and abroad. This is because Cavalier's bold gamble in shooting the entire film in a studio against a neutral cyclorama backdrop transformed what might have been a rebarbative psychological study into a work of earthy humanism by lending each shot a still-life-like neutrality, a cinematic distance. Whenever film-makers have succeeded in depicting mystical elation with such detachment they have made works of great power. But unlike Bresson or Dreyer, Cavalier's fascination for the religious is rooted in a depiction of the material world which his formal experiment liberates from the platitudes of naturalism, and which gives *Thérèse* its surprising, painterly accessibility.

Thérèse

Fifteen-year-old Thérèse Martin (Catherine Mouchet) is granted her wish to
leave her father and enter the severe Carmelite Order at Lisieux, along with
her three sisters. Her love of life and God help her to endure the privations
of the monastic life and the death of her father. She is an inspiration to those
- around her. But she contracts tuberculosis, receives no medical attention
and dies, aged twenty-four, in 1897. Her canonization follows in 1924.

**Knowing your work, I was surprised at your choice of Thérèse, the little saint
of Lisieux. Why?**
Several reasons, but I think primarily I was inspired by the photographs her sister took inside the Carmelite convent in Lisieux. These documents about Thérèse
and Carmelite life were released about fifteen years ago. They are absolutely wonderful. In the film you see Thérèse's sister with the camera. I combined this –
these pictures are published – with childhood memories of religious boarding
schools. So *Thérèse* is a combination of childhood emotions and almost cinematographic documents which tell the story of a young nun in a provincial convent at the end of the nineteenth century. All this was motivation enough.

What are the photographs like?
In those days you photographed people's professions. You showed them standing by their shop windows. Being a Carmelite nun was also a career. You see them
wearing their uniform, a leather apron and cowl. Very serious and hard-working.
They stand in a row, and pose for the camera beside a cross. You see Thérèse's
suffering written on her face. It is very moving. When she first went to the convent, she was quite plump. Her face didn't alter much, but it hollowed out. The
look in her eyes became more intense. She also seems a bit embarrassed. She had
to pose for seven seconds, so her expression is deliberately neutral, neither happy
nor sad. There is a mystery there which I find exciting.

The pictures tell her story right up to her death. I kept the last image, substi-
tuting an old lady for Thérèse. This is a wreath, and flowers all around. It isn't a
sad death – quite happy really.

**What about the photo taken by her sister where she is dressed up as Joan of Arc.
Did that really happen?**
Yes, I copied the costume, the dress studded with lilies cut out of chocolate wrap-
ping papers. But in the original photo she is wearing a wig, which I didn't put in;
it looked too much like a late-nineteenth-century pious cliché of Joan of Arc. I
hope the film is understood to be slightly metaphorical, not only religious. There
are Thérèses everywhere; now I know that, and I know exactly why, because I
researched the subject furiously, like an historian. Then I tried to forget all I knew
when I started writing. As I worked, I sifted through the material and changed

things. That's when I took out the wig. I had actually found one and put it on Catherine Mouchet, but it seemed heavy-handed, it spoilt the whole scene. With her hair short like that, the image is much more poignant – and much more cinematographic. That's my opinion, anyway. Her face is much clearer and the image is simple. That's the sort of historical adaptation I like.

You mention historical research. What is there on *Thérèse?*
Not much, frankly. You're talking about very withdrawn and solitary institutions, and in the many hundreds of years since the start of the Carmelite order not a single proper study has been done. All we have is what the Church has allowed to filter through. With three old bits of a column you can rebuild a temple, but it's not very satisfactory. Two things saved me. Firstly, my experiences in a religious school, with boys and girls kept apart, and plenty of strict doctrine. I could imagine what life would be like inside a convent. Secondly, I met some wonderful women – Carmelites whom I spoke to inside the convent, and other women who had left the order for whatever reason. So, in fact, I learnt much more from listening to people than from my months and months of reading mainly Roman Catholic material. *Thérèse* is the voice of these women.

Have you met the specialists on the subject?
No. There's Father Six and Father Guy Gaucher. Their work is admirable, but my film was to be personal and cinematographic, in no way linked to the Church. But there is a library adjoining the Convent in Lisieux where I went occasionally. I told them I was making a film about Thérèse and needed to do some research. One day I was summoned by the prioress to a small room with a table (no grilles any more) and we chatted. She had no idea what I was planning to do with Thérèse's life – I could have been a complete iconoclast and, anyway, I am a man – yet she suggested I visit the convent. The bishop had given his permission. I walked down the passages, saw Thérèse's cell and the infirmary where she died.

At what stage did this happen?
When I was writing.

Your daughter, Camille de Casabianca, worked on the script with you. You had already written Un étrange voyage together. What was it like, writing Thérèse with her?
Completely different. *Un étrange voyage* was Camille's first film. We drew on her experiences and her actual life. She acted and wrote. Here I focused on Thérèse. Sometimes I talked to Camille, as they were about the same age, and asked her if I should go on: I wasn't sure, I wondered if anyone would be interested in the life of a nineteenth-century nun from Normandy. She encouraged me. She saw clearly what I couldn't see. I was swamped by difficulties, some of which seemed insurmountable. I needed reassurance, so I gave her some scenes to look at. That's how we ended up working together.

And your visit to the convent? What did that contribute?
Strangely, it gave me impetus. Obviously, anything that happens in the preparatory stages of making a film has an effect. I knew that I had either to film there – which would be impossible, as it is a closed working environment – or find an alternative. I looked for empty convents, considered using studio sets. Then one day I was looking at the book of Manet's work and realized that it is possible to be entirely realistic and a million miles from reality at the same time: a dark backdrop with no doors, windows, landscapes, and it's perfect, it's real.

So you hadn't decided to use a studio until that moment?
No. I'd thought about it, but I hadn't made up my mind. I wasn't confident that it would work. So Manet clinched it. Combined with the convent visit, seeing his work produced a ray of light, and a confused idea that I had been grappling with for a while suddenly became clear. In the modern world we are attacked from all sides by a whirlwind of visual and aural data from the moment we wake up to the moment we go to sleep, and I thought it was important to find a simplicity, to give the film a point. Without this, one would just be reproducing the noise outside, adding chaos to chaos.

When *Un étrange voyage* was released, you talked about your striving for simplicity. You said there were too many colours, too many words, too many feelings.
There are still too many in *Un étrange voyage*, which, I finally realized, was the account of an exhausting journey taken by us, the crew. There were nine of us carrying the whole weight of it. By the end of each day I was shattered. Endlessly changing scenery, trains going by, two people arguing, searching for something, discovering. I think that in the period between *Un étrange voyage* and *Thérèse* I achieved something – a sort of breathing space. I already felt that things were too busy.

Considering that you had everything to hand, and your desire for simplicity, isn't fifty days' filming quite a lot?
For an inexpensive film – we had exactly the money we needed to do what was necessary – fifty days, ten weeks, may be slightly above average, but it's fine.

Was it so long because you had a lot of rehearsals?
Just the opposite. We didn't even have readings. A film is a secret between the actor and the process. You just have to check how the actor takes possession of the film, and what he has to offer it. It's all about focus. Total concentration. And when I talk about simplifying things, I'm also talking about concentration. So, because the film lent itself to it – which is rare – we shot *Thérèse* in chronological order. Then, because the editing was being done twenty-five metres from the set, I knew by the following day what we had shot the day before. So we watched the tree growing, and pruned and repruned it. We could reshoot bits, we had enough time. We could make mistakes and take things out. When you have twenty-five

different sets, and you're running round like a madman, hiring such and such for three days, then it's very difficult to reshoot things. So you never do. On this film, we could and did.

In this way the backdrop, which gradually became an angel, was, at first, a monster: this ten-metre-high grey wall had to be tamed, we had to learn how to use it. At first it completely caught us out: there were problems of depth of field, proportion, faces moving against a background, speed of movement – because, when someone moves, the speed is different, depending on whether the background appears fixed or not. The backdrop was like a wall, not a uniform grey colour but shifting from black gradually through to white. We had to learn how and when to light it, warm it or cool it, because its base colour was a warm reddy-brown, which meant that – by using the light – it could either be hot or cold, bringing out either the brown or the grey. It was a real accomplishment, learning to use it like a painter does a canvas. It was like the strokes of a painter's brush – it was actually painted by an artist – but on a different scale. It was alive and had a life of its own. Some days, in rushes, you could see it wasn't playing ball. It was too white, it was pale, boring. It was aggressive. The section of the wall used as background for each take was also significant. Finally, we learned to communicate with it, and from then on it was our judge; it became an integral part of the film. By the end, I loved it. I used to touch it.

Was it this progression from black to white which inspired the panning shots which move us from one room to another and from one scene to another, for example, taking us into the cell of Pranzini, who is condemned to death?
Yes. But I tried not to overdo it. It was very tempting just to move from one set to the next, without cuts. For Pranzini, I wanted to give the effect of a dream, as if Thérèse was radiating subconscious energy, and thus mysteriously communicating with him. She felt she was, anyway, so it was important to put them in the same shot without cutting.

When the collar of Pranzini's shirt is cut, Thérèse is seen touching the nape of her neck. It reminded me of Jean Rochefort fainting at the beginning of *Un étrange voyage*. Is this telepathy?
Yes, the film is entirely about telepathy, but I hope that's not too obvious.

There is also a pan, a double one, there and back, as Thérèse enters the convent.
There is a shaft of shadow, like a cloister, and we pass from one world to another. First the prioress crosses it, coming to fetch Thérèse. She is dressed in a wedding gown amongst her friends and family in the outside world. She leaves them and is led through the shadow by the prioress, where she is greeted on the other side by the entire Carmelite community. We had to film this scene twice because the cameraman found it very difficult and it didn't work. Luckily, operations like this are always saved by a little detail which you get right. On this occasion, the

detail was the lighted candle that the prioress was holding. At first we put up a sort of black panel with the camera behind it. But it looked very harsh; it took some time to work out what was wrong. For it to work, the shadow had to be a bit hazy, so we put a little bit of light in, hence the lighted candle. By doing this, the Prioress was not entirely swallowed up by the darkness; the shadow remained alive, yet intangible.

What fascinates me are those transitional scenes, of which this is an example. I think that those changes always involve passing through shadow; i.e. when you are going from one state of mind to another, from one desire to another, there is a moment of anguish and darkness. Like when you have to change shoes. I hate throwing away shoes, it's a mirror image of life: they wear out and then finally die. So, I always go to the same shop and I leave the old pair when I buy the new ones. This gives me a feeling of continuity. I couldn't put them in the rubbish myself.

Entering the convent must have been a big step for Thérèse, such an important decision, totally changing her life. It's highlighting something deep inside one, but there's no safety net, no looking back. That must have been particularly difficult as regards her father, who we see, at that point, like a commander, saying, 'I'm still here. What have you done to me?' She feels responsible for her father's paralysis and ensuing death.

Is this what brought about her decline?
I'm sure there were factors that affected her, because she became very fragile, first psychologically, then physically. Also, Carmelite life is not easy, or comfortable. It's cold, and the food is poor and not very good. So you have to be very resistant, naïve, happy and tough to survive. Thérèse was all of these things, but she was also in pursuit of perfection, which meant she was bound to be smashed down sooner or later.

It was this strength of hers that attracted you?
She was an athlete, with an engine of – heaven knows how many horsepower – a capacity for love, that she drove into the ground, until finally she had to leave the track. You can't live for eighty years like that.

You have made comparisons between her and Joan of Arc, St Just and Rimbaud. They all died young too.
Yes. My charming quartet didn't make it into old age. All for different reasons, but the root is the same. Their perception of life was too powerful, their idealism bordering on lunacy. This was how they confronted reality. And if things that seem surprising happened in a Carmelite convent, it is because it's a society like any other, in which mediocrity and stupidity reign supreme.

Thérèse: The lighted candles as Thérèse enters the convent.

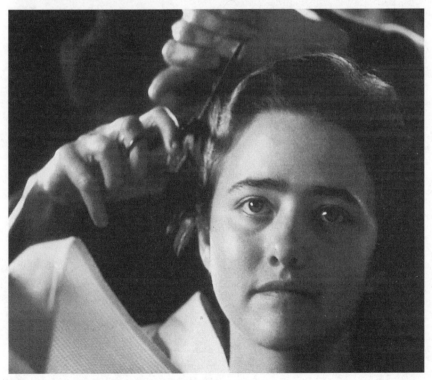

Thérèse: Catherine Mouchet in transition.

This strength, this gift – which one of the sisters reproaches her for, the one who doesn't like her – isn't it unfair, as the sister points out? Isn't there something Jansenist about it?

It's difficult to say. She tries to dissimulate. Perhaps it's true humility. I don't think she is the sort of person who feels superior and makes up an extraordinary story to impress others. I think she was blessed with this gift of humility and a love of little things which gave her strength and energy. In her opinion, nothing is ugly, nothing is stupid. There is something astonishing that happens in life, something which was very much on my mind while filming. I was telling the story of an adolescent who was going to die of TB. It's a very negative story, but I don't think people see the film as negative. Because, even though she dies, and in her death we find both light and darkness, she gives off very powerful vibes. That's my opinion, but I was motivated to make the film by instinct, not rational thought.

There are often deaths in your films, deaths which seem to leave a space for something else to follow after. Is Thérèse's death, which happens practically side by side with Lucie's running away, not a way of liberating Lucie?

What touched me – while struggling to film her death, which really shook me – was that she died partly as a result of Lucie's escape, she died in failure. Lucie is her double. She didn't really exist; I created her from my talks with Carmelites who hadn't survived the course. So, if Thérèse dies as a result of Lucie's freedom, Lucie is free as a result of Thérèse's death. And, at the end of the day, Thérèse isn't really dead because part of her has got away.

A part of her which escapes down here, as opposed to the part of her which escapes upwards; she talks of going up to the stars.

Yes, I suppose so. But that's difficult to conceive when you're struggling on set, with twenty-four women wanting to know what to do – your mind is on other things.

What is the failure you mentioned earlier?

Thérèse's failure when she refuses to go on.

There's an almost carnal element to this love of Christ. She speaks of Him as if He was her lover.

Traditionally this is what happened; it happens less today. It's obvious. When women are shut away among themselves, what do they talk about? Just men. When I was at boarding school, we talked about women all the time, fantasizing wildly and drawing on our experience with sisters, mothers, passers-by. But there was a sort of electricity – sometimes stupid and vulgar, and sometimes gentle and sensitive – whenever women were discussed.

Why would it be any different in a convent? Why wouldn't these women talk about the one man who unites them all? And from one point of view, almost for

Thérèse: body

the sake of their good health, they can't be entirely deprived of men. This concept stretches far, they see this man not only as their husband, but also as their child: the wooden baby Jesus you see is the child these women could have had. And, in a strange way, He is also their brother and father. He is the whole family.

At the moment when we see the wooden baby Jesus, we hear a baby's cry.
That was there when we filmed. Beforehand, we had discussed the little presents and the details, and then we filmed, like a documentary. If you look closely, you can see a nun, the one standing next to the one holding the baby, faking a baby's cry by pinching her nose. But you have to really look to see it, and people think it has been added after, by the director. In fact, it's just an off-the-cuff improvisation. When I saw it, I was bowled over. These women were splendid. If there had been a conscious decision to put this cry into the shot, we would have made more of it, but as it was, it simply slipped in discreetly. Sadly, for me, the viewer thinks this is a deliberate cinematic ploy. It's a pity, but it's interesting to see how things can be sometimes completely misunderstood. I dislike the fact that I have been accused of cleverly reworking this scene, as I hate insets. And I don't want cuts, because I then have to dub. There isn't any dubbing. The soundtrack has remained untouched since the original recording, made as the scenes were filmed. So there's no dubbing, no music, no insets. Just the tape running. What we call live – the sound of footsteps, fabric rustling, nothing added, nothing taken away. We obviously worked on it at the time of recording, and sometimes it's a

deliberately false 'live' soundtrack, when people are talking close to the camera but are recorded from a distance, or the other way round, when there is other stuff going on. But nothing has been re-recorded. I really like this live sound-track.

We get the impression that, over and above the fade-outs, it's these sounds that bind the film together. And the realism of this soundtrack creates an astonishing contrast to the set – the surroundings in which Thérèse lived – which are an expression, or at least a footnote, to the spiritual side. But there is also a material aspect to things; for example, the three beautiful takes inside Thérèse's cell with the rosary and the sandals.
That's just part of the whole. They are just little things which lead us to the big things – or what we believe to be the big things. This is also very much in the spirit of Carmelite philosophy. *Thérèse* is a poor film, not poorly done, but with a small budget, and the essence of it is poverty. For example, at one moment, the Carmelites receive a letter and they recycle the envelope, to avoid wastage. It's the opposite of what happens now, where people are encouraged to work to earn money, to then go out and spend it, and the more they spend, the more work there is, and so it goes on. It's an old story. The Carmelites have decided to get away from all that and devote themselves to something else. Personally, I think it's fine to devote oneself to machines and life's pleasures, but they made their own choice. Anyway, one can't do two things at once – watch television three hours a day and write a book. The danger of the choice they've made is that, sooner or later, you find the same things on the inside that you have left on the outside. You can't hear the traffic and see people charging around, but you still find faces you don't like. It's a small group and there are inevitable tensions. I think Thérèse applied some of her skill and strength of character to being systematically kind to those around her.

In her autobiography, *Histoire d'une âme*, does she mention these pressures?
Yes. Reading between the lines, I don't see why they wouldn't exist. It isn't a perfect environment. Every civilization knows that. We just pretend to discover this from time to time. Women have always shut themselves away – the Vestal Virgins, and even further back in time. It's strange, as if they were frightened that this life that they have constructed for themselves will go out like a light and disappear for ever. So they group together to protect it – it's like the graphite bar inside a reactor making the electricity; they withdraw from life in order to make a life and then protect it. Without making children, which is interesting, because they think and give off – I'm not sure about this bit – powerful vibes that enable life to continue. I think that Flaubert had the same idea, and this justified the many wearisome hours he spent writing. It's a different sort of mysticism. In fact, he spelt it out: 'If I wasn't in love with the body, I would be a mystic.' So he was one.

You too?
Me? Cinema is a game. I may have a predisposition for it, but, at the end of the day, it's a cinematic game which holds you hostage. I was really worried while working on *Thérèse*, wondering whether I was just using the film as a cinematic experiment, whether I'd left behind the one thing I was attempting to find in Thérèse's life and being. Maybe I had lost the fundamental point by using it as a work tool. And I spent hours thinking to myself: 'It's great that it's about that, but if there's nothing but that, it'll be a bad film.' Then I found the emotion again, and I felt reassured.

Is this emotion aroused by these women who draw back from life in order to protect it, and in order not to have to live in the world as we know it?
It's the emotion inspired in a man who finds himself facing these women united. There's nothing erotic about it. It's very subtle for a director, because film is so suited to transmitting erotic vibes that when you film a woman, it is automatically erotic; suddenly you find these women whose aura is not entirely different, but is so delicate and rarefied that you are enchanted. By comparison, groups of men – be it in the regiment, or in a team – appear coarse. Of course, there is tension and violence. But there are moments that had me weeping. Neither the film, the camera, me or the crew had an erotic relationship with these women. There were undoubtedly loving relationships, but no desire – or lack of desire – no 'She's pretty', or 'She's not pretty', 'She looks good'. None of that. This helped me a lot.

Who are these women, because they're not all actresses?
There is a mixture of theatre actresses and women who lived near the studio in Billancourt, for whom it was convenient and easy to come in.

You hand-picked them, they all have something special. You couldn't mistake them for each other.
That's true. I was worried that the habits would make them all look the same. But that's not the case. I knew that one would get the overall picture, and see them, but I feared that their individual characters would, from time to time, disappear into a sort of melting pot. Now, I don't believe that one could confuse them. But, at the start, as I had never previously made an historical film, never stuck a moustache on an actor, I was worried. Having said that, it's hardly a costume drama, as there is only one costume.

It's this that enables you to bring out other things – this and your attention to mundane details.
That's true, but you mustn't exaggerate the simplicity. It is coupled with a mad baroque streak. It's very baroque to portray these women whose emotional make-up is completely natural in this unreal uniform, which is completely coded – every bit of it has a separate and symbolic significance. It's a light burden. We dress to keep warm, and, less importantly, to seduce or not seduce. But these women wear

the same clothes winter and summer. So it has a different emphasis, over and beyond change; it's a quest for harmony in their life. It's their searching that is moving, not their aim – which they never attain. I don't know what they are looking for, truth or something else, but what is important is that they are looking. This gives them great joy, but, at the same time, it could kill them.

You talked earlier of a 'career'.
Yes, that's how they describe it. It's work. Let's say it's like gymnastics. To become a great gymnast is hard work. In fact, it's the same for all of us. Those calm times, those times when we sit back and soak up the past, the present, the future – they're hard work.

Is there a documentary aspect to your film?
I didn't live in the convent, I just tried to get close to it. But I also fantasize a bit. I've no idea what the Carmelites in Lisieux will think of the film. They'll see it on video, because they aren't allowed out to the cinema. I hope it will make them laugh. The smallest thing makes them laugh, they love it. Like anybody who lives within a strict discipline – it's a little transgression that I became aware of when I spent time with them. I would crack some very banal joke and they would think it was funny.

And the laughter in the film?
That was real. You don't enter a convent if you aren't a bit naïve, if you don't have some sort of insight into the bigger picture.

So you shut yourself away in order to open yourself up?
That's what I love about it. In the darkness, you find light. And yes, you shut yourself away to open yourself up.

You disturb quite a few clichés.
Yes, but they are quite easy ones. I have to say that the cinema is partly to blame, because, whenever a camera has set foot inside a convent or a monastery, it has exaggerated. This just made the clichés, already in people's minds, even bigger. Under the pretext that cinema is truth, twenty-four times a second. It is also a monstrous lie, the biggest lie there is. To think that, of the last hundred years, the only real documentation will be cinematographic – one can barely imagine the commentaries that will be made about the films of the twentieth century. The fantasy element, such as mine in *Thérèse*, will disappear. Because, once something is over, done, any reconstitution is, by definition, false. Anything that is no longer alive is false.

Who is the real Thérèse? You said earlier that there were Thérèses everywhere. You also said that your film is metaphorical.
I would like anyone who has given a bit of their life to an action, a cause, anything, to see themselves in Thérèse. Thérèse is an energy channelled into some-

thing you believe in one hundred per cent. That you know could destroy you. But that you do with joy. She is a way of being which is excessive, never giving up, right to the bitter end. The only driving force is love. There are many different forms of Thérèse, many different ways to be her.

Is that how you felt when making the film?
Yes. My reaction to it was very physical; some days I was ill, and other days I felt very light and happy. Today, for the first time, I think that I will live for a very long time and become eternal. Or die tomorrow morning. It's quite fun. It changes every day.

What is is that links the four films you made before *Thérèse*, and what will link the four that include *Thérèse*?
I'm not sure at the moment; I know there is one, but I can't exactly put my finger on it and define it. I know there is a way of filming, of dealing with the financial considerations, working with professional and non-professional actors, simplifying the texts – but I haven't yet found the underground link which brings all these factors together. As for the next series, all I know is that there cannot be five of them and that they will completely drain me. After that, I have no idea if I will ever want to film again.

Back to the present, or, more to the point, the immediate past, a last and rather indiscreet question. Some of us in Cannes were hoping that *Thérèse* would get the Palme d'or. Were you disappointed?
It's very simple. At the first screening for the critics, it was well received, then there was the next one for the public. I had been warned that when films appear strange or different, half the audience is liable to walk out. So, as soon as the film began, I left the hall, terrified, and didn't go back in until the credits, when I saw that the audience was still there. Then, they applauded, so that was great. Just the fact that the film went to Cannes was unhoped for; that the critics liked it, and then that the public liked it, was amazing. The fact that it didn't win was rather in keeping with the theme of the film, with *Thérèse*. Official recognition would have made it banal. A side seat was perfect. Like when I go to the theatre, I arrive late and slip into a corner. So I was very happy with the outcome of Cannes, and delighted that the film was there at all. I had no regrets, none at all. Working on *Thérèse* meant I grappled with the notions of pride, vanity, self-love, the destruction of the ego, the 'me', the absorption of self into the greater picture, and getting a lollipop at Cannes was not really part of the picture.

Interviewed in Paris, 26 June 1986

Claude Sautet on *Un Coeur en hiver*

interviewed by Michel Sineux and Yann Tobin

Claude Sautet, directing Emmanuelle Béart on *Un Coeur en hiver*

Born in 1924, Claude Sautet made a name for himself with his first film, *Classe tous risques* (1962), starring Jean-Paul Belmondo and Lino Ventura. He has directed many of the major stars including Yves Montand (*César et Rosalie,* 1972), Michel Piccoli (*Max et les ferrailleurs,* 1971) and, more recently, Daniel Auteuil, Michel Serrault and Emmanuelle Béart. His most recent films are *Un Coeur en hiver* and *Nelly et Monsieur Arnaud.*

Un Coeur en hiver
Premièred at the Venice Film Festival in 1992, *Un Coeur en hiver* is an acutely observed romantic triangle. A violin maker, Stephane (Daniel Auteuil), wreaks emotional havoc on the lives of his old friend and partner Maxime (André Dussolier) and Camille (Emmanuelle Béart), a gifted and beautiful young violinist with whom Maxime has fallen in love. Stephane develops an unconscious attraction towards Camille and his way of resolving the emotional turbulence he feels upsets the delicate equilibrium of all three lives.

What is the genesis of *Un Coeur en hiver*?

The link between *Quelques jours avec moi* and *Un Coeur en hiver* is tenuous. When I hired Daniel Auteuil to make *Quelques jours*, I made him read to improve his reading skills. He found long sentences difficult, and wasn't good at reading for reading's sake. Philippe Carcassonne had given me a wonderful book by Lermontov called *A Hero of Our Time*, with a story in it called 'Princess Mary', which had a dramatic quality which was ideal for Auteuil. After reading it, Daniel said that he understood what I was getting at. Later, when I was looking around for ideas for a screenplay, I told Fieschi a very imaginary tale based on my memories of Lermontov's story. Not having read the book, he was struck by the plot, in which the lead, who is a darker, much more troubled character than in the original, aims to seduce his friend's girlfriend, in order then to tell her, once he's won her over, that he doesn't love her. We then forgot all about it, only to come back to it later. My son had just given me a recording of Ravel's sonatas, played by Jean-Jacques Kantorow, which are beautiful. As I listened to them, I thought back to the story, and wondered about transposing the plot into the world of violin-makers, with the Princess Mary as a violinist.

At first it wasn't the main character that preoccupied us, but the one played by André Dussolier, Maxime. In Lermontov's story, he was someone who was totally despised by the hero, whereas for Fieschi and I, Stephane couldn't exist without Maxime. Stephane is wary of Maxime, nevertheless he is his friend. The girl's arrival on the scene engenders an unfolding of the characters. Early on, we decided on the setting, and decided that the link between the three of them would be the old music professor. The idea that Stephane would kill the sick old professor came early on, but then, when it came to working on it, we felt ill at ease, worrying that maybe it was just a sub-plot tacked on. Then we gradually realized that it was a valid part of his character. As Stephane is incapable of any positive action in a conformist sense, it's the only compassionate and loving thing he does. In moral terms, obviously, his action is bad.

Are Stephane's solitude and lack of sensitivity representative of our age?

La Rochefoucauld says: 'There would not be many lovers if people never talked about love.' I'm not so sure. I don't know if this character has been like this since birth, or if this is just a period of his life. I remember going through periods like this in my own life. Stephane relies on postures of self-protection and disillusionment. But he's happy in this state, and what happens to Maxime, this love affair, upsets him, so he decides to play a little game, to create chaos and upset something that doesn't seem authentic to him.

Did you do the casting early on in the writing of the screenplay?

No, at the last minute. I thought of Emmanuelle Béart first. I saw her one day, with her hair tied back, she was strong-willed and young: she suited the character, but she needed to learn to play the violin. As she then studied it for nearly a year, by the end I was confident that she could play Camille. I was stunned by her work on the violin. She was ready to fight, and this dimension comes across in her acting. The violin played a big role. All the practice, night and day, gave her confidence and a certain strength. The thing that I always wonder about with actors is, how do they get self-confidence without resorting to the rather unpleasant tactics we all know about?

After choosing Emmanuelle Béart, who did you find next?
I was embarrassed because of the media attention given to the relationship between Béart and Daniel Auteuil. I knew Auteuil could do it, but I didn't want the couple Béart/Auteuil. Then I thought, this is ridiculous!

How did Dussolier come on to the scene?
I went through all the actors. I had thought of him right at the start. I had an image of him as a handsome, seductive man, but in fact he brought a certain credibility to the role. At the same time, it was his character in Alain Resnais' film, *Melo,* in reverse. This worried him a lot, he wasn't sure if he could be as confident in this role. But we spent a lot of time together, so that he could really get to grips with the character, and understand that he was a sort of cosmic force. Auteuil and Dussolier are completely different as actors. Dussolier is used to the theatre. He questions everything, every position, every movement, before the shoot. Auteuil, on the other hand, absorbs everything you say like a sponge; he just takes it shot by shot. But they got on really well, they spent a lot of time together on the shoot, they played squash. When we were editing, I realized that they were much closer than I expected. When Maxime comes to see Stephane in his new studio, Auteuil's reaction is totally childlike, as if he hadn't believed it could happen. And the fact that Dussolier has the upper hand over him makes any confrontation over Camille unthinkable. As we filmed, we realized that Stephane couldn't escape the friendship with Maxime. As he says to Camille: 'You've missed me, and I've lost Maxime.'

It must be satisfying to see that underlying ideas in the screenplay come to light during filming, and even later, while editing.
This happened more to me in this film than in any previous film. I had planned the mounting tension, but I had no idea there would be such an emotional torrent. The last scene in the café was so intense that we shot the whole thing in two takes. Mostly, when you are filming, you don't feel any emotion, you are just fumblingly trying to achieve what you want.

There are fewer background shots, minor characters, less general polyphony, than in any other previous film of yours. Everything is focused on the protagonists, filmed in close-up. Is this why you filmed in 1.66m rather than in 1.85m?
I left it up to the cameraman to do what he wanted. Personally I preferred 1.85m, but he felt that with this, what we gained in width, we would lose in height, and there were not enough wide-angle shots to justify it.

Un Coeur en hiver: Daniel Auteuil and Emmanuelle Béart

Un Couer en hiver: 'Auteuil absorbs everything.'

How did you prepare the visual aspects of the film?
As always happens, when you are talking to the cameramen, your thoughts are not very coherent, you are just conveying impressions formed by the different locations you've chosen. Slowly you make decisions about framing and the light. The more compact the space, the elements, the colours, the easier it is for me to focus on the essentials.

Even though you are not known as someone who focuses particularly on visual effects, it is striking that some of the same colours, tones, and materials are to be found in several of your films.

It is important, if only subconsciously. It's also quite a test, to produce something that you aren't aware of seeing, but that you can feel.

Do you ever look through the lens?
Yes, but I never operate. Strangely enough, I looked through the lens less in this film than I usually do, because the osmosis between Angelo and me was such that it wasn't necessary. He understands music, he got the Premier Prix at the music academy at eighteen. He's very cultured and understands without having to be told. But I do play an important role in the photography.

You also play a big role in the construction of the dialogue. There is a poetic style to the dialogue that is very much your own.
In musical terms, it's about harmonizing, chords – just to give you an idea, we spent four months on the first third of the dialogue, getting it right.

Was the music already there when you were working on the screenplay?
I made my co-writers listen to Ravel's sonatas and trio before we started. Fieschi, who claims to know nothing about music, understood something from listening to them, and I was haunted by that music.

Did you know in advance which bit of music would accompany which scene?
Yes, especially as we had to do the recordings before we shot. Emmanuelle Béart practised the playback for three months. I had decided that the 'Perpetuum mobile' from the Sonata for Violin and Piano should be performed in a very energetic manner, demanding an enormous effort of concentration, and that this tension would enable Camille to throw herself on Stephane in the car.

That's why it was even more important that she was convincing as a violinist.
The professor who was teaching her said, after three months, that at least she could now hold a violin and bow. No one believed that she would possibly be able to play 'Perpetuum' – including me – but it was essential. She buckled down to it during filming, and cracked it in a week.

Like Max in *Max et les ferrailleurs*, Stephane is masochistic, misogynistic and a handyman. But his choice of profession, violin-maker, plays an intrinsic part in understanding his inability to communicate with others. He's an autistic who heals himself, who applies his own therapy by assembling the different parts of his instruments.
Absolutely right. Having chosen this musical setting, I didn't want to put proper music in the film. Ravel's sonatas and trio are perfect, because they aren't particularly stunning, and they show the work involved. People who aren't especially into music can see the energy, the work involved, without being distracted by the music. Stephane is often hidden, he likes watching and hearing, and being out of sight himself. And when he is in the picture, he clearly 'disappears' at times. It's all part of his game. When, occasionally, Camille is face to face with him and asks him

about himself, he's uptight. He tries to fade away completely, as if he didn't exist.

You've never used this kind of character before.
No. A character with a past, reminiscing, yes. But never this, someone with no plan, no strategy, no motive.

There is a symmetry between Camille, Regine and Maxime on the one hand, and Stephane, Maxime and Camille on the other: two trios which shift. When this happens, Regine and Stephane are unsettled, the first by Camille, the second by Maxime. Is Regine's character (played by Brigitte Catillon) in the screenplay from the start?
In my memories of Lermontov's story, 'Princess Mary', she was more or less looked after by a mother. When we thought of the violin, we realized there was always someone around, an agent or a teacher, so that's how Regine appeared. She is Camille's mother's best friend, and she lives with her. She protects Camille, who depends on her. In the film Camille grows up, and becomes an adult, hence the problem with Regine.

Isn't there a vaguely homosexual relationship between the two women?
It's conceivable; it exists, but it doesn't happen. Most people who live together find themselves in this situation at some time.

There is another example of symmetry, on a larger scale between this film and _Quelques jours_. Auteuil is in both films, one is fairly positive, the other fairly negative. The first has a group forming, the second a group disintegrating. These are like games with numbers. All your films have a musical structure.
I use numbers to reassure me, and calm down my emotions. I am obsessed with proportion. When I watch other films, I perceive their faults by eliminating worthless numbers.

In this film, everything focuses on the essential. Everything is purified, but the emotions remain powerful.
I think Stephane's character, if ostensibly scheming, is fairly impenetrable, so all the nuances were to be found in Maxime's and Camille's characters.

What was Etienne Vatelot's role?
I asked him lots of questions, and his answers were what I expected. He sent along one of his instrument makers, who stayed on the set with us. Auteuil was beside himself with excitement at having so much to learn – some actors gain strength from using their hands. When you see the closing of the violin, it's symbolic. Everything, all the work that has gone on underneath, is hidden. The skill of the craftsman is such that it takes two people to close up the instrument.

Interviewed in Paris, June 1992

69

8   Maurice Pialat on *Van Gogh*

interviewed by Michel Ciment and Michel Sineux

Maurice Pialat

Maurice Pialat is one of the most respected film-makers working in France today. Originally a painter, his first feature, *L'Enfance nue* (1967) was a searing, near-documentary autobiography. His most famous films are *Nous ne vieillirons pas ensemble* (1972), *Passe ton bac d'abord* (1978), *Loulou* (1980), *A nos amours* (1983), *Police* (1985), and *Sous le soleil de Satan* (1987), which won the Palme d'Or at Cannes. Pialat is famous for directing such actresses as Sophie Marceau and Isabelle Huppert. He discovered Sandrine Bonnaire aged fifteen (*A Nos amours*) and directed her opposite Depardieu in *Sous le soleil de Satan*. His *Van Gogh* (1991) is a major achievement, a considerable improvement on most biopics, including Vincente Minnelli's attempt at the same subject.

As is clear from this interview, Maurice Pialat has regularly expressed dissatisfaction with the way his films are received critically and commercially. He runs a famously bad-tempered set. *Van Gogh*, for instance, has three director-of-photography credits, evidence of successive sackings. Yet it is the extraordinarily limpid lighting of the outdoor, 'impressionist' scenes – a picnic by a river, a summer lunch at Dr Gachet's – that sets the film apart from run-of-the-mill biopics. If ever proof were needed that very often it is the director, not the D.P., who determines photography, this is it.

Van Gogh

The last three months in the life of Vincent Van Gogh, May–July 1890. Van
Gogh arrives in Auvers-sur-Oise, befriends physician and art enthusiast Dr
Gachet, and eventually commences a difficult affair with Gachet's daughter
Marguerite. He is visited by his brother Theo (to whom he is profoundly
indebted) and Theo's wife Jo, and calls on them in Paris in turn. But there
Vincent rows with Jo and later with Marguerite. Back in Auvers, Gachet
tells Vincent that he excels as a painter, but fails as a human being. Van
Gogh shoots himself, refuses aid and dies, holding Theo's hand.

Bitterness. Not bitterness. It's not anger either, unfortunately. You can't go on
hitting out, if there's nothing to hit out at.

What happened on this film is what happens on all my films. I don't like always
being the scapegoat, but it goes on happening. It was the same on this film, but I
suppose someone had to take the brunt – it's symptomatic of today's cinema. The
film was stopped because it was costing too much, because it was under-budgeted.
Some of the costs could have been avoided totally, and others reduced. It should
have cost about 40 million francs, whereas we spent over 60 million francs. About
15 or 20 million went up in smoke, spent on sets, things we didn't even use. As a
result the film was stopped, to save 3 million francs and three weeks of shooting. It's
not very logical, saving 3 million on a film that's costing 60 million. The 3 million
that were then found, and now represent three quarters of an hour of the film. I am
partly responsible, but it all seems odd, I didn't believe it was going to stop and
leave everyone in limbo, with no one taking any decisions, least of all the decision
to put a halt to the enormous sums of money being swallowed up in set designs that
were finally never used. We even had to finish the film twice. We resumed filming
knowing that we couldn't go through to the end, and then filmed again a month
later. All this enabled people like Dutronc[*] to claim that we filmed for eight
months, although in fact it was only four, which was already a lot. He said other
things as well, while claiming it was nothing to do with him. I realized that, out of
the ten films I'd made, five have been stopped during filming, one of which, *Loulou*,
was stopped for over a year. Can you imagine making a film, all the time knowing
that you're almost bound not to finish it? With *Loulou*, it wasn't my fault. Isabelle
Huppert left for a year to go rollerskating with Cimino. Then the producers went
bankrupt, so for months we screened the film with chunks missing. So, all in all, ten
films, five of which were filmed in two parts. You must admit that it's sod's law that
it always falls on me, who has a reputation for causing trouble. Do you believe that
for one minute? It's masochism, it doesn't make sense. Right from the start I had
problems, as I was up against a wall, I felt like a reject. One day, when I'm calm, I
should write all this down like a police report, objective and without bitterness.

[*] Jacques Dutronc, who played Van Gogh.

Which are the sets you didn't use?
All of them. A team of set decorators spent a month doing nothing. Twenty people being paid. Did you notice that you don't see any exteriors in the film? That's another thing, critics who know everything. Like at school, when you did something, and then someone, who was usually ignorant, took your hand and told you what you were trying to do. For instance, I was told that it was intentional that you saw nothing of Auvers. Or that you don't see Van Gogh painting. In fact, I had no choice in these matters. But I cracked it. I work best when everything is going wrong. That's not to say that things must go badly for me to perform well, and that I deliberately cause trouble!

Why were these sets built?
Because I was having problems. There was also an element of incompetence. People were employed to do jobs that they weren't capable of doing. There are people, even people not in the world of cinema – my mother-in-law for example – who question me, saying that, as I'm the director, it's up to me to deal with these things. We should have changed the sets. I didn't do anything for weeks, because I thought that, with the team I had, it wouldn't be possible, and that if I got a new team, it might be even worse! With my assistants, it was the same thing. This can be seen as weakness, but in fact it's a sign of strength. For weeks I turned my head away every time I had to walk past those dreadful sets. I'd walk past a pile of stones, and wonder where everyone was, and then be told that they were at the station. So I'd go to the station only to find it just as it was when we first picked the location. Where they actually were was in a workshop in the Richelieu station, where all the railway equipment was, and where they were apparently working on things. But they were actually doing nothing. Obviously, if I'd been the boss, I'd have done dreadful things like stopping shooting for a week, sacking everyone and getting things on to a saner footing, which would have worked out much cheaper. But I wasn't the boss. The boss took no decisions, and so wasn't really the boss, either. He just signed the cheques. Judgement was then passed on the film as it is. And it shouldn't be as it is, there's so much missing. It's OK, but you don't see all that should be in it, and isn't there.

Did this problem with the set design result in your changing your mind en route, and going for natural sets rather than studio sets?
No, because my sets would have been realistic, natural anyway. But these are lifeless, if slightly less so than *Tous les matins du monde*, in which there isn't even a fly! You can hear signs of life in the soundtrack, but you see nothing. I feel this way about *Liaisons dangereuses*, despite its qualities. There's none of the life of the times, although we know perfectly well that a chateau at that time would have been bustling with people, and animals from the adjoining farms. It's the first thing to put in if you are a film-maker, even if you take it out later on. Because of that lack, *Tous les matins du monde* is on a par with a TV soap opera – sometimes

there's more life in a soap. But I'm getting away from the subject.

Despite your protestations, we get the impression that this lack of life is deliberate. For example, the fact that we don't ever see Van Gogh painting. Most films about painting fall into the trap of showing someone painting. The only two that don't are Tarkovsky's *Andrei Roublev* and your film.
I think we still show too much of it, I cut some shots in which he was simply holding a paintbrush, not even painting. I find it all so false. Sadly, in some scenes, such as when Marguerite is posing for him at the piano, we see him painting outside. It's dreadful. Resorting to using the hand of a real painter is awful too. To make it credible you need a look, a feel. I just had to let the piano scene ride, I was so stunned by the child's performance, and I thought that if I said 'Cut!', she would think that she wasn't doing it right. Anyway, no one sees anything. I could have put in some link shots, but putting separate shots into a sequence like this is very unsuccessful.

You mustn't forget that most people see a film only once, and they aren't aware of the details that worry you.
That's true. That's something interesting about the cinema. It's worth thinking about. There is no reason why people shouldn't see films several times, but fewer and fewer people are really capable of, or interested in, discovering things. Those who have this awareness and knowledge, this desire, and who go back again and again to see a film – these are the people we should primarily be making films for. We make concessions all the time, but it never pays off in the long run.

You manage to avoid a trap by not mindlessly showing us the painter producing his pictures. Remarkably, however, you seem to lend the landscape which Van Gogh is about to paint an indefinable quality which enables the viewer to sense the inner metamorphosis which transforms a panorama into a painting.
Thank heavens for that! I wish I did it more. Your remark is an indictment of Minnelli and Huston. In *Moulin Rouge*, he had living characters in the foreground and *tableaux* in the background, which makes everything look like waxworks. By the way, I have to say that wide-angled films don't really work these days, never mind what's in them. The films that work are shot in close-up. That means cinema is dying. Which is a relatively new phenomenon. Great pre-war film-makers, even post-war, made wide-angled films that moved. For instance, yesterday, I was watching *L'Auberge rouge* again, which is full of defects: it stinks of design and cardboard skulls, it's heavily over-acted. All the same, it's in a different class from today's films, which look like they're taken out of a how-to-make-8mm films manual. I've told myself so often, 'Why don't I just go and make a film like that? It will be less trouble and maybe it'll do well. Then I can shut my gob, I won't say a word, I won't say I copied their style.'

Take the extras in *Van Gogh,* they're not right yet. Like the set – only things weren't quite as bad. There was a girl, Marie-Jeanne Pascal, who worked with me, she was very good. But I didn't have the time to direct the extras properly, to mix them up. That's happened to me before, in several films. You can't imagine the work involved. I've been making films for twenty years and I've never liked what I do. For instance, when we reach the water's edge, with the family – that was shot very fast. When you see what it was like just before we started shooting and then the result, which suggests that the camera was there just by chance, not like it's in 1890 at all but as though something living had been recorded – when I contrast that with what others are doing, then I see that they beat you at the finishing-post, I mean from a commercial point of view.

Actually, I don't think *Tous les matins du monde* is all that bad. It gets by, it's an honest attempt. I often compare films with sport, even though they have nothing to do with each other. But the fact is that it is always the best – those who run the fastest, who jump the highest – who tend to win. If Carl Lewis is in a race, he doesn't come eighth, like French runners do. He comes in first or second, he's there. With films, you're there, you're doing well, and suddenly a bloke shows up, he's there with you, you have no idea what he's up to, it's as if he'd appeared on a moped, hopped off ten yards before the finishing line and then, bang, beats you. You can't believe your eyes, you wonder what it means.

If you were to be compared with a painter, you'd be more like Degas or Cézanne than Van Gogh. You're closer to bathing and the Montagne Sainte-Victoire than to sunflowers or a starry sky.
Yes. They're pretty awful. When I started to paint, I was twenty years old, I adored Van Gogh. I grew to like him less and less. A long time ago, I wanted to make a film about him, not out of admiration but because the story his sister put together was good raw material. Otherwise, I'm more interested in, say, Seurat's last year. Just as, other things being equal, if I was going to adapt Bernanos, I'd have been better off doing *L'Imposture* and not *Sous le soleil de Satan*.

To return to Van Gogh, I've just mentioned Seurat. What beginners like about Van Gogh, is the ease with which he works. You couldn't buy pictures like that at the time, it would have been unimaginable. It was out of the question. To answer your question about my choice of landscape in which to show Van Gogh painting, I'd already made a film at Auvers. Loads of painters went there. Which is why it seems a haunted place. There is a legend. There are those two oddballs buried side by side. But I didn't try to establish a connection between the pictures and the place as it appears in the film.

So you opted for Van Gogh rather than Seurat for narrative reasons.
In the first place, it would have been hard to find an actor to play Seurat.

And a producer to produce a film about him.
Listen, Toscan de Plantier has many failings, but he'll do anything. The proof is *Sous le soleil de Satan*. That was loony. You're probably going to say I'm obsessed with the box office, but Seurat would have sold thirty thousand tickets, no more.

Sous le soleil de satan: Father Donissan (Gerard Depardieu) and his temptress Mouchette (Sandrine Bonnaire)

Anyway, films about painters never work. Though, for the first three weeks, we thought *Van Gogh* was going to do well.

The film's been seen by 1.4 million people in France. That is remarkable. People don't go to the movies now the way they did in the 1930s. Everyone went then. Now it is a matter of choice. People go to the movies now the way they go to the theatre, the way they choose a book to read.

I am disappointed in that I expect a great deal of my audiences, I am too demanding. People are facile. Like it or not, cinema needs commercial success. The difference between me and Jean-Jacques Annaud is that if I need a budget as large as he got for *L'Amant*, he can raise the money and I can't. On the other hand, up to a few tens of millions, I can do as I please, which isn't bad but doesn't mean all that much, given that I know a chap who's just made his first film and who got 15 million to make it. I can't remember what I got to make *L'Enfance nue*, but in today's money I'm sure it's much less. The only film I've made which was not for a general, all-ages, audience, was *Nous ne vieillirons pas ensemble*. *Loulou* and *Police* might have made it, I really needed a hit. I really needed to be up there, at least once, with the three or four top films of the year, because you can live off that for a while, like Blier did. *Van Gogh* could have been up there with those.

How did you come to decide to focus on Van Gogh's last seventy days. Was it Toscan's idea? Or yours?

In 1964, I made a short I could show you. It lasted six minutes. At the time, I was making *Chroniques en France* for television, short programmes for French-language broadcasts worldwide, not shown in France. I made about ten of these bread-and-butter projects. One of them was a little film called *Auvers*, which was not just about Van Gogh but about Daubigny too; there were landscape shots of the area, a little rostrum work, not much, in black-and-white. I thought of a film called 'Van Gogh's Last Seventy Days'. It came back to me later. It was one of those ideas that don't go away. I've made two of those running, *Sous le soleil de Satan* and *Van Gogh*. It was meeting Daniel Auteuil which got me going. I should have known better. When an idea lies around for a long time like that, you mustn't touch it.

What you say may be true in general, but it isn't in this instance.

The idea came to life when I met Auteuil. He called me and said, 'I want to work with the best directors, with you.' He'd met Bernard-Henri Lévy and wanted to shoot his Baudelaire. Just as *Tous les matins du monde* has a faint air of warmed-up *Amadeus*, so Auteuil wanted to star in a kind of *Camille Claudel* revisited. Baudelaire had a faint air of that. I started to read the thing, but I didn't get to the end. I couldn't see myself doing a period piece with all those top hats. I didn't feel like doing another costume drama, even if I did end up doing exactly that with *Van Gogh*, though in this instance we were fairly restrained. We can discuss that later. The exception is the two dance-hall scenes, which were a bit hasty, a bit 'let's get it in the can'.

I'm giving you a psychoanalytic interpretation here, though it may not seem like that. You're the one on the couch, but I'm the one suffering. This is how I make a film. I meet a nice chap who commissions me, but doesn't put money on the table. He does bring a bit in though, because with his name someone like me can get a bigger budget. So I say, 'I've got something I want to do.' This is exactly what happened with Granier-Deferre's *Le Fils*, scripted by Graziani, and *La Gueule ouverte*. Graziani wrote *Le Fils* for Montand, a story about a son returning to see his mother who is dying. So I said to Graziani, 'I don't see it like that. If I were to make a film about my mother dying . . .' Which is how it all started. I made *La Gueule ouverte*. With Autueil, it was worse because I got commissioned and was persuaded to do something I didn't particularly want to do anyway. But I don't mind. What you do counts at least as much as what you intended. And when we eventually agreed to make the film it was like stepping back in time. I wanted to make 'All Van Gogh', or 'The Tumultuous and Passionate Life of Van Gogh'. We wandered about Arles a great deal, which I finally discounted because the fact that Gauguin was involved bothered me. Then I decided I would include the Saint-Rémy phase and stuck to that for a time. But it no longer fitted. The project had changed. So I looked for a new place. The production designer had found an old people's home at Carpentras, which is magnificent. It is going to be preserved and renovated. The residents – who are not mentally ill – would have made brilliant extras. They could have occupied the screen for whole minutes at a time. Daniel Toscan let me know the script needed pruning. So then I saw the film as a kind of Simenon: Van Gogh steps off the train, he calls on Dr Gachet . . .

Auteuil at first believed the film could be made the year we met. But it was summer. Everything was all dry. There was nothing. In August, we abandoned that plan. We would have had to put it off for a year. And I had done the screenplay. But Auteuil had agreed to do *Les Fourberies de Scapin*, so there was a bit of a struggle between us. I said, 'You can't do that, it's Molière's worst play. I ought to know, I put it on. It's incredibly dull, it doesn't raise any laughs these days.' I feel sorry for him. If he'd done Van Gogh, it would have put Ugolin [the character Auteuil played in Claude Berri's *Jean de Florette*] in the shade.

Why open the film with a shot of Van Gogh painting? And the hand is yours.
It's an admission that something is missing. There's so little painting in the film, we had to start with that. When we were preparing the film with Auteuil, I tried to find him a drawing teacher, who could teach him to draw plaster casts. In the old days, at the Beaux-Arts, everyone learnt off plaster casts, even the architects: it was a way of getting the proportions right, of putting down what one sees. Well, I discovered that no one teaches that way now, which is hardly a surprise, given the painting one sees these days. So there is no one to teach that method. Even today's 50 year olds weren't taught that way. Just like I, at my age, am one of the last people to have a certificate of education, a real one. Auteuil was quite talented, even though he cheated. What I wanted was to see the way a painter or a draughtsman sees. That was the crucial thing. I'm sorry, once again I've failed to answer the question.

The striking thing about *Van Gogh*, regarding both costume and dialogue, is that though it's a period film, you focus on the most concrete aspects of everyday life so that there is nothing anachronistic in relating the action to 1990.
As far as the dialogue is concerned, the reason is really simple: I didn't think about it. The language is not really contemporary. What people forget when they make museum films, the huge anachronism, is that people never speak old-French. I believe that if you start using period terminology, you might as well give up. As far as the costumes are concerned, things are even simpler. There are plenty of photographic records of the period and it would have been easy to use them. But I wanted to avoid stiff collars and top hats. I was haunted by that. We had some made in London, which were OK but – surprise, surprise – they are not in the final cut. But the naff things – the ones we hired – do appear a couple of times.

Almost every scene has its comic side.
That's not really an element of the writing, it came during the shoot. This may

Van Gogh: a portrait of the artist (Jacques Dutronc)

sound immodest, but I think one of my talents is turning fuck-ups to my own advantage. Which isn't to say I seek them out. When something goes wrong – and this is part of my theory that the real true moment in film-making is the shoot itself because what counts is what's in the can – then I always find a way out. I believe I steered the film towards those comic moments, to the extent of my ability to do so. I've been wanting to make a comedy for a long time now, but I wouldn't know how to write it, I have neither the wit nor the sense of dialogue to write the screenplay. People like Woody Allen, even Audiard know how to do that. I'd need to shoot someone else's writing, though with that person's permission, I'd have to stick my nose into his work. It's true that this is one dimension of *Van Gogh*, but then the expectation is of something heavy and dramatic. I wanted to inject some humour, some fantasy, without – I hope – being too heavy-handed. During the shoot, I kept saying, this isn't *Van Gogh* it's *La Vie Parisienne*. I steered the movie in that direction to make it more fun to watch. Basically, the natural audience for *Van Gogh* are the people who never went to see it. Anyway, I don't think life is all that dramatic. We've all seen people die. Well, to the very end, life hangs on in there. Just because someone's a painter, it doesn't mean they have to go around with this inspired, affected expression on their face. Painting is technical, you do it as well as you can.

I do think that *Van Gogh* was more driven than my depiction allows. That's a weakness in the acting. Just think all he managed to paint and draw in those seventy days! I read in Zweig's bad book about Nietzsche – it could only be bad, given what Zweig is like – that Van Gogh painted really fast. That sounds right, I'm sure it's true. Actually, it's something he could be criticized for. The idea that painting is about gesture came later. It's in a different class. Some of his contemporaries, like Seurat, went on preparing their canvasses and meditating. Cézanne needed up to sixty sittings for a portrait and redid the picture from start to finish at each sitting. In terms of portraiture, the result is not always as good as Van Gogh's portraits, even if purely in terms of pictorial achievement there is more to it. Van Gogh, on the other hand, could do up to three pictures a day.

There is a lot of you in the character of Van Gogh, for example in what he thinks of Aurier, the critic, who wrote a complimentary piece about him but also about other, minor painters, and in his harsh, connoisseur's opinion of colleagues' work, such as the comment that Cézanne was bad at painting the sea. It sounds just like you!

Yes. It's like *Positif*. I'm sure you write flattering pieces about Tavernier and Jacques Doillon! Having said which, I may express opinions through the character's mouth but he is quite unlike me. I exercised restraints in the remarks about critics, I could have gone much further. As far as I'm concerned, the best pieces are demolition jobs. I prefer negative criticism of my own work. When someone who is reasonably silly and not very well-educated – I mean critics in general – decides to lay into a film, he turns quite nasty, he seeks out the flaws and often gets it right. Whereas praise . . .

The film treats female characters with kindness whereas Gachet and Theo get off less lightly!

Which didn't stop some critics saying the film was misogynistic. But you are quite right. Perhaps I had to wait till I reached an advanced age before I could show men and women in a relaxed relationship. Before now, I have depicted the bitches I came across in my life.

The relationship between Marguerite and Cathy is entirely fictional.

Nothing is known about them. There may not have been any contact between them at all. I felt that there must have been some kind of love interest, though this might come across as quite feeble. There's nothing hard, nothing like Blier there. Nowadays people worry that if you don't go for, 'Come and have a butcher's at your mother's arse, get those buttocks apart', they are not really moving with the times, they feel they are being backward or soppy. I could be a lot tougher than Blier, but one exercises a degree of restraint, especially as one grows older. Richard Brooks died yesterday. I remember when he was making *Looking for Mr Goodbar*, he was sixty-two at the time, I felt the subject wasn't right for someone of his age. At the time, I was a lot younger than he was. I felt he overstepped the mark, there was something embarrassing about the old goat having a go past his sixtieth birthday. Now I'm that age myself, I feel differently! Because I feel that if you aren't up to treating certain subjects, you may as well give up. If you can't tackle one area of interest, you're probably past it in general.

The striking thing about *Van Gogh* is that you alternate between using leaps in time – like with the suicide scene – and using real time, or even expanding real time.

I have a feeling that leaps in time are a sign of weakness. Incidentally, people are thought to be good at dramatic construction when they are good at duration. No one except Tolstoy – I advise you to read him on the subject, it's quite something – ever dared criticize Shakespeare. Well, I've played in *Julius Caesar* and I don't like it much. There's nothing like acting in a play to get to know it because you repeat it over and over again, you end up knowing it almost by heart. I only had a small part – Ligarius – and one scene with Jean Chevrier at the Nîmes festival. I have been accused of not treating the most significant scenes in a story. I have to admit that I don't know the difference between strong moments and weak moments. As to the suicide, you know how Minnelli dealt with that. Van Gogh is painting a crow, a cart drives by, and Bob's your uncle. He's lying dead beside a tree-trunk. That's what people expect. Everyone knows Van Gogh didn't die out in a field and definitely not during that famous picture of crows. The letters don't tell us what he was painting two weeks before he died. There is one unfinished painting which might be the one he was working on at the end. There are several versions of the suicide story: there's a peasant who is said to have seen him talking on a road, then killing himself in the farmyard. There's the unbelievable story of a load of toffs who used to come down to the water's edge and who were friends of his: one of them is supposed to have let off a shot and mortally wounded Van Gogh by accident.

As to the leap in time, it came quite naturally. I felt there was no need for explanation. That was a mistake. People know nothing about Van Gogh's life and nothing about his work. Nowadays – and this is truly a sign of the times, we've been in major decline for decades – only one thing matters, and that's money: a picture is worth 400 million francs, so that makes him the greatest painter in the world. That's all they know. This is a good time to tell you a story. We had a meal in a good restaurant which recently closed, unfortunately. One of the waiters had seen *Van Gogh*, like quite a few people who know me. Well, there was one thing he didn't really get and that was the death scene. He wasn't sure if he'd followed it properly or not, but he reckoned that the prostitute had sent one of the men to kill him out of jealousy. When you hear that, you know he's right. Audiences that know nothing about Van Gogh are accustomed, because they watch TV series, to know exactly who kills whom. And if there's a mystery, it's always solved at the end. The funny thing is that I was going to call the film, *Who killed Van Gogh?* I also liked *Dr Gachet's Daughter*. It wouldn't have made much difference.

80

The other nice idea, at the end, is the landlady who gets her leg stuck in the staircase after Van Gogh dies.

That should have fitted in before the death. I'll probably recut the film to make it work like that. It will make Theo seem hateful. It will mean he comes to pay the rent before his brother dies. And he is not particularly nice as it is. The episode came quite naturally and I believe that if I hadn't told people about it, they would have got it. The point is, life goes on. It's like the contrast between the guy in pain and all the people dancing. It's the same sort of thing. But when that sort of thing comes at the end, the effect is different. Especially, now that we've added a 'He was my friend.' It should have come when he was still upstairs with someone watching over him.

The music is very discreet. Then at the end it gets very loud, with the Honegger.

At first, the ending came like an axe-blow. Perhaps it was better, but there was something unsatisfactory about it. Theo appeared at the window in a room we'd never seen him in before. Consequently, one wasn't sure where he was – some people thought he'd gone back to his apartment in Paris, to put his tie on. The soundtrack – with the woman getting her foot stuck – made sense of it, but it wasn't all that clear. So I added the scene with the painter at the end, which was never very convincing. The original thought was that Marguerite would appear thirty years later and that the scene would be longer. But as she hasn't aged, people didn't understand, they thought the scene took place the next day, which made no sense. We even had a van drive by to show time passing. Now, it isn't very clear. People wonder what is going on. I was fond of, 'He was my friend', I didn't want to lose that. It's a quote from *Moonfleet*, but it works better in *Moonfleet* because it comes over a wide-shot. I think I'll cut that shot out. The film will end with Theo shutting the door.

It is now one year since *Van Gogh* was shown in competition at Cannes. With hindsight, what do you think happened?

I've got a cuttings-book from the festival. The press is bad, which is incredibly unfair. I don't mind telling you that by the end of the edit, I thought *Van Gogh* was the best film in France since the war. When a film is released, you need to believe in it and the fact is that, to an extent, *Van Gogh* was up to my expectations. But now I know it's not good enough. If I was the only judge, but I am not. There are lots of reasons why no one can make the best film in France since the war. In any case, those kinds of competitions are a bit like the Tour de France, I don't much care for them. I really feel that you can't let the kind of press coverage that we had at Cannes pass – it's unforgivable. Editors should sack critics for writing that kind of article; that's assuming editors are any better than their journalists, which is often not the case. Usually they're worse since they have to play the guard-dog. I hear that one woman journalist was sacked, but I don't think that was the reason.

People wrote that the film was ill-received at the public screening at Cannes, which is untrue. That kind of thing has no impact on the box office, but it would be nice if people got it right. Anyway, there was one thing at Cannes. The sound mix was only temporary. The sound, as I'm sure you know, is awful at the Palais. During the mix in Paris, I'd gone off for a few days. That's the kind of silly mistake I often make – really one should stay around. They muddled through by themselves interpreting the sound after their own fashion. It wasn't too bad, but I wanted something very loud. And suddenly, during the Cannes screening, in the waterside scene, I heard the sound vanish, the music was inaudible. The theatre didn't help. Anyway, after that, I couldn't concentrate. When we stood up for the applause, at the end, I knew there were a few alterations that needed doing, childish little things. We went up to the actors, kissed them, shook their hands. That way, you getting the clapping to last a bit longer, there are always people timing these things, though the timings they get are always wrong. I like playing that sort of trick, I'm a bit of a ham, really. A big ham.

Interviewed in Paris, 13 March 1992

Bertrand Tavernier on *Un Dimanche à la campagne*

interviewed by Michel Ciment, Jean-Pierre Jeancolas,
Isabelle Jordan, Paul-Louis Thiraud

Bertrand Tavernier

Originally a film critic, Bertrand Tavernier is one of the few French film
directors of his generation with an established international reputation.
Films include *L'Horloger de Saint-Paul* (1973), *Que la fête commence* (1975),
Le Juge et l'assassin (1976), *Coup de torchon* (1981), *Un Dimanche à la cam-*
pagne (1984), *Around Midnight* (1986) with jazz musician Dexter Gordon,
La Vie et rien d'autre (1989), *L627*, *L'Appat* and *Capitaine Conan*.

This interview refers to several of Tavernier's films, notably a documentary
on jazz and the American South; *Coup de torchon*, adapted from a Jim
Thompson book and set in Africa; and *Un Dimanche à la campagne*, made
three years later, which is an intimate portrait of an elderly painter sur-
rounded by his near relatives and which exhibits the elegance, the accomplished acting and sensitive writing that typifies the best of Tavernier's work.

Un Dimanche à la campagne
Seventy-six-year-old artist Ladmiral (Louis Ducreux), a widower, wiles
away the time in his country home, ministered to by a housekeeper
(Monique Chaumette). One Sunday in 1912, he receives visitors: his son
Edouard (Michel Aumont), his daughter-in-law (Genevieve Mnich) and
their grandchildren, followed by his unattentive but adored daughter Irene
(Sabine Azema), of whom Edouard is frankly jealous. The day passes, the
family leaves, and Ladmiral returns to his easel . . .

The striking thing is the diversity of your work. You don't lock yourself into any one particular brand of film-making. Every new film opens up new territory. What is it about you that makes this so?

I need every new project to be the opposite of whatever preceded it, and yet to draw on what preceded it too. I always want to head off in a new direction. And I feel strongly that I want to express so many different things. For instance, I'd like to try another period piece, set in the Middle Ages.

***Coup de torchon* was ironic and grotesque. *Un dimanche à la campagne* is quite the opposite.**

Just as *Coup de torchon* was the extreme opposite of *Une semaine de vacances*. And yet I think my last three films have a great deal in common, in terms of how they are directed, in the way the camera moves – which is always governed by my stubborn notion that human characters must be depicted in relation to the environment which contains them. I see camerawork as melodic rather than strategic. I have a feeling that sets, locations, design are unusually significant in my films. They are not on a par with the extras, but organically connected to the actors. People have commented on the Ardèche landscapes in *Le Juge et l'assassin*. In fact, there are only fourteen minutes' worth of exteriors, out of a total of two hours and five minutes. And yet the impression of being out-of-doors is very powerful. Similarly, I feel that Glasgow is very present in *La Mort en direct*, though there are few actual shots of the city.

Coup de torchon

84

In *Coup de torchon*, there was also the pleasure of having a Steadicam to play with.

On that subject, I would like to make something clear. Referring to *Coup de torchon* in *Cahiers du Cinéma*, Michel Chion wrote that Steadicams 'meant that it is now no longer necessary to have a sense of what is going on off-camera'. One day, I discussed this with Chabrol. We decided we had no idea what he meant. Anyway, depending on one's opinion of a director, or of a film, one can prove anything one way or another. The photography in *Coup de torchon* is restless, all right, but that is a deliberate effect. I adopted this style because it was diametrically opposed to that used in the films that I was using as a reference: French colonial films of the 1930s. The design of these films is entirely based on a symmetrical design built around a diagonal axis across the screen. The eye is drawn to the centre of each shot, regardless of whether what you see there is the star, or a mere horn-player in the band. There was always a notion of 'composition'. But what I thought was interesting about Steadicam shots is that they have no centre. They give an impression of floating. Besides which, they give one a great deal of freedom with the actors, which long tracking shots don't allow – at least not under African conditions. The texture of Steadicam images also distinguished the style of the film from that of certain pre-war films, which are otherwise very similar to *Coup de torchon*. Also, the Steadicam effect was reminiscent of the world of Jim Thompson's novels,[*] in which you seem to have your feet on the ground, but you are always stepping into a minefield.

This is a form of madness, but calculated madness

That's precisely it, and you never know whether it's simulated or not. You find this mental instability even in characters that do not speak in the first person, being described by someone else, who is sane. Thompson expresses this effect by his use of italic sentences, which seem to contradict what was said in a previous sentence, and also by abrupt changes in tone. So using a Steadicam was justified for narrative and dramatic purposes, not just as an experiment.

We didn't apply very much theory. The fights are filmed with a portable camera, because that was the best way to do it. Two different reactions to this film moved me: the first was Fuller's, who, not understanding the French, screamed 'Twin brother!', at the moment where Marielle comes back. Later, at dinner he said, 'Your character is a success. Normally a schoolteacher, dressed in white, climbing on to a train, is a turn-off, reminiscent of *Dodge City*, with Olivia de Havilland and Errol Flynn, or *The Virginian* with Gary Cooper and Mary Brian, which was the inspiration for *Dodge City*. But when I really identified with your character was when, in the train, Philippe Noiret stretches his legs out, forcing you aside so you end up sitting so uncomfortably. That's what I call directing.'

The other moving reaction was Genet's, with whom I was going to make a

---

[*] *Coup de torchon* is based on Jim Thompson's *Pop. 2000*.

film. He said that the subject of *Coup de torchon* was the most beautiful theme ever: martyrdom by abjection, a religious paradox which made it the first ever Chestertonian film.

Did you approach the photography of *Un dimanche à la campagne* in the same way as in *Coup de torchon*?

I asked Bruno de Keyzer, whose first film it was as director of photography, and Jean Harnois, the camera operator, to make sure that none of the camera moves were functional. They had to be designed to augment the effect of a particular action, or emotion. When two characters are walking together, the shot would have to be fixed, or a pan. The only exception was an unavoidable one, when they walk the whole length of the street down to the church. I gave them Altman's *Come Back to the Five and Dime, Jimmy Dean, Jimmy Dean* to watch before the shoot. Because, although it is totally unlike what I was attempting, the camera work is remarkable. Altman had originally planned to cut all the panoramic shots in the film, because he was using several cameras, but finally, they came at such strong moments in the film that he kept them all. At first I didn't like what Jean Harnois was doing, so we did some retakes, and from then on everything went smoothly. The idea is that camera movements should connect characters to their environment and at the same time lend a sort of musical effect, so that the film acquires a kind of rhythm. We often played the Fauré theme before doing a take in order to determine the right pace.

Why did you change your camera crew for this film?

I just felt it was necessary. I have nothing against Peter Glenn, who helped me enormously, but I just felt that I needed a different atmosphere. Glenn knew me so well by the end that he could anticipate my wishes, whereas, in a muddled way, I would have liked to explore other avenues. So I needed a different personal and working relationship. After being used to the very easy and smooth rhythm of Glenn's team, and his moral support, I discovered a silent team, who didn't know me and were marvellously available. They forced me to talk things through and allowed me to make things up as I went along. If I ever work with Glenn again, which I am sure I will, the relationship will be a different one. We have had a lot of fun, but this film required greater serenity. Furthermore, despite the low budget (about 6½ million francs), this is, with *Coup de torchon*, the film I have pre-produced most intensively. We did lab tests, we tried out various lighting styles, we did make-up trials. I owe a great deal to Yvonne Sassinot de Nesles (who was recommended to me by Schlondorff, after she did the costumes on *Un Amour de Swann*), because, for a period film, given the size of her budget, what she achieved was miraculous. The costumes and the sets were carefully planned round lighting and cinematography, so that we were able to manage with a 33-day shoot.

Was the weather a specific problem?

It gave us trouble with lighting. The technique we used, without the white bath, which bleaches all the colours, replacing reds with ochres and golds, served to strengthen blacks and whites. As soon as the light began to fail, from our point of view it might as well have been night, so there were only four or five hours a day in which we could shoot, and ensure continuity. On top of that, the weather in the Vexin changes every half-hour. One day we had to start filming very late because of the local elections, which annoyed Bruno de Keyzer. The challenge was trying to keep up a constant level of invention despite the atmospheric conditions.

In spite of this, you deliberately fade to black...

Yes, and I do the fades in camera, because I don't like noticeable special effects. I don't like the last shot of *Coup de torchon*, because it's too green in comparison to the rest of the film. I think there should be a return to the methods of photography and set design invented by those wonderful prewar craftsmen that modern technology has made us forget. Even with the sophisticated equipment we use today, we can't achieve some of the effects they obtained.

***Un Dimanche à la campagne* could be entitled 'Portrait of an old man as a second-rate artist'.**

Hearing that pleases me, because that is the subject of the film. Pierre Bost's book took a more ironic approach, which is the way he and many others saw that sort

Un Dimache à la campagne: artist and daughter (Louis Ducreux and Sabine Azema)

of artist at the time. Now they are being rediscovered and appreciated in their own right.

Reading the book, we weren't sure how you would be able to deal with discourse on painting, which is by an inner voice in the novel, while the old man is washing and getting dressed. From this point of view, the scene at the open-air café is very convincing. The fact that it comes at the end makes the comments about art seem all the more significant.

I didn't agree with Pierre Bost, who I felt condemned the old man far too soon, in the first ten pages. I knew Pierre well, and I'm sure that he would be happy with the changes I made. He was an extraordinarily humble man, but I think the book was very autobiographical, he saw himself as a novelist and playwright, who despite several successes – plays produced by Jouvet, and discovering Queneau, Giono, Marcel Aymé – was not really successful overall. Out of a sort of puritanical modesty, he chooses to depict himself and his appearance in a comic light. During the war, the Germans released him, because he was so appallingly thin.

Bost saw himself as a minor figure, and I felt good talking about someone in that way. I'm not sure the word 'minor' is correct, but I feel he saw himself as having missed out on a movement. I don't know that he would have been capable of joining if he had tried. I found that touching.

Where did the idea of using Ducreux come from?

The French casting director, Dominique Besnehard, was wonderful, and we had a discussion one day about the actors available to play the old people you need to cast. He mentioned Ducreux, and I told him that I saw him every Thursday morning, at the Société des Auteurs, where authors' rights are discussed. I couldn't see him as an actor; what struck me was the impression he gave of always being half-asleep, he never spoke. Could he act?

I had seen him at the theatre, in *Un monsieur qui attend*, which Losey adapted as *Time without Pity*, in which he played the character that Michael Redgrave played in the film. He was very impressive. He had translated several plays by Emlyn Williams. So, I went up and spoke to him about La Société des Auteurs, and he confided to me that he never opened his mouth, for fear of being chosen to sit on a committee!

That's understandable!

I realized that he was, in fact, extremely attentive, he followed the arguments, the votes, and the speeches. I told him that I had him in mind for a role in the film, and, when I went to his flat, he showed me his picture collection: he was the perfect choice!

He gave us an enormous amount – the benefit of a long, artistic career. He is a very cultured man, splendidly knowledgeable, all of which contributes a wealth of gestures, infinitesimal reactions and behaviour. He embodies the character without actually having to act. The painting which he is supposed to have painted as a young man is one of the pictures in his collection.

In many of your films, there are references to the paternal figure, and strong fatherly images.
There is something in that. Family relationships are important in all my films. I've noticed that, in my films, there are a lot of widowers, single people, or abandoned characters. Noiret is unmarried in *Le Juge*, and is in a very strange situation in *Coup de torchon*. I find this loneliness, and these strange family relationships more and more interesting. *La Soeur perdue* opens with the death of the father.

And *La Mort en direct*?
The father figure we are waiting for throughout the film comes at the end: Max Von Sydow.

It's a new thing for you to alternate between making documentaries and features.
I've been wanting to do this for a long time, but didn't dare. I started, but filming *Soupault* was a shock. My brief was to make a 52-minute film, but there were such wonderfully happy moments that we ended up making three hours.

In the same way that *Soupault* prepared you for Ducreux, and *Un Dimanche à la campagne*, perhaps *Pays d'octobre* can be seen as an extension of *Coup de torchon*?
Definitely! I really wanted to make *Pays d'octobre* to discover Jim Thompson's characters, to find out what Southern people are like, to hear them talk. And when I did, it felt like I was rediscovering my own dialogues. If you delve into Southern literature, you see the incredible connections between people like Thompson and people like William Faulkner or Eudora Welty. This journey was all about tracing roots, I think all my films are about this.

Pays d'octobre is a project which changed course. At first it was about Faulkner, then we realized, Bob Parrish and I, that we were assembling a ton of anecdotes about Faulkner, and we started think maybe it isn't all that interesting to see people say on film that Faulkner thought rats were incredibly intelligent creatures. So we decided to do something different.

We were filming in Oxford, Mississippi, for three reasons. Firstly, Faulkner lived there, and set all his novels in and around there, in Lafayette County. Also because that is where James Meredith came from. Lastly, because there was a great guy there called William Ferris, who runs the Centre for the Study of Southern Culture and has done an amazing amount of research. He took us to dozens of different places that it would have taken us three or four months to discover on our own. He arranged for us to meet loads of people, because in the South, getting an appointment is a nightmare.

One of the few people we had a definite arrangement with was a blues singer called Son Thomas, and he had left for Germany when we arrived. So we had to film his uncle and neighbours. Hence we have the scene with all the unemployed singing the blues in a shed, completely improvised.

The film gradually loosened up, and then came together around a few themes, such as religion. Bob and I were struck by the sense of an evolving world, the world of the South. Everyone talked about the past, but also of the deep desire for change. The South makes much more of an effort to change than the rest of the USA.

Pays d'octobre started out as a very organized project. We had two themes: Faulkner, and the relationship between Bob Parrish's childhood and the South as it is now. But gradually, those two ideas became less important.

Did you choose Parrish because he is a Southerner?
For that reason and because he is a friend. Thanks to him, people were very friendly. As soon as he said, 'I come from Georgia,' people opened up. When Marcel Ophuls came to view a cut, I asked him if I ought to use voiceover and he said, 'Definitely not, the sound is amazing, the accents are all different, don't cover them over.' And he said that what struck him was the fact that there was no condescension on our part towards our characters. Usually, when French people make films in America, they always look down on their subject-matter. 'Hey, we're French, and we've come all the way here . . .' Whereas Bob and I and the rest of the crew really got on with people. The crew gradually entered into the thing.

The crew appears in the film. French people learn about the South not just in terms of what they see through the lens, but also through the characters in the crew.
That was Bob Parrish's idea. At first, he used a second camera and started shooting the French guys. The baseball party was his idea. But Parrish lacks confidence, and when we got to the edit he wanted to cut out most of his ideas. He wanted to cut references to his childhood and was in denial about much of his work. But to answer your question, yes, I decided to put the crew into the film.

Your documentaries are in the first person, unlike your features.
Really? I think *Un Dimanche à la campagne* is hugely subjective, as is *Une Semaine de vacances*. I identify with my characters. I need a mask to talk about myself, it makes things easier. What can I say? It's hard to say what is subjective because I have so many different interests. Calling a film-maker's work autobiographical is facile.

What if he's obsessed with himself?
Obsessed? I don't think I am. Only if he keeps describing episodes from his life. In *La Difficulté d'être*, Cocteau has some wonderful things to say about that. People complained that he was not personal enough because, according to him, 'I have too many hairs in my hair.' Too many interests, too many passions. French people find it hard to understand how a historical movie can be personal. People

have this idea that an autobiographical film is a film in which the film-maker talks about his childhood, or his sexual misadventures, or his military service. But the idea that one can completely identify with a character from another century in order to explore oneself or one's own time . . . After *L'Horloger*, Bost said something I'll never forget. He said, 'You've made a more personal film by adapting Simenon and using screenwriters than if you had written an original screenplay yourself. We got things out of you, we forced you to use them, things you would have censored if you had been on your own.'

In the filmography in the press leaflet for *Un dimanche à la campagne* you go straight from *Coup de torchon* to your most recent movie. Does that mean you don't really rate your documentaries on a par with the rest?

No. It's a mistake. I am more than happy with both attempts, *Soupault* and *Pays d'octobre*. There is no pecking-order. There are some things in *Soupault* which are among my best work, like the last half-hour in which he starts to open up, or some of the times when he gets angry – with Dali, for instance, saying, 'I hope he dies, the quicker the better.' I have a feeling that working on this film has really taught me something. All my recent films have enriched me as a human being, in emotional terms. I learnt something from Soupault. As I did from the people I met in Senegal when I was making *Coup de torchon*. I learnt a lot from an old African with whom I discussed religion and death during the tea ceremony. I am sure those moments are powerful in the film.

Talking about working in film, there's something which has been appearing in the press recently which has shocked me, namely the way Godard and Pialat vilify their crews, saying, 'These people won't do anything, they think only about money.' That's scandalous! Crews reflect the director they work with. An article about Renoir describes everyone having a great time, a stimulating time. I've seen technical crews give all they've got. Personally, I hate confrontation. I need people to feel comfortable. I don't mean it's the only way. I would never say that Pialat's work is terrible because he likes a battle, likes a row. He is made for conflict, with people telling tales on each other, it's ghastly. Though with *A nos amours*, the shoot was not as horrible as usual and the film contains some deliriously happy scenes. Godard, today, is self-tortured. But when I knew him, around the time of *Les Carabiniers* and *Pierrot le Fou*, the atmosphere was pretty relaxed and jokey.

You've adapted four novels and written four original screenplays. Do you see any difference?

None. Both are equally hard and equally personal. I'm writing a screenplay with David Rayfiel which is an original story. It doesn't have a name yet. I'd like to steal a title off a script he's written and not sold yet, *Welcome Home, Well Done*. It's a story about a jazz musician who comes to Paris to die.*

* It was eventually made as *Round Midnight*.

The two films you've made based on 'contemporary' stories are perhaps your least successful, as if plunging into the past, or projecting yourself into the future gave you a kind of beneficial detachment.

Les Enfants gâtés, I agree, is not really a success. I lacked detachment. I didn't like the charm and I was wrong. But I don't agree about *Une semaine de vacances*. It's one of the films I'm proudest of. I wouldn't change a thing. On *Les Enfants*, I made some mistakes. And then there is the fact that it was shot in Paris, there was none of the adventure. I need a sense of adventure in making a film, I need a break from everyday life. Fictional characters are so invasive that I need to do documentaries to take a break, to return to reality. Making a feature film is taking a trip and never coming home.

Interviewed in Paris, 20 March 1984

10   Claude Miller on *Garde à vue*

interviewed by Françoise Aude and Michel Sineux

Claude Miller

Claude Miller was assistant to Marcel Carné, Robert Bresson, Jacques Demy, Jean-Luc Godard and François Truffaut. His first film was *La Meilleure Façon de marcher* (1975) and his third, *Garde à vue* (1981), was a major commercial success. He went on to specialize in films about female adolescence such as *L'Effrontée* (1985) and *La Petite Voleuse* (1988), which starred Charlotte Gainsbourg and was based on a Truffaut script.

Garde à vue (in English, 'The Inquisitor') describes the detention of a wealthy lawyer in a child murder case on New Year's Eve. The film revolves round his interrogation and the cunning way in which Miller plays with the audience's sympathy for, alternatively, the suspect (Michel Serrault) and his interrogator (Lino Ventura). A parallel sub-plot provides a harsh description of bourgeois married life and gave Romy Schneider her last role (before she committed suicide after the death of her child) as the suspect's wife. The three principals are – or were – huge stars.

Garde à vue
New Year's Eve in a provincial police station, and an interrogation is being conducted. Cop Lino Ventura engages in a game of cat and mouse with his witness, wealthy lawyer Michel Serrault, who has fallen under suspicion of the rape and murder of a child. Exposed, in parallel, is the hopelessness of Ventura's marriage to Romy Schneider.

Who gave you the novel, *A Table*, which is the source material for *Garde à vue*?
Jean Nachbaur who worked with Ariane Films, which was Mnouchkine's and Danciger's company. They owned the rights to the book, which had been recommended to them by Michel Audiard. So Audiard is really the original source. Audiard reads a lot of the Gallimard *série noire* thrillers, often at proof stage. He'd loved this book. Which is how they came to be looking for a director. Nachbaur called me. But the whole thing had been set up before I got involved. If I'd turned the project down, they would have found another director.

So you had to deal with Audiard.
He was part of the package. That sounds ungenerous, but I know I'll make it up to him later in the interview. If I was going to take the project on, then that meant I had to take Audiard on too. There is nothing wrong with that. The history of cinema tells us anyone can be responsible for getting a project off the ground: a writer, an actor, a director . . .

And the others came later? Like Jean Herman . . .
Audiard is really a dialogue specialist. He has written screenplays and adapted novels; he's been a director and I know he wants to go on directing, but he's not really good at dramatic structure, he doesn't enjoy that part. What he likes is to have another writer or the director adapt a story. Sometimes, at that stage, he participates in general discussions on how to proceed. But he really gets involved at a subsequent stage. So in this case, I started working with Jean Herman. We wrote an eighty- or ninety-page treatment, without dialogue, and then Audiard used that as a basis for a screenplay.

What about the actors? Were they chosen by the producers or by you?
By me. I chose them before the screenplay was written. The book was strong on dramatic structure and we knew we'd stick to that. So that gave us enough to go on to start casting. No one put pressure on me. I'd been wanting to make a film with Lino Ventura for ages. And I just knew that Michel Serrault would be right for the other character. The producers said OK.

Was it *Pile ou face* that made you want to work with Serrault?
No. In fact, that was a problem. The deal was done while *Pile ou face* was on general release. They were worried it might seem like a follow-up. Yet another film about a cop and his suspect. I insisted, knowing that when the film came out, one year later, *Pile ou face* would be long gone. Anyway, I knew my film would be quite different.

In *Pile ou face*, Serrault's character is small-time. Is that why, in *Garde à vue*, you made him different and grander?
Naturally. In the book, Martinaud comes across quite differently. He's small-fry, a humble employee, a faceless loser, timid, a bundle of nerves, hen-pecked. He's got

a twisted side, but he's an introvert. He's got a black spot in his past which is not dissimilar to Camille's in the film. In other words, his appearance is close to Michel Serrault's in *Pile ou face*. So that led us to think about what we could do with Martinaud. He had to be capable of sustaining a confrontation with Ventura. Otherwise, it would just have been a story about a loser's collapse. The character was born out of Serrault's refusal to be cast in the same type of part as in *Pile ou face*, as well as out of our own determination to do something different.

Audiard gives the impression here of not working for himself; for once, he really seems a part of a team. And Serrault gives the impression of having written his own part.
That is because of the way Audiard works. He cannot write dialogue until he knows the cast. It so happens that he is friends with Serrault. He digs deep into Serrault's personality. He provokes him, by writing lines that Serrault will react to quite profoundly. Some of the lines were suggested by Michel on set. For example, when he's having a go at Guy Marchand about the stickers on the magazine cover. That's something we needed to get the scene going, and to irritate Guy Marchand's character. Since his days with Poiré, Serrault has been a gifted improviser. We needed that skill, it fits the character.

Up till now, you have tended to use actors who innovate, and thus force writers and directors to find new ways of doing things too. Patrick Dewaere, Depardieu, Miou-Miou come from cabaret, but Michel Serrault's music hall background is not dissimilar.
That's right. Michel Serrault has tried his hand at everything. He's had a go at every kind of French comedy. And some drama as well; he was in Clouzot's *Les Diaboliques*; he even played Molière's *Le Bourgeois Gentilhomme* on television.

Were you intimidated? Your actors are such stars.
I was. But it's no different to ordinary stage-fright. When I made *La Meilleure Façon de marcher*, I was intimidated by Patrick Dewaere who was a kind of star, compared to me at least. I was intimidated at the thought of working with Miou-Miou and Depardieu. And in this case too. It's a question of temperament. I'm a timid person.

Who was the most malleable? Ventura or Serrault?
Their physical appearance is deceptive. Lino Ventura is much easier to control, more disciplined that Michel Serrault, who, as he says himself, needs to take risks. He enters into a peculiar relationship with his characters, which is hard to communicate. It's hard to talk about a part with Michel before you start, and if you do, it's pointless because he's quite capable of doing something completely different the next day to what was planned. His genius is that he acts on impulse. He doesn't know in advance what he is going to do. He'd be very unhappy if he was told what to do in advance. He's very inspirational, that's why he's hard to

Claude Miller (centre) with Michelle Serrault (left) and Lino Ventura

control, whereas Lino Ventura is very dependent on his director. Lino needs to see the logic of his character's behaviour, or he feels uncomfortable. Either the director goes along with that, or he pretends to, without openly cheating. What I do with Lino is try and make sure that there's nothing bothering him. If I know that a scene has to end up less cut-and-dried, more ambiguous, less rational, then it's up to me to find a way of getting that. I don't approve of putting actors into a strait-jacket.

You've just expressed a moral conviction. You've said actors shouldn't be put in a strait-jacket. Yet you worked with Bresson.
You're right. Bresson puts people in a strait-jacket, but they are not professionals. I exercise much more control over beginners.

The other key player is Romy Schneider.
In terms of screentime, it's actually a small part, but it is true that the part is crucial. The others discuss her from the very beginning, and when she appears, the whole film changes course. I was doing a Hitchcock, I think. The point wasn't to find a decent actress. There are plenty of those, less famous. But in order to generate suspense, I needed a star, someone who could get top billing, so that the audience would know in advance that sooner or later Romy Schneider was going to appear in the part of Chantal Martinaud. Audiences have lost their innocence. They wait for the star to appear. I took care to show her picture before she appears in person. Hitchcock taught us that suspense is to do with

desire. The audience wants to find out what Madame Martinaud is like, and all the more so because Romy Schneider is playing her. When someone says, 'Madame Martinaud is here', and Lino Ventura goes into the next room, I bring out the full works. She is in the dark. The light is switched on. She turns round. I am showing off.

Lino Ventura with Romy Schneider

It's a bit like Preminger's *Laura*. She is an apparition.
Quite so. Though when I first mentioned Romy Schneider, the producers weren't quite sure. They said we've already got Michel Serrault and Lino Ventura, it would be a bit like spreading caviar on foie gras. But if you're going to use stars, then you have to stick with stars, they become like a means of expression. Romy Schneider was part of the grammar of the film. You mention *Laura*, but actually whenever I thought of Romy's character, the film that always came back to me was *Angel Face*, even though I don't remember it all that clearly. All I can think of is a car driving off in reverse, Jean Simmons at a piano. It was my reference, a way of taking in that smooth, American film noir quality that Gene Tierney epitomizes.

Romy Schneider is somewhat out of character in this film. In Sautet's films she comes across as a generous and warm, almost gushing person. Here, it's the opposite.
True. She's often shown either in a positive light, or as a victim. Even in *La Banquière* she has to struggle against people who are even worse than she is. She has a Christ-like quality.

Combined with a *femme fatale* streak.

I was interested in the way she intimidated me. I was scared to meet her. Seen from that angle, she's a perfect Madame Martinaud. It was her star quality that I wanted, more than a character in the usual range of her parts.

To what extent do you devise your characters' entire biographies, as do some film-makers? We only see a fragment of their lives.

I tend to believe that before and after the film nothing exists. As *Garde à vue* is an interrogation, I knew there would have to be times when the characters would discuss their past, dredge up things from another time, which as a member of the audience I always find somewhat frustrating because these are things I am not allowed to visualize.

Martinaud remains opaque to the end. Does the audience need to know whether or not he is guilty?

He is not guilty of murdering the little girls. Some members of the audience may have doubts, but by that stage attention is supposed to have shifted to Camille's story. I'm not interested in knowing who killed the girls on the beach and in the wasteground. Martinaud cannot legally be held guilty and that is the end of the film.

The question of guilt then shifts to Chantal Martinaud. Why does she kill herself? Is it because she is a potential murderess and that she has failed to obtain the death penalty for her husband? Is it because he is a free man and that she is going to have to live with him again? Is it because she is ashamed?

I thought of all that. She kills herself for all those reasons. Either she commits suicide because her revenge has gone wrong (which would be fairly small-minded of her), or because she lacks the courage to face Martinaud. What can they say to each other? Her death is the consequence of a life that has gone all wrong.

So she kills herself for the same reasons as Martinaud confesses to murdering the little girls?

Yes. They are failures. Martinaud's final words, 'Gallien! Gallien!' prove he is hopelessly in love with his wife. She is very beautiful, more beautiful than he is, and his love for her is fetishistic. She humiliates him. Their home life must be unbearable. His last words mean, 'Gallien, what is left? What has happened? The horror!'

Chantal's behaviour is that of an outsider too. Your films have all these outsiders inclined to murder. Martinaud's release, from Chantal's point of view, means that he might go to Camille again, and she might therefore end up rejected again.

Certainly, feeling an outsider, feeling guilty and punished for it, are feelings that make me violent. Chantal is, in any case, rejected on moral grounds. She accuses her husband of making a gesture towards a little girl. This gesture is not shown, it is off-screen. 'I won't tell you what he said, but he was speaking to her as to a woman,' she tells Gallien. Then the child smiles and we return to Chantal saying, 'He had no right to make her smile like that.' The notion of right has a sexual connotation. Legally, one is not allowed to interfere wtih children sexually, but here one is not even allowed to make them smile. In Nicholas Ray's *The Savage Innocents*, Eskimos talk about 'laughing together', meaning to make love. Chantal's reason is puritanical, but that doesn't mean that all perversions are legitimate. Having said which, the trouble is everything that precedes such a gesture, not the gesture itself.

There doesn't even have to be a gesture. Verbal fascination suffices. On the other hand, one can see Chantal as just jealous. She hates her husband, but she wants revenge as though he had betrayed her.

As you say, it hardly matters whether Martinaud touches the child or not. As far as Chantal is concerned, she won't have him having a relation with anyone else that he can't have with her. That means she is frustrated and frustration makes outsiders of us. I emphasized the images of Martinaud with the little girl, making them as moving as possible, in order that the reverse on Romy Schneider's face can be a picture of frustration. I wanted Romy Schneider's character to have some hope of redemption, and not be confined to the realms of informing, jealousy, envy. Frustration softens her a little.

What about the set, the claustrophobia of it? It's like an aquarium, the colours. How far was all that planned?

The more I make films, the more I calculate. I have noticed I prefer lenses longer than 50mm.

You go without depth of field.

That is something I both like and regret. Sometimes, the staging requires depth of field, which means I have to work in a studio because I have to move a long way back. I have discussed this with Claude Sautet, who uses them too. He said, 'Oh yes, the aquarium effect.' Without going so far as to quote Bachelard, I feel the form must be at one with the content and I seem to return to that particular form. It gives the characters greater presence. I use lenses which probe facial expressions. That is what gives my films their formal coherence.

In an earlier interview you talk about Bresson and Godard more than Hitchcock.

I am more and more interested in the erotic dimension of Hitchcock's work, in his Grace Kelly films and in *Notorious*. He uses a smooth and glamorous image to make the sexual dimension more explosive. Grace Kelly's and James Stewart's kiss in *Rear Window* is masterly. It's a subjective, personal matter, but I personally rate Hitchcock very highly as far as sensual suggestion is concerned.

What about morality? Bresson and Hitchcock are sensual moralists – Godard less so.

Sauve qui peut (la vie) is very sensual from a cinematographic point of view. Jean-Luc wants a theory for every situation, but he is always on the brink of an outburst of emotion: that is the contradiction in him and what makes his films so moving.

Childhood is important in your cinema.

In my films, children are part of a sexual theme. One day, I'd like to make a film about children's sexuality. Childhood is a time when sexual feelings are strongest and most repressed. They are strong because a child has no moral qualms and repressed because the parents are there, along with a whole set of other blocking mechanisms. Sex is better and trickier later. There is also the issue of children's feelings about adult sexuality, which is taboo, alien and exotic. The moment when a child discovers his parents making love is a fundamental event in human life.

When Camille observes Chantal Martinaud, does she know she is entering the sexual intimacy of two adults?

Children's innocence is relative. A six-year-old child knows that a remark has a sexual connotation even if he does not respond in the same way as we do. If Martinaud makes sexual remarks, in some way or other, when she sees his wife, Camille knows she is the third element in a triangle. It is a map of a primitive scene in which the roles are reversed. Romy Schneider should be in the child's shoes.

Your male characters are complex, but not the female characters. Why?

They are passive elements in a story which is about men. My subject is masculine desire. Feminine desire is a mystery. I tend to see women as objects of male desire. They are a function of it. I don't see how to change this, other than by working with a woman.

Another reason which explains this aspect of your films is that they are about power struggles between men. In contemporary social practice, women are only just beginning to be allowed to take part in the power play.

Perhaps, though I am writing a screenplay in which the two main characters are women, and I have noticed that relations between them are governed by the same rules of power struggle. Is it that they behave like men? How do film-makers well-known for their depiction of women, like Ophuls, Cukor and Bergman, solve these questions? Anyway, the time to talk about that will be with my next film, with its female leads.

What about your work method? Do you prefer working in the studio?

Garde à vue is entirely shot in the studio – even the lighthouse, which is a brilliant model by Eric Moulard. Everything – except the police station and police head-quarters courtyards. Each of my three films was made the same way. I work like a composer who writes music he hears in his head. I write formal shooting scripts, which describe exactly what I visualize. But first, I produce a straight script, with dialogue, which takes no notice of technical, shooting problems. Producing a shooting script is visual work. The producers of *Garde à vue* allowed me to have a proper storyboard made up by Lam Lê. I talked him through the screenplay and he drew up the scenes for me. Which is how I got the pace. Usually, you only get the pace when you get into the cutting-room, which is fairly haphazard. Hitch-cock, Kubrick and Boorman all use storyboards. It's normal practice in the States. In France, Clouzot used them. For my early films, I did without them, against my better inclination. I had the swimming-pool and murder scenes in *Dites-lui que je l'aime* drawn up. In point of fact, this practice is welcomed by producers because it saves money. For instance, the Christmas scene with Camille might have required parents, guests, a proper set. When the designer asked me about the apartment, I was able to tell him that only a few significant or indicative ele-ments needed to appear. I'll take the storyboard a step further with my next film, make it a real piece of art direction so that the drawings give the film's aesthetic.

What function does music perform in your films? You've used Alain Jomy twice and a gentleman named Schubert.
I even forced Alain Jomy to use one of Schubert's themes for *Dites-lui que je l'aime*. I like film music. I know Eric Rohmer says it is dishonest because it expresses too much. Well, why not? Encouraging people to feel emotion is not in itself reprehensible. What matters is the nature of that emotion. I don't see why one should make moralizing judgements about music rather than cinematogra-phy or acting-style. I watch films instinctively, for their sensual emotion and, as it happens, I feel the same about music. For narrative reasons there is not much music in *Garde à vue*. Delerue and I looked for something which would evoke childhood and popular fêtes. The fête theme is 'coherent', it is a part of the nar-rative. We wanted the 'Camille' theme to swamp the whole film. It is present right from the start, as the camera moves on to the glass wall. I wasn't going to have organ-grinder's music, I told Delerue, so we mocked something up out of five recorders, a kind of improvised organ made up out of five natural sounds. Delerue's *ritournelle* sounds innocent and insolent at the same time; it suits Camille's personality.

What are your plans for the future?
I want to alternate between personal films and commissions. If a commission has some kind of personal resonance, like *Garde à vue*, there's no reason to turn it down. I hope that the success of *Garde à vue* will give me a little leeway to do what I want. It is getting quite difficult to maintain some kind of artistic credibility and at the same time attract finance. I hope that my film's commercial success will

give people more confidence in young film-makers. But things are not always that simple. Anyone wanting to make *La Meilleure Façon de marcher* will take three years to set the project up, and it may not come off.

What about discrepancies in the way films are distributed?

I was unhappy with the way *Dites-lui que je l'aime* was distributed, but not with *Garde à vue*. Two French films came out this week: mine and Gilles Béhat's *Putain d'histoire d'amour*. I've got stars, he hasn't, which is a disadvantage. But there is also a discrepancy in the advertising budgets. It takes money to make sure products are displayed in the same way. And it's the more expensive films that get the biggest promotion budgets. It's the law of the jungle, it's capitalism. The promotion budget for *Garde à vue* was 1 million francs ($180,000), which is 10 per cent of the overall budget. There ought to be some kind of subsidy which ensures that all films are released on an equal basis.

Interviewed in Paris, 27 September 1981

interviewed by Yann Tobin

Patrice Leconte

Patrice Leconte, the director of *Ridicule* (1997), *Le Mari de la coiffeuse* and *Monsieur Hire*, all released in the UK – an unusual hat-trick – started out in cabaret. His first film was a major hit comedy entitled *Les Bronzés*.

Ridicule marks a departure for Leconte, better known for his rumbustious comedies and melancholic portraits of loners: the film is a major costume drama which opposes the affected value system of the court of Louis XIV with the concerns of a sensitive, provincial nobleman. The film is accomplished in the English tradition. It is mordant and well shot, well written and well cast. All this craft was rewarded at the box office.

Ridicule
Versaille, the 1780s. Ponceludon de Malavoy (Charles Berling) comes to Louis XVI's court at Versailles seeking approval for a drainage scheme which will alleviate the blighted lives of his peasants in the marshes of Dombes, Lyon. In Versailles, he encounters corruption in the shape of courtiers the Abbé de Vilecourt (Bernard Giraudeau) and the Comtesse de Blayac (Fanny Ardant), and quickly learns that wit is the fittest weapon with which to intrigue and win influence. He falls under the sway of de Blayac, but because of his growing attraction to the fair Mathilde (Judith Godreche), he risks incurring her wrath and losing all.

Your last three films have all come about in very different ways: *Le Parfum d'Yvonne* is adapted from a book; *Les Grands Ducs* is an original screenplay; and *Ridicule* was a commission. How did *Ridicule* come about?

Jean Rochefort told me about this wonderful script he had read, and said that no one knew who was going to direct it. The author, Remi Waterhouse, was going to do it, but he decided, together with the producers, Gilles Legrand and Frederic Brillion, that the project was a bit ambitious for a first film. So they looked around for a director, and pulled my name out of a hat. I thought the screenplay was brilliant, and told them not to look any further! I was seduced primarily by the quality of the script and its title, but also by the idea of making a film in which I hadn't written one single word! I had been wanting to work like this for ages, but nothing had come along. It's exhilarating, being able to be objective, as you would be of a book you had bought and loved. At every stage, the preparation, the casting, the filming, you can refer back to the impression you received when reading it. It's someone else's possession, not yours. During filming, I hoped I would be able to make a film that would give others the same intense pleasure that I experienced when reading the script. All that gives you wings . . .

How did the writing go on *Les Grands Ducs*?

I worked with Serge Friedman, and, for the first time ever, I didn't pick up a pen once! We discussed it day after day, but he did all the writing. Previously, when I had worked with Patrice Dewolf, we shared the writing.

And on *Le Parfum d'Yvonne*?

I wrote alone, using Modiano's book.

So are you moving slowly away from the whole writing process?

For the moment, yes. I have no pretensions about being a writer. If, for the rest of my life, I was offered screenplays as brilliant and desirable as *Ridicule*, I would quite happily make films without writing. This 'writer-director' business isn't very smart; since the 1960s we have assumed that people make films that they themselves have written, and the result is that when you need a scriptwriter, they are thin on the ground. Then, when a producer who has bought the rights to a screenplay needs a director – and we have loads of talented directors – they say they can't do it because they haven't written it. It's the opposite to what happens in England and the US. I remember Stephen Frears saying that he had been sent the screenplay of *Accidental Hero*, and, having read it, decided straight away that he wanted to make it. At the time, I thought how incredibly lucky he was. Now the same thing has happened to me!

Did you draw on real experience in *Les Grands Ducs*?

No, not at all. I don't believe in this need to know all the facts on a subject. Just leave it to the imagination, and if it ends up being the real story, all the better. It's the same old distinction between the real and the plausible. The real is boring. Those actors who spend three months in a police station, or a hospital before filming . . . At the same time I have never made a film on a subject about which I knew nothing. If I had to make a film about the Stock Exchange, I'd have to research it, which is why I never will!

Do the scenes and the dialogue sometimes change during shooting?
Not very often. Particularly not in *Ridicule*, because I so admired the screenplay, and I didn't feel that I had the right to change anything. Plus the fact that it is very stylized dialogue, which is difficult to play around with. As for *Les Grands Ducs*, everyone loved Serge Friedman's dialogue and no one wanted to change anything.

Did you frame your own shots in *Ridicule*?
Yes, I usually do. It's essential to my style of directing. It's a means of achieving a degree of intimacy with the actors. I don't know whether my films are any different since I've been framing the shots myself, but it has certainly changed the way I work. I do sometimes worry that maybe my directing is limited by it. The pleasure I get from it is about lay-out, not the actual execution of the shots.

Where did you learn how to do it?
Making commercials. On publicity shoots, there are lots of takes and you've got quite a bit of time, because you're filming thirty seconds over two days.

In *Ridicule*, the cinematography is very different to that of *Les Grands Ducs*.
That's putting it mildly! Looking at both films together, it shows how each film you undertake has to be shot in a particular way, each has a specific concept. As the advertising men would say: 'How will I film this?' The idea of *Les Grands Ducs* is obvious, it's like a documentary, camera on the shoulder, no light, fast film. That style works for that script, but I couldn't possibly have done *Ridicule* the same way. Each project is individual, and has to have its own individual style.

How did you go about finding the style you wanted for *Ridicule*?
Easily, I just kept saying to myself all the way through 'The film is set in the eighteenth century, and although I'm not a historian, this enables me to rub shoulders with a different period in history to my own. I'm not interested in filming carriages, castles, dresses, wigs, and flounces, but as the characters have to wear dresses, and travel in carriages, I just get on with it. I have no strong views about period films, but I didn't want to have to ask anyone's advice on how they held their forks at that time and so on. I didn't want this film to be a lesson in eighteenth-century living. When I see that sort of stuff in other films it makes my hair stand on end. The eighteenth century has been filmed every which way. Who needs another lesson? So I tried to discipline myself not to be caught up in the fun of filming the costumes, the colours, the gold. Having said that, you can't imagine how invasive the classicism of the time is. Even in the most intimate, simple scenes, it leaps out of the screen at you.

Ridicule: Bernard Giraudeau performs to an admiring Fanny Ardant (seated)

So does this mean you have to get very close up to the characters?
Not necessarily, you just have to focus on what's going on in the scene, and not on the set, if it's not what is relevant.

You still had to work very closely with those responsible for wardrobe and set design, who had to respect a minimum degree of authenticity.
Of course. But it was up to them to make sure that nobody sat in an Empire chair with the wrong wig on. I just trusted them to get it right. Equally I infused them with a light-hearted approach to the period, so they didn't feel the need to be either dogmatic or respectful. I had a discussion with the boy who was in charge of the wigs, because I hate the white wigs that sit on characters' heads like cow pats. I suggested to him that we use different colours, like real hair, to get away from those sinister white ones.

Le Parfum d'Yvonne **was also a period film.**
Yes, but a period I remember, so it was nice to be able to get into it with the cars, the cigarettes, the clothes – all very evocative. *Ridicule* works in a completely different way.

Did you laugh when you read the screenplay?
Yes, but I was also frozen by suspense with what was at stake in each scene. I was fascinated by the venomous, sharp side of these courtiers, beneath the powder and the smiles.

It is actually a very dark film.
Yes, a serious film. That's what I liked about it: the protagonist who doesn't know

what to do any more , and who is tempted by that court world, but frees himself. There is an inner turmoil for him, as he discovers this strange, chaotic, corrupt world of people who would kill their parents for a 'bon mot', and who commit suicide when they are dismissed from favour. All this powdered brutality is terrifying.

The film tells us that ridicule kills.
For sure. Jean Rochefort, who frequently hits the nail on the head, described the screenplay as a western in which the guns are replaced by witticisms. The seriousness of the film is made tenfold by the fact that everything is always masked to save appearances.

The characters in your last two films develop in opposite ways: In *Les Grands Ducs* they appear ridiculous at first and then, by the end, are making us laugh, but intelligently; in *Ridicule*, the characters are supposed to be intelligent and witty, but end up totally ridiculous.
People often say that I have a chameleon-like quality that enables me to make very different films. You can't imagine two films more disparate – and, at the same time, complementary – than these two, and that's what I like. If I ploughed the same furrow all the time, I might burn out. To come out of *Les Grands Ducs* and throw myself into *Ridicule*, a completely different world, was very stimulating. It made me question everything about the cinema, and directing.

I get the impression that the work with the actors is the same.
Yes, always. I don't chat with them, I just calmly lead the actors towards what I'm looking for. It sounds stupid, but when you love someone, they give you the best of themselves. When I feel that we are slightly losing course, it's easy to put things right again, if there is mutual trust.

Do you see the actors before the shoot?
Not much. On these two films, we met up for the costume fittings, which gave us a chance to play around with the characters. I saw Fanny Ardant quite a bit before we filmed, because she was worried that I wanted to make the Countess of Blayac into a sort of nightmare killjoy. I said that, on the contrary, the Countess was a dazzling, shining character fighting for survival in a pitiless world. Fanny is excellent in the role, we just both needed to feel reassured that we weren't recreating Cruella in *101 Dalmatians*.

It's often said that actors fight tooth and nail to defend and excuse the characters that they portray.
I'm totally behind actors who go into roles with this attitude. However black the character is, what's interesting is to find a side to him which saves him – not spiritually, but in human terms. All you need is a weakness, an excuse, anything. The most pushy and unattractive character is the Abbé de Vilecourt, played by Bernard Giraudeau. He's pleased with himself, a snob, generally unpleasant. I told Bernard to go as far as he wanted in making the character awful, because

we both knew that, in his last scene, in which he is disgraced and rejected, there are fifteen seconds in which he moves us, as does an abandoned puppy. If the character moves us for his last few seconds, that's good enough. So, prior to that, he can be monstrous. You don't need to spend a lot of time with actors, it's not helpful to try and rationalize and intellectualize everything, just keep it simple. The cinema is all about gut feelings, emotions – life!

The lead in *Ridicule*, Ponceludon de Malavoy (Charles Berling), appears to be a deeper version of the character played by Hippolyte Girardot in *Le Parfum d'Yvonne*.
I don't agree. I find the character in *Le Parfum d'Yvonne* very cerebral. An observer, a voyeur, like the film-maker or the author. A Parisian! Whereas Ponceludon is provincial, a man of the land with naïvety and innocence. He doesn't hide behind a door, he pushes it open and goes through, and then puts his foot in it. He's idealistic, and driven, because he wants to save his region of France, and he will use whatever means are possible, even those employed by the courtiers. He can use the same arms as them. At one point, Mathilde (Judith Godreche) says to him: 'You've changed, it's as if you like this comedy, you're becoming one of them.' That's the danger, there's a wonderful duality in his personality. Is he really attracted by the Countess of Blayac, or is she just a means to an end? Both, obviously.

This enigmatic side to him is similar to the character in *Le Parfum d'Yvonne*.
That has a lot to do with the personality of Charles Berling, who I very much like. He is always on the fringe, so when things are too straightforward and predictable in a scene, he can always be counted on to be slightly off-centre.

How did you find him?
I had spotted him in Celine's *L'Eglise* at the Théâtre des Amandiers in Nanterre, and in a few other things, all under the direction of Jean-Louis Martinelli. I couldn't take my eyes off him, his acting was so wonderful. He's never boring, because he always does something unexpected. He reminds me of Depardieu when he was first discovered – that way he has of almost sounding false sometimes, but that's the real him. We looked everywhere for someone to play Ponceludon, someone younger. Charles Berling is in his thirties. Then, suddenly, it became clear that the youthful personality of the character didn't reflect his age, but simply his provincial simplicity. I didn't like the idea of him being twenty-four, because it would distort the relationship with the Countess of Blayac, I didn't want any notion of virginity creeping in. In the film, he finds himself happily balanced in years between the two women.

The film has wonderful moments where we can escape from the constraints of language: the deaf and dumb scene, and the underwater scenes...
It's great to be able to put the words away for a bit. Bellegarde's character (Jean Rochefort) becomes immediately more human, calm.

Like the pastoral scenes in westerns!
We went into those scenes in the most natural, impressionist way possible, with Thierry Arbogast, the cameraman, and then Dominique Hennequin, the editor.

Do you do a detailed scene breakdown before shooting?
No. On *Les Grands Ducs* it was very straightforward. We acted out the scene, pulled it all together, and then brought in the camera. On all my other films, including *Ridicule*, I had the impression that I was a spectator. I want to have the camera watching what's going on, placed to get the best view. Whereas *Les Grands Ducs* was filmed from the actor's point of view. This kind of camera style, on the shoulder, meant the camera became like an additional character in the scene.

Did you do a more detailed scene breakdown for *Ridicule*?
I had an idea of what I wanted, but I didn't want to commit it to paper, for fear of being held hostage to it. For *Tandem* and *Monsieur Hire*, the first two films where I chose the framing, I had written a shot list, just in case I suddenly ran out of ideas. Then I let myself go on *Le Mari de la coiffeuse*. I just decided to take it day by day, depending on the mood of the scene, of the light, of the set. And because this approach worked, I gave up once and for all the hassle of writing scene breakdowns. But on *Ridicule*, I gave it a lot of thought. You can't work out how to break up a scene at the last minute, you have to think well in advance. To begin with, I read the script over and over until I know it off by heart, and try never to lose the overall picture.

Are you interested in the sound and mixing process in your films?
Yes, it's gripping. I had more fun mixing *Ridicule* than I've ever had on a film. At every stage, we had to decide what we wanted to hear in each scene: 'What's this scene saying?' A barouche arrives, stops, and a young girl gets out. Which sounds are the most important? The wheels and the horses' feet on the ground, the snorting of the horses, the door opening, the steps being put down, the feet on the gravel? In fact, the most important thing is that this girl, whom we are seeing for the first time, gets out and looks up. So, in the mixing, the carriage must arrive through the greenery as if on air, with the horses completely silent, to make her appear more mysterious. The mixing process enables us to lead the spectator through the film aurally, being as selective with sound as one is in real life.

And the music?
I don't think I could make a film without music, I'd go demented. I can change musicians with ease; it was Antoine Duhamel who did the music for *Ridicule*. I told him at the beginning of the shoot, I didn't want any neo-classicism. We decided to give the film its own music, not remotely eighteenth century, but to get a baroque orchestra to play it. In *Les Grands Ducs*, I played a nasty trick on the musicians. As I need music to edit the film, we put in temporary bits. In this case we used two Django Reinhart 'swing' numbers. The poor musicians found them-

selves crushed under the weight of this glittering reference. Finally, they wrote a very spirited number which was played by Didier Lockwood, the jazz violinist.

How did you organize making your last two films at the same time?
Knowing that the two films were to be made one immediately after the other, I did the preparation for both at the same time. I had organized the costumes and sets, and done the casting for *Ridicule* before we started filming *Les Grands Ducs*. It was all a bit mixed up. During the shooting of *Ridicule*, I would see the rushes, and then go off to the editing of *Les Grands Ducs*.

So the lives of these two films are intertwined.
Yes, they're a couple, divided by the Berlin wall! There is no overlap. The harder I worked to make the two films as different as possible, the better I felt, and the happier I was that they were coming together at the same time. The funny thing is that *Les Grands Ducs* could easily have been called *Ridicule*, and the other way round!

All your films could be called *Ridicule*.
So could my whole life! But this title could give the impression that I was denouncing the characters I portray, whereas in fact I love them all to bits.

Including those in *Ridicule*!
I basically find ridiculous characters very touching.

The character who hangs himself, after being made to look a fool, played by Albert Delpy, is dreadful. Even for the actor.
The most dreadful character is the old man at the beginning of the film, the Countess of Blayac's husband. He's a wreck, but a noble one. He has to be dumb, expressing himself by grunts, paralysed by a stroke, glued to a wheelchair, and wrapped in blankets to protect him from the cold. And, to top it all, the Chevalier de Milletail is going to come in and piss on him! It's a difficult deal to sell to an actor. And in his second scene, he will be on his deathbed! I found a wonderful actor, but he read the script and refused. I then met him, and explained how embarrassed I was to offer him such a part, and that I completely understood his refusal . . . And then he said he would do it!

In *Ridicule*, did you also feel that you were talking about people around you?
Of course, but I didn't want to make it a film in which people one knows appear as fictitious characters, I can't bear that. The film is set in the eighteenth century and that's fine. I would never have done this of my own accord, as I'm not a historian. So it was great that somebody else suggested it to me. Even though I didn't want to be seduced by the costume drama aspect, I also didn't want *Ridicule* to be timeless, or contemporary. It's a film that is solidly anchored in its time. Courtiers exist now, but they also existed in Merovingian times!

Interviewed in Paris, April 1996

Marcel Ophuls on *Hôtel Terminus*

interviewed by Jean-Pierre Jeancolas

Marcel Ophuls

Son of the well-known feature-film director Max Ophuls, Marcel Ophuls is one of the greatest documentary film-makers in the world. His four-hour *Le Chagrin et la pitié* (1969), about occupied France, was picked up by the BBC after being banned from French TV until the Socialist government came to power in 1981. Subsequent major productions include *Hôtel Terminus* (1988) about the trial of Klaus Barbie, *November Days* (1991) about the fall of the Berlin Wall, and *Veillée d'armes* (1995) about foreign correspondents in the Holiday Inn in Sarajevo.

Perhaps the secret of almost all documentary film-making is how the director chooses to allow the audience to divine his own opinions and temperament. In this respect, Marcel Ophuls is a master and *Hôtel Terminus* is a key film in his career. Repeatedly, he allows himself to be seen knocking at doors that won't open, poking fun at old Nazis or chasing round the back of buildings in dogged, Marxian (Groucho) pursuit of his prey. That the respected author of *The Sorrow and the Pity*, himself the scion of a persecuted Central European Jewish family, should choose to make merry with his investigation of the head of the Gestapo in Lyons adds humanity where there might otherwise be none.

Hôtel Terminus

Ex-Gestapo chief Klaus Barbie, the notorious 'Butcher of Lyons', fled to Bolivia in 1951, having been of some service to the Allies after the war's end. But he was extradited to France, subsequently tried, and imprisoned for life in 1987. Marcel Ophuls' film is composed of interviews with a diverse assortment of witnesses to Barbie's life – friends and enemies, victims and collaborators.

The film seems to me to belong to the same lineage as *Le Chagrin et la pitié*. I see them as two parts of a work on France in the dark years. Perhaps there are more parts to come. But *Barbie*, let's call it that...
I'd rather call it *Hôtel Terminus*.

I don't think you're going to get away from the Barbie name.
I'd like to though because – well, you've seen the film, you know why. There has been a lot of good stuff on Barbie, good investigative work, even on French television. But my foible is to feel that this is not especially a film about Barbie's life.

Which is precisely where the difference with *Le Chagrin et la pitié* lies. *Le Chagrin* starts from an open-minded premise. With this film, there is a single detonator. So you work in a different way.
Naturally. I had no choice in the matter. In neither instance, as it happens. With *Le Chagrin* we were still all at the old ORTF television network, and I was making a sequel to a programme I had made for French television: *Munich ou la guerre de cent ans*, no, sorry, *Munich ou la paix pour cent ans*, it's a Freudian slip. It was a programme which lasted three and a half hours, spread over two evenings on what was then called Channel Two; it was a great success. At first, I was only going to make a sequel. I decided to focus on one town and I chose Clermont-Ferrand. It was going to be a very open affair. I've fallen into the habit of saying that the seven and a half-minute difference between the length of *Le Chagrin* and *Hôtel Terminus* can be explained by the seventeen- or eighteen-year interval between the two films, and, as they are two films about the same period, the surviving witnesses have grown older so they speak more slowly.

To get back to the point, there are many differences between the two films. And a certain similarity, apart from the fact that they are two films about the same period in the same country. Both films are a consequence of the circumstances in which they were made, obviously. Regarding *Le Chagrin*, I used the sincere and honest memories of people who were attempting in 1969/70 to evoke a period which perhaps had traumatized them and which they had not, up till then, wished to discuss. The date is significant in that it was after 1968 and people were speaking in the spirit of those times, which is say an honest and sincere spirit. They were happy to let me try and reconstruct the past. With the Barbie affair, we are dealing with a festival of lies, given that a celebrated criminal trial and a Nazi war criminal are at the centre of things. Under the circumstances, the film became a kind of police investigation leading up to a trial which was likely to take place. But we were not absolutely certain, when most of the interviews were conducted, that the trial would definitely happen. So there is a turning of the tables, which may give the audience some pleasure and certainly gave me some. That is something I tried to build into the edit, the feeling that we are swapping roles, that professional interrogators were under interrogation. Which is why there is often that good cop, bad cop thing, which is so funny. And as I am older, as I am the boss, I often played the part of the good cop, the one who gives the witness a cigarette and says, 'Don't worry, don't worry . . . Didn't you hear him say he can't remember? Leave him alone.' Sorry, I am getting a bit carried away.

Not really. You've introduced a question I wanted to ask. *Hôtel Terminus* seems more controlled to me and you've just confirmed the fact. This affects both your own part and the way in which you edited and built your story. The cutting is faster, the interviews are chopped up, it's more like a cross-examination in an American trial.

It is an American film and a large part of the film takes place in America. That was a result of circumstances. *Le Chagrin* was about personal reminiscences and adventures, each character took the film in a different direction, discussed what he had done, searched his memories, speaking for his children, or for people in the street. The only cross-referencing necessary was when we passed from one character to the next. With this film, apart from acting as investigator and lawyer and plaintiff (I hate the idea of being a plaintiff or a judge), the reason for my being in the film was that I did not want it to seem like I was giving an objective account of events. If I had not taken part and claimed objectivity, apart from seeming pretentious, the film would have acted as a substitute for the trial. I didn't want that. I realized as I proceeded, that I could not have got the film made unless the trial had been about to happen. It would have been indecent, immoral. The only people who could judge this business were the citizens of Lyons, democratically chosen jurors. Representatives of the Republic, the French Republic, had to act according to their conscience, take note of what had happened, judge the facts of genocide, deportation and torture which had taken place at that time on French territory.

Right. I am digressing again. Let's get back to why I appear in the film. There is also the fact that, unless we were going to be boringly chronological, the film was going to leap from one continent to another, quickly, coherently, in such a way as to cover the ground covered by twenty-four witnesses. It would have been a shame to lose one of Barbie's childhood friends, to lose the secret agents. If you look, I think you'll find every one of those participants is necessary. Sergeant Taylor and his German wife are quite different to Lieutenant Kolb, and different again is the Head of the Secret Services, John G. McCloy who is visibly dying and yet still has the courage to lie to protect his boss. I admire him greatly. He had multiple sclerosis. I expect he is dead now. He is attempting damage limitation, as are all the former American agents who appear. I am certain that before seeing us, they all rang Washington, rang the CIA, and that in the evening, as soon as we left, they rang in their report. Everyone plays a role, and the roles were attributed by the powers that be. I had to find a way of communicating all that, of suggesting that *Hôtel Terminus* was not a mosaic of genuine reminiscences but rather a polyphonic tale based on manipulation, lies, half-truths and connivance. Of course, things are different in France, there is the Resistance. But there is plenty of uncertainty and half-truth about the business at Caluire. People are cautious. That had to come across too. One of the curious things about the Barbie affair, and the Barbie trial, is that it begins with the man who tortured Jean Moulin and ends with the children of Izieu. That is very exciting and positive. That trajectory had to appear in the film. The reason it went like that is that war crimes are proscribed after a certain time, whereas crimes against humanity are not. But French and world public opinion evolved in that direction too. There were some very positive, very remarkable developments.

Caluire plays a very important part in the film.
I have to say that I was not especially keen on that. I have this image, I am the man who made *Le Chagrin et la pitié*. One day, at the Brasserie Lipp, Claude Lanzmann asked me, 'So are you going to do for Lyons what you did for Clermont-Ferrand?', meaning are you going to shit-stir, are you going to try and pick holes in the Resistance? Which is a highly contentious thing to say because actually *Le Chagrin et la pitié* is not like that at all. In *Le Chagrin* the heroes all belong to the Resistance. The only thing the film does is to try and show that people who took part in the Resistance were in a minority, which is what they were saying themselves at the time. All the film did was help destroy the Communist/Gaullist myth of the Resistance. That myth is dead and when Chaban-Delmas went to Lyons to try and restore it, he came a cropper. He is an honourable man, his testimony was remarkable but it has had no impact twenty years later. On the contrary, by showing that there were not many Resistance heroes, one points to the merit of those who genuinely took part. This time, of course, by force of circumstance, because of everything involved in the Barbie affair and the Barbie trial and the fears it provoked, we were bound to come across spy stories and political rivalries which perhaps gave rise to treachery. One could hardly avoid mentioning René Hardy's story. But I swear I was in no hurry to go into all that because I knew what would happen, given the fact that I am a German Jew with a French passport, somebody without a country, whose reputation is founded on a film which some people have called anti-French.

But given that I was making a film about Barbie, France, the Barbie affair and everything that goes with it – themes which the trial would have to investigate, if it took place – it was inevitable that I should cover Caluire. And as I am a bit of a maverick, as I seek to be polemical when necessary, I soon saw that the mysteries of Caluire were far from being resolved, and that the behaviour of certain well-known Resistance heroes in that business was far from being above suspicion. And it is not because the trial did not cover Caluire, when it eventually took place, that one can forget the whole business and say, 'It was all a bluff of Vergès.' Things are not that simple.

Did you never consider interviewing Bénouville?
Of course. A request was put in by Claude Bourdet, who is an old friend, with Noguerès. They corresponded. Bénouville refused, unless we were prepared to let him make a statement under his lawyer's supervision, the questions being submitted in advance, in the knowledge of what Vergès and the others who were going to contradict him would say. In other words, he behaved like a French grandee. A powerful French grandee. And I behaved like someone who doesn't like censorship. I sent them packing.

Let us return to the American aspect of the film. What role do you feel you gave the female student from Lyons? It seems to me that as far as American audiences are concerned, she plays a part not unlike that played for French audiences by the chemist's daughter in *Le Chagrin*.
She is a student, a girl from Lyons, who was with Richard Bernstein, the *New York Times* correspondent, in Lyons. She speaks English with a beautiful Maurice Chevalier accent. What she says is, 'Don't for a moment believe that we young people have fallen into the trap of accepting the Gaullist myth of Jean Moulin and a united Resistance. We know the different factions were at each other's throats.' Why include that scene? So that I could return to Daniel Cordier and the questions about the Resistance which arise in connection with the trial. And then the meal has its own function. It's upstairs downstairs. Downstairs is the Lyons restaurant owners and the memories of which we were unfortunately able to use only a very small part, because they are very sarcastic and awkward and funny – for instance Madame Vettard's story about crayfish, the three-star point of view on serving the Nazi occupying force. Upstairs is the new occupying force of the international media, American and Jewish, who, during the Barbie trial, enjoyed slap-up dinners in the same famous restaurants. That was the idea. During the trial, there was a deal of uneasiness and I tried to find a way of communicating that uneasiness. The uneasiness was in the local community in Lyons, 'The world has its eyes on us. What are they going to make of us?' And as is often the case in France, that became a resentful feeling: 'It's none of their business anyway.' But of course it is their business. The Holocaust is everybody's business, and Nazi war crimes too. It so happens that these crimes took place in Lyons.

There is another aspect to the international dimension, something I was conscious of all the time, including when I was feeling paranoid on some German or French or Latin American street. I sensed that some people would say, 'Oh, yes, another Jewish film.' And that affected me as a director and as a participant in the film. If I'd only stood on one side of the camera, I could have dealt with that fairly swiftly, but as I was on both sides, it drove me intermittently crazy. We were discussing internationalization. It is true that I have at least one thing in common with Barbie (maybe there are more, I shout a lot too, though I don't torture people), which is that we are both cosmopolitan, both born in Germany and then driven into exile. In his case, with the torturers, in my case with the others. I don't know the man, but I know that the idea that he is in some sense narrow-minded, or stupid, is obviously utterly wrong. His IQ is high. He understands the people he is dealing with and uses his knowledge professionally. I do too.

I'd like to go back to the paranoia you were talking about. Did you ever feel threatened?
Not in Germany.

I was thinking about Bogotà, not Marburg.
Yes, yes. It's a mystery. See here, I've a hole in my head. Coming back from La Paz, I was in a Bolivian plane, we were re-routed, our plane was inexplicably changed for another – it all seemed entirely set-up. Anyway, the result was that one day a briefcase containing all my documents found its way to Buenos Aires, while I went to Rio. Two or three French consulates were involved in retrieving it, and when I got it back I found that it had been searched and everything inside photocopied. I remained in Rio and there it would seem I was mugged on the beach. I say 'seemed' because I would appear to have lost consciousness for about a quarter of an hour, and when I came to I found myself on the Avenida with a ten-year-old boy trying to explain in Portuguese, with a lot of hand gestures, that I was wounded and bleeding. I was looked after at the hotel, I took two days off and went back to Paris. Two weeks later, an ambulance took me to the Pitié-Salpêtrière Hospital because I had internal bleeding. Which is where the hole in my head comes from. The amnesia remains. I still have trouble with my memory and other problems. The question is, what happened? Muggings are common in Rio, but not on the Meridien beach. Everyone knows, all the petty thieves know, that no one in Rio brings a watch or money on to the beach. So one does wonder whether after the planes being re-routed, the loss of my bag, this was all part of . . . If so, it's nothing to do with the government because at the time the government of Bolivia was democratically elected and it's still more or less in power. But it is possible that Banzer's mates or some mates of the neo-Nazis tried to settle a score. At the same time, one wonders whether real mercenaries wouldn't have done a better job. I believe Lanzmann had much more trouble. He was beaten up several times.

I've grown a little more impatient, a little pessimistic. Listen, from that point of view, too, *Le Chagrin et la pitié* was misunderstood. It's an anthem for France, an optimistic film, naïve even. It's like a Western, it shows goodies and baddies.

Both films end with a baddie, a woman.
Not *Le Chagrin*.

I mean the hairdresser, Madame Solange.
She does not come right at the end. There's Maurice Chevalier and de Gaulle too. But it's fair to say hers is the last big interview.

I see a connection between her and the middle-class lady from Lyons – Madame Hemmerlé, I believe – in *Hôtel Terminus*.
Of course. It's a remake. In colour, colourized. Except it's not quite the same. I think Madame Solange's story is a love affair. In this instance, we're dealing with a woman who was convicted of being an accomplice of a man called Max Payot, who was one of the Nazis' great friends, a gangster, a pimp, a member of the Lyons mafia and also a double agent, a registered member of the London Intelligence Service, who was executed at the end of the war by the Communists before he could go to court. I was introduced to this woman by a writer from Lyons, an expert on that period. He brought me Madame Hemmerlé's book, which was published by Alain Moreau at *La Pensée Universelle*, which means that she paid her own costs. The interview is interesting in that she always downplays her part compared to what's in the book. And as I had read the book the night before, another example of my interventionism, my police techniques, I kept having to intervene to get her to confirm at least part of what she had written.

Both women are shot in a similar way, using their spectacles and the shadows thrown by their spectacles.
Not on purpose. The cameraman was different. I gave no instructions. I play a great part in what goes on in the cutting-room, which is where the tale is constructed. Editors matter a great deal. Albert Jurgenson is a great editor and Catherine Zins comes from a similar background to mine, she's a young woman of Austrian parentage. After the moving testimony of the trial, she encouraged me to make use of that Central European humour which is an essential part of the narration. One has to get one's own point of view across and inevitably one relies on sarcasm or irony. She gave me the courage to do that. Both these editors came to the project late, but they played a greater part in structuring the film than my former editors; previously, I alone had been responsible for the structure of the film. But to get back to cameramen, they are necessarily very free to do as they please, because I concentrate on the person I am speaking to and on interviewing them. I give them certain instructions: for instance not to shoot very close up, to give me lots of different types of shots, to zoom or pan very fast so it can be cut out if necessary. Aside from this, I ask only that they should not disturb the interview and the lights should be set up very quickly. People said about the hairdresser in *Chagrin* that the sight of her fidgeting with the buttons on her jacket was a deliberate intention of mine, but it wasn't. The reason we see her doing that is that as the interview happened very fast – so that she wouldn't have time to call

her lawyer or friends who might have advised against speaking to us – we did not shoot any cutaways. André Gazut, the cameraman, knows that I hate hand shots, but he had no option. I have to admit that as far as photography is concerned, my films are poor; they are dry and careless. There is no time to devise a style. In fact, a thought-out style would be wrong. In *Hôtel Terminus*, the only stylistic device is the use of comedy and this is so obvious that people see the point. There are times when I stand in front of the camera and say 'Yes, we're still in Bavaria' and there's another time when we're with De Castro when he's in one room and we're in another and I'm wearing a dressing-gown. Needless to say, it wasn't shot at the time. I cheat it, and the editing shows, in a way, my contempt for the character.

Our friend Luc Béraud, who saw the film at the Cinémathèque the other night left me a long message on my answering-machine, which is the first time I've had a film review on an answering-machine. He told me that because I have a beard in that shot in the hotel in La Paz, I reminded him of Professor Siletzky in *To Be or Not to Be*, the scene with the two beards. It has to be said that is in two rooms as well. I told him I hoped he saw me as Jack Benny playing Siletzky rather than the real Siletzky. Enough of that. Is childishness allowable in a film about Barbie? The crucial thing, I hope, is that the audience gets Simone Lagrange's and Lise Lesèvre's testimony, as well as Favet's at Izieu. They tell things as they are. The crucial thing is that this mayonnaise made of black comedy, sarcasm and an itinerant set of subjective, police-type interrogations comes together with what happened in Lyons in a coherent and, if possible, artistic manner.

Vergès plays an important part in the film. Did you direct him in the scene in his study?
He directs himself. I'll you something about this scene. There are some things one does on purpose, you could call it directing, though it's a very odd form of directing, a very documentary form of directing. I've never told anyone this. We arrived three hours late. On purpose. We weren't wasting our time during those three hours. We interviewed the Aubracs in the morning. From time to time, the production manager would call Vergès on my behalf to say, 'We're still at it, we'll arrive at such and such a time.' The first call said we'd arrive at one, the second at two, then at three. When we eventually arrived, I went into his office and said, 'This is a wonderful office, we need to light it, it will take at least an hour. Please forgive us. I shall go away and come back again and if you need somewhere to work, please go into the next room because it will take us an hour. He made a very surprising remark, he said, 'Of course, Monsieur Ophuls, you are in conquered territory here.' And that's the reason we started the interview with a phone call, which is absolutely genuine, something he did to impress us, but not set up by us, where he tells a crew from Radio Monte Carlo to wait. Where is the stylistic device? In the use of a very wide shot. We took the time to do a wide shot. That's all. He is at his desk. The camera is at the right height, not too low, not too high. As in Hawks's films, the camera is always at eye-level.

But perhaps your discomfort with the Vergès scene is elsewhere. You were saying that I gave too good a part.

No. Too long a part.
He is a very important character – especially once Barbie is gone and has disappeared. He is an important character because of what he represents and because he plays the relative card. He says, 'Why that particular torturer when there are so many others, in Algeria, in Israel and elsewhere?' He is a link with the kind of hostility and indifference one feels elsewhere, in Bolivia. He is also a connection (though he would utterly repudiate this if ever he were to read this interview) with Le Pen's speech about the Holocaust being a detail of the history of the Second World War. Of course, he says he is not anti-Semitic. I am not sure he is, but he is a man of conviction and yet a cynic, and who, right or wrong, is in the media spotlight. He has been said to have Machiavellian tendencies, right or wrong. I'm not sure he is such a good lawyer. During the trial, when the witnesses for the defence were called, he completely collapsed. His case was hollow. And his summing-up was unexpectedly populist. He said, 'Let us allow these wounds to heal, it is the internationalist lobby which is continually re-opening them.' That is a reference to Jewish people in the media. During that speech, I felt he was referring to me personally, especially as he often looked over at me and we had got to know each other well.

It has to be said that Vergès is an interesting, likeable character. Some witnesses, such as Madame Lagrange, found him repulsive; but in the film he collapses twice. The first time is when we deal with the Dannecker circular about the Final Solution and Barbie's subjective knowledge of it. He collapses on camera and relies on his old trick, namely that the prosecution has failed to let him see this document, which is absurd. It only means that it is a part of the case which is of no interest to him, which is revolting in itself, since when one is defending a Nazi criminal one ought to take an interest in the Final Solution and in one's client's presumed knowledge of it. I think Vergès is someone who needs bringing down to earth.

The film hardly does that.
Yes, it does. In what I'm talking about. And at the end, when he is confronted with Favet, where his cynicism is evident. The film shows he is man who knows how to make a good appearance, who loves the limelight, and who has no relevant arguments to put forward in relation to the Barbie case.

You know, all this is highly subjective. It's the same as with Christian de la Mazière in *Le Chagrin et la pitié*. I quite like de la Mazière, but I really don't see how Simone Veil could say several times, in public – until I told her to shut up – that Christian de la Mazière was the only likeable character in the film. One day, in private conversation, I asked her whether Mendès-France, d'Astier de la Vigerie, the Grave brothers meant nothing. She gave this wonderful reply, she said, 'Huh!' And then she went giving interviews in which she said the same old thing. That's politicians for you. They can have an intelligent conversation in private, then when they go public they come out with any old vote-canvassing rubbish. I'm sick of it now. I'm showing her up. Surviving death-camps to become a Minister doesn't mean to say you're unimpeachably respectable. Her current problem – which is to find a way of moving to the left – hardly warrants our total admiration. After all, given that she is Jewish, which more or less determines the nature of her electorate, she can hardly have anything to do with Le Pen. There is no merit in her refusing to do so. There might have been merit in refusing to join a government in which Papon held office. But there is no sense in listening to one's conscience in an era when the RPR and its allies are dealing with Le Pen in Marseilles. After all, she's the one to have said that her parentage is what makes her. Michel Noir has merit. She does not.

I would have thought the film was a difficult one for French schoolchildren to comprehend, and even more difficult for American schoolchildren. It presupposes considerable background knowledge, or that one has followed the Barbie trial very carefully through the press.
There hasn't been any problem to date, but then the film has only been shown at Cannes and at the Cinémathèque, i.e. in front of quite specific audiences. There has been some criticism already from people who did not follow the trial, who were not in France at the time. I believe we have achieved something fairly miraculous. I've often come across the line of argument you are using in our profession and I am suspicious of it. Producers love saying, 'I know I understand, but will the audience?'

It is not a question of understanding but of information.
I agree it is necessary to be very careful that one is clear, that one cannot rely on information which people may or may not have access to. But I don't believe this film has that problem. I admit I don't stop to think about my film's educational aspect. If there is such an aspect, that's all very well, but a film has its own rules, determined by the complexity of this man's journey, with all the help he got, the double agents. I have never used voiceover commentary, not since I started making documentaries. My stories are polyphonic, based on interviews. This reminds me that when *Le Chagrin et la pitié* was screened by the BBC for the first time, the director of programmes was a wonderful man called Robin Scott. He had me go over to supervise the voiceover and subtitles. He used to say, 'Marcel, the film is crystal-clear but you must realize English people don't know French history. They don't even know there was such a thing as a Free Zone and an Occupied Zone.' So what could I do? He said, 'What I suggest is that I introduce the film in person, and that I have a map of France and a ruler and I indicate where the line between the two halves ran.' I said, 'Fine, that ought to solve your difficulty' and that is what he did. It was fine, except that it added three minutes to an evening

that was already four and a half hours long and it only solved that one specific problem, it didn't solve the problem of those people in the audience who had never even heard of the war. Do you know that studies in the United States on schoolchildren's grasp of geography have shown that young people have no idea where Tokyo is. Art Buchwald wrote a funny column about that. 'The next time there's a war,' he said, 'the boys will bomb Kansas City.'

My reply is very long-winded and it doesn't answer your question. I am sure we could have made some things clearer. *Hôtel Terminus* is easily the trickiest film I have ever made. I am delighted and confident to have emerged from it alive; I really believed that I would end my days in that far-flung edit suite in Billancourt. It was a real delight not just to finish the film, more or less, but also to have good reviews, to be invited to Cannes, then New York, it's like a dream. There were 120 hours of rushes, 80 witnesses, because we could not tell, as we were shooting, what was going to happen. So we had to try and cover every eventuality. Would the trial happen? Would someone die before? Would the trial be dismissed? Would the Moulin affair come up? I think I wrote five different structures. I write by hand, with different-coloured felt-tip pens. I get transcripts of the interviews, copy out everything of interest and annotate it. Other people do this with scissors and Sellotape, but I find that using Sellotape is abstract, I don't really get into the structure of the sentences. I need to identify every comma, every pause in the transcript on paper. I wrote those five structures and I started finding the trip from Neuilly, where I live, to Billancourt exceedingly difficult. There were tough times. I had to change editing crews.

You've just said that the film was more or less finished. When did you decide that the shoot was over?
There was one person we were unable to meet, because he died, and that is something I regret very much.

Hardy?
Yes, René Hardy. Given that we had a mutual friend in Nicholas Ray, and Michel Kelber, and that he was something of a man of cinema, I feel that I would have got something out of him that others did not get. And then there is the fact that his book, which no one has read, *Les Dernières Minutes*, is full of talent. Perhaps it was ghost-written, he was at death's door, an alcoholic and sick, but it is a brilliant and carefully researched book.

Your question is when did I know I'd finished. I thought I'd finished when after the trial I did my last three interviews. With Pierre Truche, the state prosecutor, whom I could not interview before because he was not allowed to give interviews. With Madame Zlatin when I realized that I did not have enough material on Izieu, that Favet alone was not sufficient and that Favet required the support of another witness. And with Rappaport, the lawyer, who says that though the trial was entirely to France's credit, it was, none the less, in spite of its fairness, not perfect. Izieu was a mini Caluire. We could not go into the details of the business at Izieu because there must have been other informers and Izieu is an entirely French matter. We tried not to treat the trial as an entirely French matter, which is why we excluded certain elements.

Another person whose absence is critical is Lea Feldblum, because she is in Israel and we could not get there. It was she who accompanied the children of Izieu. And Bourdon is not there, we've got his address and we could have interviewed him, but the production company could not, or would not, go on. I believe that I might have got more if fatigue had not set in. I had had enough. You see, I am saying that the film is unfinished. It is not finished.

Interviewed in Neuilly, 20 June 1988.

13   Otar Iosseliani on *Les Favoris de la lune*

interviewed by Michel Ciment

Otar Iosseliani

A Soviet exile of Georgian origin, Otar Iosseliani produced his first French
feature film in 1984: *Les Favoris de la lune*. His previous work focused on the
Caucasus and its history, including *La Chute des feuilles*, *Il était une fois un
merle chanteur* and *Pastorale* (1976). His most recent production is *Brigands
(chapitre VII)* (1996).

The interview focuses on *Les Favoris de la lune*, a burlesque in which a
group of Iosseliani's friends play twelve thieves whose paths cross and
recross as a variety of different kinds of booty passes from hand to hand.
The film is almost without conventional dialogue or narrative structure,
although it was co-written with Polanski's French screenwriter Gerard
Brach. It exudes a comic, futuristic quality, which may stem from Iosseliani's relative lack of familiarity with the French society he is trying to
criticize. The net effect is of a return to a more primitive style of film-making, harking back to the days when life could be summarized as a series of
madcap sketches whose unlikely effectiveness was impressionistic rather
than logical.

Les Favoris de la lune
The separate paths of dozens of Parisian thieves (and lovers) constantly criss-
cross as money, paintings and objets d'art are passed from one to another.

Your last film has a title which is surprising, *Les Favoris de la lune*. When you are preparing a film, do you sometimes have a title already in mind, or does that come later?

I always choose the title after the edit is over, sometimes much later. Finding a title before you start shooting is half the battle, but I've never managed it. As this film is all about theft, plagiarizing someone else for the title seemed like a sensible thing to do. The only problem is, I don't like it. It's too pseudo-romantic, pseudo-poetic. I wanted something better, but then I ran out of time, the film was just about to be released.

I found *Les Favoris de la lune* helping my daughter revise for her exams. It's *Henry IV*, Part 1: ' Let us be Diana's foresters, gentlemen of the shade, minions of the moon; and let men say we be men of good government, being governed, as the sea is, by our noble and chaste mistress the moon, under whose countenance we steal.' I would have preferred a double title, such as 'Douze Voleurs ou les favoris de la lune', which would have played down the poetic aspect, and underlined the fact that it is a comedy. Actually, the international title ought to be 'French Comedy'.

You got the idea for the film in Georgia?

Yes, I'd been asked to make a film for the Italian television network, RAI. I'd had this idea for a story about different destinies crossing. I wrote an initial twenty-three-page treatment, which outlines the basis of the story as it is now. When my Italian funding fell away, Gaumont came and asked for a project. I showed them the treatment. They couldn't make head or tail of it. They asked for a three-page synopsis, outlining who loves who, who fights who and who dies. I couldn't do that. But then, Pierre-André Boutang introduced me to the writer Gerard Brach, and we started working together. He produced a very impressionistic draft based on my treatment. The Avance sur Recettes rejected this,[*] but asked us to submit a second draft. So Gerard and I put our heads together again. In the end, we got the grant. Then we produced a third draft and I drew up a storyboard, as I always do, with 320 sketches.

The structure of the story didn't really change through the edit, except that we shortened a few sequences to tighten up the pace. I'd deliberately filmed these sequences in such a way that they could be cut down later, if necessary. In the storyboard, everything is drawn in detail, the actors' movements and the camera's. Everything has to be worked out before I start filming. The shoot was very tense because there was so much to be shot in nine weeks.

You had been living in Paris for a year before you started shooting. That must have helped in finding suitable locations.

* The 'Avance sur Recettes' is a subsidized loan scheme managed by the French National Film Centre, a part of the French Ministry of Culture.

I started writing this story two years ago. But I work in a very strange way. Nothing happens for months, then it all comes together in a few weeks. I find myself in a vacuum, with nothing down on paper. But that's a character trait. I'm incapable of routine. Which is a nightmare.

How do you actually pull together a screenplay?
I begin by working out a kind of skeleton. On *Les Favoris de la lune*, there were two difficulties: first, I had to find a way of making sure all the characters reappeared continually, so that the audience doesn't lose sight of them; and second, I had to give each a proper story of his own, regardless of whether that story was going to be gripping or not. It's like playing patience: you've got to decide in which order to turn the cards over.

Once I've got an outline, I elaborate each sequence, each one around a fable of its own. It is the details that give life to a film. They are the flesh on the skeleton. I gradually add in all the little things I like, the things that make me want to shoot.

I'd rather do it this way than develop a screenplay in a linear fashion, as one would a novel. My method is closer to writing music, or mathematics. I often apply mathematical methods, particularly that of the shortest length between two given points. People who've studied the arts create great curves between points, but the application of algorithm, which is a discipline in itself, allows you to organize things better.

Did you feel, after making *La Chute des feuilles*, *Il était une fois un merle chanteur* and *Pastorale*, that you'd had enough of a certain kind of film? *Les Favoris de la lune* is structured in a very different way.
Maybe. At this point, I was less interested in the kind of narrative continuity which focuses on either a single protagonist or a group. And I felt I had done as much as I could to describe the habits and morals of specific social groups. In *La Chute des feuilles*, I dealt with factories; in *Il était une fois un merle chanteur*, the city and its intelligentsia; and in *Pastorale*, the countryside, and the conflict of attitudes between townspeople and country people.

So with this film, I wanted to explore my own experiences and opinions. I'm fifty years old, and it's time I started to think about things seriously. That is what dictated the form of *Les Favoris de la lune*. If you analyse the decline of modern culture, it can be explained only by the growth of individuality. If you break away from society, you're alone, and, to fill the void, you turn to material objects. In a way, it's as if people communicate with each other through their possessions, and this creates different social levels. The barriers between people aren't created by different attitudes, because the attitudes themselves are dictated by the different social levels at which people find themselves. The fact that people draw away from others like themselves is a serious problem, but the best approach is through comedy. So the film is ironic, farcical. The idea was that we leave this world empty-handed, and regretful. Perhaps that is not true. But regretting the error of our ways at the end of our allotted span seems like a good idea. What we wanted was to provide an analysis of such errors.

Is this what gave you the idea of using theft as a metaphor for life?
Theft is the result of individuality. The more you steal, the more you forget that you are stealing from someone else; the whole concept becomes abstract. The chain of thefts is the main thread of the film, and, by following it through, we find out who loses at the end. When an object – or a woman, or a man – changes hands, it gets worn down. So things get broken, or they shrink, and people get colder, more desperate.

You are more on the side of the thieves than the owners.
Everybody deals in theft. But professional thieves are naïve, simple and straightforward. Those who steal something believe that it has some sort of significance, whereas in fact it's nothing. They are the opposite of my singing blackbird.

You yourself are a thief. Your film is very personal, it's coherent. And yet you poach from Tati, Clair, Bresson and Godard. How did you reconcile the France of your cinematic memories, and the France that you were seeing?
One is never solely responsible for one's actions. We are all the product of things happening around us. I am what I am because of my grandparents, who brought me up, and my parents. Even their absence was sometimes an example, perhaps an even more significant one than their presence. There were also my neighbours, my playmates, my teachers, the intellectuals that I spent time with at university. Such people influence one, as do figures from the past – in my case, Pushkin, Mozart, Rabelais and Homer. They help you choose friends and lovers, and they help you find contentment. In my opinion, there are two sorts of people – those I would like to share a meal with, and those I avoid, using work or whatever as an excuse. From this point of view, I don't find French cinema very exciting, especially in recent years. There are those that I feel very close to culturally, such as Vigo, René Clair, Carné, Renoir, Tati, and Bresson. But not all the time: I find *Le Déjeuner sur l'herbe* stupid and depressing, but some of Renoir's films are wonderful.

You tend to use friends rather than professional actors in your film.
My aim is to create a world that is unique, and set apart from the rest of the cinematic world. If I use professional actors, they bring to my film their acting history, their methods, their trade marks. Especially if they've worked a lot, their face has been seen around, and evokes all sorts of other associations. This is damaging to my film. It's no longer my character – it's Catherine Deneuve playing my character, it's Belmondo who plays the thief, and so on. I restrict the actors' performances by shooting simple movements and actions; there are no dramas and tears, no long psychological searching. I try to express passions or emotions by contrasting differ-

ent bits of film, using contradiction rather than psychological unravelling.

Cinema is a superficial art, we only show what happens on the surface, we don't go into people's minds. That's the strength of literature. It's distasteful when the cinema tries to go deeper, taking a keyhole approach to film intimate scenes, those things that people wish to hide. It's not possible to completely avoid this sort of thing, but I still think it's better to keep a distance. Wanting to know how the neighbours live is the motive of the petty bourgeoisie – that's why they go to the cinema, to see the blood and dirt of others. Producers know what's needed to sell tickets. I prefer to stay on the surface of things when I'm filming.

I try to use non-professionals as much as I can. I ask a tramp to do the same as he does everyday, he just has to be sufficiently talented to be able to repeat things in front of the camera, and not turn to stone. I did think that only Georgians could act without being actors, and so I used lots of my countrymen. But then I found hundreds of Frenchmen who could do it too. I'm surprised that the amateurs in Bresson's films seem a bit wooden and lifeless, as if the director is behind them pulling the strings.

Les Favoris de la lune: 'I use non-professionals as much as I can.'

How did you find your actors?

They are all friends of mine. I knew they could act. You have to be gentle and attentive with them, because they aren't used to the camera, or to being watched while they act. So you have to get them to relax, then gradually add little bits of colour here and there, building on their personalities. They love doing it because it's a game for them. The crew must be gentle, smiling. For a shoot like this to be fun, no one must be cynical.

Did you rewrite any of the dialogues after choosing the actors?
The dialogue plays a very small role in the film. We knew what they were talking about. It's basically rubato – improvising on a given theme. Nothing was learnt by heart, the words came naturally. The tramp wasn't capable of saying the same thing twice, he just knew what it was all about, so he said the right thing.

If you had filmed in Italy, would the people and the situations have been different?
It could have been more spectacular. The Italian personality is quite similar to the Georgian personality. It would have been more theatrical, crazier. I would have preferred to film in Germany or England, because the colder it is, the more suspense there is. The more ceremony and good manners there are, the more distant the tone of the film can be.

There isn't the same degree of tenderness in this film as in the films you made in Georgia.
I don't agree. My other films were considered to be anti-Georgian by my countrymen, but seen from the outside, they appear very tender. I've visited a lot of countries, and I see Georgia as completely out on a limb, like a tin of preserves – if all else disappears, you could open it and find certain things still intact. Within its borders, you can find all the different ways man has lived since Antiquity, and which make up our culture. It's all linked to a history of war, and so it's very serious. A boy is brought up to be a man, and to die honourably in combat. We don't send idiots to the front line, a man must know what he is dying for. So, education is very important in Georgia, and this hasn't really changed with the passage of time. It is good to be faithful; to give is the greatest pleasure in life; everyone endeavours to invite in the passer-by; to grow fruit either to sell or to keep is bad; and respect for the woman, whose destiny in life is the hardest, is natural. In fact, the first Georgian Constitution, in the 1920s, gave women equal rights. These values are totally different from those we strive to achieve elsewhere in the world today. But I see my country gradually becoming more and more individualistic, and its culture slowly breaking down. Shooting *Les Favoris de la lune* in France was like making a science fiction movie in my country: it's the future in store for Georgia. The characters in *Les Favoris de la lune* are the same as those in my previous films, except that they have become unhappy. They suffer because they don't live as they should. In France I found a group of friends who were suffering, and I made the film with them.

It should be full of tenderness. It's true that it is quite dramatic and ironic, but it has hope. The characters are all lost, they don't know where they're going, or what they're doing, they have no aims. In French cinema, I find terrible coldness in the films of Coluche and de Funès; they contain such hatred of the people and their country. But when the spectator laughs crudely, the hatred goes unnoticed. I think you have to differentiate between tough love and cruel laughter.

You came to France several times for short periods. Did you feel a change over the years? Did your attitudes change as a result of your long stay to make this film?

The first time I came, I was surprised because it wasn't at all as I imagined. I felt that the France I knew through literature, paintings and films no longer existed: these were images from the 1930s and the post-war period. I imagined everybody – whores, artists, tramps, philosophers – sitting together in cafés, a gay, welcoming world. I visited all the areas where these cafés were, and found drawings and poems on the wall, carefully covered in transparent plastic. That world no longer existed. What the people do is eat, eat, eat . . . They don't know each other. The only thing that was left was the Closerie des Lilas, but it's snobbish, and cold. I also discovered, sadly, that the French have no sense of humour, they take everything so seriously, creating unnecessary problems, and taking offence at the slightest thing. They love gossip; as soon as someone leaves the room, they bitch about him. It's all very bad-mannered.

But I also found people who stay quietly at home, modestly or not, who do not calculate everything, and who welcome people into their home with an open heart. Getting to know the tramps was a revelation to me. I lived with them for a while, and discovered that they are very honest, with clear concepts of good and bad. It seems to me that they are the only social group which is completely honest and free, except that they do have to beg to survive. Each thing they do is discussed among them.

I think that the problem the French have is that they do less parenting. The warmth that human beings know as children disappears gradually, the children grow up, marry, and leave their parents, and find themselves alone. The grandparents, who have the time and desire to give them tenderness, are also separated from the family unit, so, as there are no bridges crossing the generations, the relationships, without being mean, are just cold.

Are the black-and-white sequences in *Les Favoris de la lune* inspired by the Golden Age of cinema?

Nowadays we tend to feel, understandably, that things were better before. We know that's not true. There was the Inquisition, torture, famine, tyrants, the guillotine, the Plague, serfdom, as in Russia. We prefer to think that things were better then because they probably were, in terms of lifestyle, due to the absence of all the technological amusements around today. But giving ourselves time to live together, to play the piano or the guitar, is something that we did better before. Showing this past gave the film a perspective. The same actors appear in the past and present scenes. I wanted to emphasize this more, but there wasn't enough time. I would have liked them to undress and change their clothes before moving into the colour sequences.

And the music?

I wanted to use old French songs, romantic songs from the 1920s and Rossini's Quartets. The composer, Nicholas Zourabichvili, is very talented and wrote three or four pieces for me, including a waltz. He understood what I was looking for, we understood each other. The relationship between the director and the composer is very important. Nino Rota's influence on Fellini's films is enormous, he rendered them tearful and burlesque at the same time, in true clown tradition. After he died, Fellini made *Et vogue le navire*, which is really depressing and sad.

I don't like it when you can see the workings of a musical score. All the music I want to use is already written. I use music which helps me express myself culturally. The music mustn't be complicated. Folk music has travelled down through the centuries, and is solid and worthwhile, so that's what I use. Zourabichvili understood this, and didn't want the core of the musical script to be original, because he also preferred popular music.

How did you work with Philippe Theaudière, your cameraman?

He had already worked with me on *Lettre d'un cinéaste* and *Euskadi*. He usually works on documentaries. I didn't want any complications with the images because I knew what I wanted to do, I just needed someone who was flexible enough to realize the shots. He concentrates on the job, doesn't bother you with suggestions, doesn't feel obliged to have an artistic temperament, which makes it easier to focus. Some cameramen interfere, suggesting their own ideas for strange takes. I don't like 'beautiful pictures'. Cinema isn't painting. Beautiful pictures kill the momentum. When you watch Eisenstein's *Ivan the Terrible*, you come out more interested by the images than the storyline.

Did you do lots of takes?

No, very few. Two or three at the most. I did as many as twenty shots a day. If everything is clear and simple, filming is easy. This film could have cost a fortune, but we organised our time well, the crew was responsible and skilful. Some people don't know how to work at all. I discovered a phenomenon I'd never known in Georgia – people who come to work on a film as employees. In my country, I can depend on people's love of cinema, but here it's rare. The unions kill everything. Someone working on a film is paid five times what you earn working for Renault, it's very unjust. I earn five times less, but that's my problem, it's my film, and I would do it for free. In France, cinema technicians are always asking for more money. In Georgia, they earn at most a hundred roubles a month, but they know that they can't earn any more, so they make no demands. You take on a job because you love the work. When the driving force is money, attitudes change. What is also very important in Georgia is that everyone drinks, during filming and after filming. So you are always slightly jolly. That's not the case here.

The mixing also really surprised me. I found myself with a mixing technician who was considered a great professional. But what is mixing? It's just a great big amplifier, with lots of buttons. Sharps, flats, different volumes, and sixteen columns. That's all. The people who do the mixing see it as all very secretive, and you're not allowed to touch the buttons – only they know what to do. I think it's rubbish – all my life I've mixed my own films, and done it perfectly well. But by the time the technician's understood what I want, got his head round it, corrected it, then I've corrected it – so much time has been wasted. Especially as he's never seen the film, and doesn't know where he's going. But he's very happy to be paid a thousand francs an hour. I had to remix the whole thing with him by my side. It still wasn't any good, so I had to start all over again with a new technician, and do the mix a third time. French mixing technicians are used to dialogue firing back and forth throughout the film. They like perfectly audible sound all the time, the gentle murmuring of emotionally evocative music, and the loud banging of doors and car engines. That's all these brilliant technicians know how to do, they've lost touch with their craft.

As to editing, I managed to win out over French work practice. Normally, the editor sits at the table, and the director stands behind her. He tells her to stop and start, and asks her opinion, but only she cuts. Another big secret. I must touch and edit myself, and my editor was very understanding and accepted this. For me, an editor is a friend who talks with me, not someone who edits while I walk around.

It's the same thing as with a scriptwriter?
Yes. Gerard Brach was first and foremost someone I enjoyed talking to. He helped me enormously because he knew which things could take place in France and which couldn't. For example, in my original script, there were lots of bribes, like in Georgia. Bribery exists in countries where everybody is corrupt, so no one's frightened. It creates a form of confidence, because you know that you won't be immediately denounced. The first time I went through a red light in Paris, and got stopped by a policeman, I pulled out a hundred francs. Luckily he didn't understand, he was astonished, and simply thought I had pulled out the wrong papers!

Interviewed in Venice, 5 September 1984

14

Olivier Assayas

interviewed by Olivier Kohn

Olivier Assayas

Olivier Assayas is a well-known screenwriter and director. He wrote the
script for André Téchiné's seminal film, *Rendez-vous* (1985), which
launched Juliette Binoche's career. His first feature film as a director was
Désordre (1986) and his most recent, a contemporary adaptation of Louis
Feuillade's vintage vampire movie *Les Vampires*, entitled *Irma Vep* (1997).
As a writer, he is known for writing.

Unlike the other interviews in this anthology, Olivier Assayas is not here
analyzing a particular film but rather discussing the general nature of his
work as a writer. Long regarded as one of the most interesting directors of
the 1980s generation, particularly for his camerawork, he has always insisted on the equal importance he attaches to writing, and has nearly always
written his screenplays unaided. Like Raùl Ruiz, he has developed new
forms of narrative which depart from conventional dramatic structure,
while using a variety of reasonably well-established casts. But Assayas'
experimentation has always been more discreet. He often seems to be offering himself up for consideration as a contemporary film artist. And his
sense of himself as a screenwriter has always formed an important part of
that claim.

You wrote screenplays before becoming a director.

My greatest wish always was to be a director. My father was a scriptwriter. He wrote for the cinema in the 1950s, and then for television. As a child I couldn't understand why a film that he'd written was always attributed to someone else, and he would explain that the 'someone else' was the director who made the film. So I decided that that was what I would do. It seemed more interesting than writing the film. As I lived in the cinema world, I was lucky enough to work on films during my summer holidays. I did it out of curiosity, but I didn't enjoy being an assistant. I was particularly interested in the visuals, I painted a lot at the time, and I was studying literature. All this wasn't leading me towards scriptwriting, but then one day, my father, who was old and ill, asked me to be his secretary. As I was a student with free time, I accepted. He was beginning to get fed up with churning out stuff for television, and gradually he started to off-load certain projects on to me. So, I was writing scripts for TV series when I was quite young. They weren't very good, but I still got a kick out of seeing something that I'd written on the screen. Then friends of mine who were directing their first short films asked me to give them a hand, so I moved into a more 'normal' writing context, with people of my own age. This was a million miles from the television stuff I had been doing until then. I ended up writing and directing my own shorts.

Before doing cinema criticism?

Yes, I started writing reviews when the guys from the *Cahiers du Cinéma* came to see a film I'd made. At first I thought it was quite a prestigious thing to do, but I surprised myself by enjoying it, and I realized that I liked writing. Later, I understood that it helped me to be objective, and to stand back from things. Until then, I had done lots of things but in a rather chaotic fashion, and with hindsight, it's clear that writing the reviews was enormously helpful.

The first feature film you worked on was *Rendez-vous*.

The first to be filmed. I had worked on some projects earlier, some of which were filmed after *Rendez-vous*. Writing for Téchiné was a breakthrough for me. It was the first time I worked for an established director whom I admired enormously, and I learnt lots of new things which were very helpful later on.

Have you ever written a screenplay on your own that has then been made into a film by someone else?

Never. I don't understand the concept of the screenplay written by the scriptwriter. For me, the screenplay is the expression of the desires of the director. The scriptwriter's job, when he is working for a director, is to help him succeed in his chosen idea, and to support and encourage him. The scriptwriter is at the disposal of the director's inspiration. His role is not to impose his own personality. Often, you find that bad scriptwriters are in fact frustrated directors, who try to impose their own ideas, but that's not the point of it. The aim is that the director pushes himself to his limits and, in doing this, achieves something worthwhile and precious. So the scriptwriter, if he isn't the director, is a co-writer, helping the director. That's the perfect scenario.

How does it actually work, writing with the director?
On *Rendez-vous*, which was originally commissioned by Alain Sarde, André Téchiné and I decided on the structure of the script, and the scenes, and then wrote very quickly. From time to time, I drew up a sort of numbered framework, which we looked at together. Then, at the next stage, we just shared the scenes – we each wrote a few and then got together and went through them. André's opinion was obviously more important than mine. If one of us felt ill at ease over a particular scene, he gave it to the other to try and get right. All this to-ing and fro-ing gave us a fairly chaotic package that we then went through again, and pulled together. We were even working on some scenes during filming. Working with someone else is odd, each time it's different. Every director has different needs and ways of working, so the osmosis is obviously different as well. The screenplay is the product of the desires of the director, and the methods used are dictated by the needs of the screenplay.

Do you employ different methods when you write a film for yourself?
Certainly. When you write with someone else, you have to justify what you've done. However close the relationship with the director, you have to explain why you have put in such and such a scene. When you write for yourself, you can do exactly what you want. The approach is much less rational, you can create a scene just because you want it, only to realize later that it's essential. You can wander away from a scene just to see where it will lead. When I write, I lay myself milestones which I then do my best to avoid. I think of a screenplay as the outcome of characters' paths that cross. I prepare the characters individually before, make notes, and then put them together in situations, and see what happens. This is particularly obvious in *Désordre*, in which the initial murder loses importance and fades into the background, after it has thrown the characters off on their chosen paths. It was the same for *L'Enfant de l'hiver* and *Goutte d'or*, which I'm filming at the moment, and taking even greater liberties with. In *Désordre*, my first film, I put down quite solid markers. It was as if I took down the scaffolding on *L'Enfant de l'hiver*, and gradually threw off conventional dramatic restraints, in order to get more and more into the characters and what they inspired in me, and to give them greater autonomy. The working conditions on this last film were perfect: I wrote the screenplay in two months, and started the preparation immediately after. For me this was an achievement, because the sooner I can get the characters that I've created face to face, as actors in costume, the more coherent the whole process is, and this manifests itself in the film. This sort of freedom is impossible when you're working for someone else.

Do you write all in one go, without stopping?
I scribble down notes about people and situations, until I've got enough materi-

al to make a film. This can take a bit of time, but once I start writing, I go right through without stopping. The only exception to this was *L'Enfant de l'hiver*, which I wrote twice. Between the two versions, I worked on a project with Edouard Niemans, which never came to fruition. It took me a long time to give it shape, and the second time I needed completely to restructure the film.

Do you lean more heavily on the prose or the dialogue in your writing?
The dialogue. I feel that a scenario is like poetry or music, it's all about rhythm and precision, and a certain sparsity. So, I use as few descriptions and set indications as possible. I write like a playwright, only without the peculiar language employed in the theatre, where the dialogue forms the basis of the action. As the cinema is all about rhythm, I give instructions concerning people's movements: 'He sits down', 'She runs'. I don't elaborate, I don't write 'The glowing bronze sunlight, peeping through the wispy clouds . . .' The reason I talk about music and poetry is that it's all about metres and rhythm. The script must be easy to read, but must also include all the necessary information for filming. I refer back to it constantly during filming, because I know that it has everything I need to build a scene – here it's slower, here it speeds up – I try to find a sort of natural rhythm inside me, to know that what I'm writing is right. I'm capable of spending two hours deciding whether someone should be sitting or standing to say a particular line. It's vital to get it right at the writing stage, otherwise I'll be stymied when filming. In this aspect writing is very similar to music – it must be 'in tune'.

So there isn't a later rewrite, a more technical one giving camera directions and so on?
No. When I'm writing, I don't spend hours thinking about what the camera should be doing, I just have an overall idea of what's needed, which I then apply scene by scene, and the decisions are made on the set. I need to ignore the director's problems when I'm writing. I don't visualize the scene as I write it, I use the space I've got, and create round it, finding ideas that are, I hope, all the more powerful and unexpected for the discipline I've imposed.

When you write, do you have specific actors in mind?
Not always. It can happen and be useful, even if, at the end of the day, the actor I thought of doesn't do it. I never have an actor in mind before I've created the character, but, gradually, as you write, actors come to mind. Then, if an idea sticks, the actor becomes an important factor: for example, in my last film, Jean-Pierre Léaud became more and more of an option for a particular character. Then, there is a sort of interaction between the character and the actor you are thinking about.

Do you ever change the script during filming, despite the discipline and intensity at the writing stage that we discussed earlier?
Never. Some directors anticipate the occasional improvisation, but I'm not one

Désordre: Corinne Dacla and Wadeck Stanczak

of them. But I do leave the actors a lot of freedom to do what they want, which is why I am deliberately sparse in my written descriptions. I never mention the psychological elements of a character, it's up to the actor to put in as much of himself as possible. I believe that an actor has a sort of intrinsic understanding of a character, in a way he knows the character better than I do, he can't just do any old thing. So, I leave him room to manoeuvre in the script. The reason I hardly change the dialogue at all is that I feel strongly that the rhythm of the text must remain intact, it's a sort of safety net. The things that can change on set are almost anticipated during the writing stage. That's not to say I worship the screenplay. On the contrary, it's something that is dead, just words on paper. Then, all of a sudden, this thing that was created within four walls, comes alive, people appear, it gets dressed up and goes out into the real world. It gets a life of its own. Everyone involved brings in something different of their own, which makes it richer. But I have never radically changed anything on set.

And in the cutting-room?
Even less so! The same problems arise in editing as in writing, the same doubts and, often, the same solutions. The editing is a quick process. Obviously, the odd bad shot has to be taken out, but I always regret it, because I think that the equilibrium that I painstakingly established in the screenplay is going to be upset. Having said that, since the writing is so precise, the editing is easy; the definitive version of *L'Enfant de l'hiver* is one and a half minutes shorter than the first version.

You keep saying that a screenplay is a dead object, but it's clear that you feel it to be primordial, and focus a lot of attention on it.

136

Yes. It's like a piece of music that is dead until it's played. The screenplay is an absolutely vital part of the whole creation, as vital as the direction, but I can't see it as a creation in its own right, because it is, above all, a search for the structure that will accommodate my film in the way that suits me best. The screenplay – and the scriptwriter – do not have an independent existence – that would be an abomination. One shouldn't speak of the scriptwriter on the one hand, and the director on the other – the two roles are inextricably bound and inseparable, there should be one name for both. Even with my own scripts, it's sometimes hard to create on film what I'm trying to say. I don't understand what other people's scripts are trying to say, I would find it very difficult to work with one. Obviously, this doesn't apply to American films, in which directors are more illustrators than painters. There are directors who are wonderful illustrators – you just give them a script, and an instant visual imagination kicks in, strong and autonomous. They find themselves face to face with characters, dialogue, images, stories, all at one go, and succeed in bringing all these different elements together to make a coherent package. They aren't inferior as directors, it's just that they do a completely different job to mine, and the product reflects this difference. I feel like a child given access to a whole lot of props, using them to create something that's deep inside me, that means something to me.

Interviewed in Paris, 22 March 1991

15

Catherine Breillat on *36 fillette*

interviewed by Michel Ciment

Catherine Breillat

In 1988, Catherine Breillat's *36 fillette* burst on the French film scene like a ball of flame, inventing a new genre: the Frenchwoman's sex film. She had made only one previous film, *Tapage nocturne*, in 1979. Her most recent production is *Parfait amour* (1997).

The critical and reasonable box-office success of *36 fillette* would appear to corroborate the old adage that sex is just about the only thing that lifts independent film to prominence. But the film's raw power comes from a real understanding of the importance of what happens on the spur of the moment, right there when the camera is rolling. Though Breillat is also a writer, a novelist and occasional screenwriter, it is the near-improvised quality of her scenes that impresses, alongside her ability to get her actors to go beyond what they think is possible.

36 fillette
Sullen teenager Lili (Delphine Zentout) is holidaying with her family in Biarritz, and bored to tears. Then she meets Maurice (Etienne Chicot), a middle-aged man of dubious virtue, who makes concerted efforts to seduce her. Eager to be relieved of her virginity, hesitant nevertheless, Lili has a fit-ful, unsatisfactory tryst with Maurice, before finally surrendering herself in cold-blooded fashion to an unremarkable young lad.

36 *fillette* began as a screenplay, then became a novel, and lastly a film. How did this happen?

The screenplay sat around at the Commission d'Avances sur Recettes. First, it was read by the Jacques Perrin committee, who gave me some money for a rewrite, then it went on to the Adolphe Viezzi committee, who rejected it after the third reading. I had completely given up, when Lise Fayolle, who loved it, suggested that she submit it again with a different title, because Christian Bourgois, who had been my first publisher, had taken over as chairman of the committee. He rang me to say that he had loved the work I had done on Pialat's *Police*, but that this script was awful, and that I had to rewrite the whole thing.

Initially, I was really fed up, especially because, contrary to what most people think, I see no point in rewrites. People say that a film is in the writing, but when the director and writer are one and the same, I believe that the film is made on set. So I was furious and wrote them a snotty letter, saying that I would explain the text to them in the form of a novel. A screenplay is just a ghost of a film, because, in the most important scenes, it's the silences which count. The words are there to soothe the more violent interactions between the characters. The novel was even more extreme, and I thought to myself, 'If they were shocked by the screenplay, they'll be even more shocked by the book!' I thought they would faint with horror. At the same time, I believed that if people censor something, and you give them something even stronger, that can seduce them. Their rejection of what you do makes those very same people ready to be won over. I mean, all my life I have been put under pressure to look feminine, do my hair nicely, make myself look pretty . . . and, on the few occasions that I have given in, feeling dreadful, the very same people who had bullied me into it weren't happy. The same thing happens in artistic situations. You have to highlight differences, not hide them. I wrote the novel *36 fillette* from the original screenplay, because everything I had rewritten was just done to please others. I had tempered it down because some people, who had my well-being at heart, found the film far too harsh, because there is no hope for the young girl. I felt as if I was working for Mosfilm, offering hope for a whole generation, guaranteeing a future and Social Security to my heroine. I prefer the first version. And anyway, once you are filming you end up cutting a lot because you are adapting to the actors, who really make the film, even if they're not always the ones you originally thought you wanted.

This explains why the film does not feel like a literary adaptation. It's very elliptical.

When you read the novel a film seems unimaginable, and that appalled the committee. As it is written in the first person, everything appears to be imaginary, therefore unfilmable.

Usually writers-turned-directors create very structured scenes. In your case,

it's the opposite, the literary element is underplayed to give priority to the passage of time, so that gestures and situations can unfold.

That's the point. I always thought that the subject of *36 fillette* was better suited to a film than a book, because it all happens visually, not verbally. It's about a duality of emotions. The actors can express both shame and desire at the same time, and it's very moving. When you have to express those kinds of emotions in words, it's endless sentences full of 'ifs' and 'buts'. The more verbal detail there is, the less strong it is. The silence on people's faces is wonderful; and if you are going to use film, you have to exploit that to the full.

The hotel scene is very powerful, because it's practically played out in real time.

This caused lots of problems. The screenplay was not at all suggestive or elliptical, and everyone wanted me to change it. They regarded the twenty-five pages of script as a mistake. In a way they were right. If I had been writing to order, I wouldn't have done it. But I wanted to film an event as it happens, which is usually never done.

Here you use very long shots.

When we prepared the set of the hotel foyer, the whole production team was in hysterics. It was the last week of shooting, and they thought the film was already too long, so they wanted to time the remainder. I said you couldn't time the film, because the pace changed from scene to scene. It's only when the actors come on that I know what speed they're working at. So it made me laugh, because I got them to set up tracks and then said, 'Look, she comes in, and then stands still, it says in the script, "as if nailed to the floor". And then there's the long passage inside the hotel, which isn't in the script, which makes it even longer. Then there's a second door and she circles round the sofa to gain time.' Delphine and Chicot started the scene and were delighted. Then the continuity girl said, 'Three minutes twenty seconds!' Just for a scene shot as a single shot in which nothing happens! In the evening we all met up, and everyone was furious. I reckoned that if no one found it long while we were filming, because of the atmosphere, then why should it be a problem on screen?

Having said that, if the film consisted just of the scenes in which they go out, she shouts, they laugh – action shots – it would have been an empty little package, but probably a more commercially successful film. Its audience was restricted by the fact that the film's content was three scenes – the bedroom, the grotto and the villa. What people find difficult to take, and what I love to show them (not out of a cheap desire to attract audiences, contrary to what people might think) is the reflection of their own discomfort in certain situations. The most violent thing life has to offer is neither violence nor sex, but the shyness we feel in certain situations. We are all naturally timid, and we struggle against it. Whenever the shyness becomes too strong, our personality falls apart, and we find ourselves doing things we don't want to do. When people fall in love, they behave like idiots, because they suddenly start trying to please the other person, which isn't necessary because they already please that person. At the beginning of a relationship, the feelings are always mutual. What happens afterwards is that, because you desire someone, and they desire you naturally and instinctively, you then lose your integrity by trying to please them, and you do stupid things. This is what I try to show in *36 fillette*. We want to see good things or bad things in a film, not things that are discomforting, however common these situations are.

In these scenes, do you shoot many takes?
Yes, and I'm very violent with the actors, when they get everything wrong and don't dare throw themselves into the scene or do it properly. I insult them. You have to shake them up a bit, and dare to tell them what you want them to do, which I find hard. I am quite shy, and they lie in wait for you round every corner, it's quite threatening. Often I filmed hiding my face behind my hands, or raising my T-shirt over my eyes, because some scenes are very intimate and voyeuristic. I never just say, 'Roll!' I talk to the actors, and then, when everyone is ready, I make signs to the crew. If you start being authoritarian, you spoil the atmosphere. And when the magic happens, when it's very intimate, everyone on the set catches their breath, blushes, looks at each other in astonishment, and then you know that the take was good. I told the actors that I make a film in the same way that I write a book. I realized that on *36 fillette*, where I felt very isolated. Very early on, the actors and I hated each other. When I sacked the cameraman, they all turned against me, because he was a popular leader. They should have seen the rushes. They were too dark, which was hardly surprising, as the crew were out partying until six o'clock in the morning. The problem is that people treat film shoots as if they were Club Meds, especially shoots in holiday locations. So, I was completely alone. Chicot sulked, he decided that I was incompetent, and made fun of me, with all the young actors round him like in a barracks. He nick-named me 'Latrine Breillat'. I didn't know what to say to that! So, I shut myself in an office for three hours and wrote. I came out like a Fury, ready to go; whereas they were all enervated, having done nothing during all this time. I told Chicot that I would film him from the back because he was so bad, and that when he got better I would film him from the front! I spent my nights sobbing, but finally, the crew accepted my loneliness and came back towards me, one by one.

Do you feel you belong to a group of directors: Rozier, Eustache, Pialat, Stevenin?
Pialat and I have a similar way of working, and we worked together on the script of *Police*. We both like taking little things out of life and inserting them in our films. I wanted Jean-François Stevenin right from the beginning. He wanted Chicot's role, but I managed to convince him to play the father, by showing him the test shots of Delphine where she looks just like him: the same round forehead, the same small bright, deep-set eyes, the same mouth, the same build. That made

36 fillette: Maurice (Etienne Chicot) and Lili (Delphine Zentout)

him realize he couldn't make love to his daughter! I got on so well with Stevenin that I started to wonder if I had gone far enough. He's someone who can come down to the beach and turn his back instinctively to the camera in order to look out at sea! A different actor asked to do that would sulk and squirm around and turn his head to be in the shot. A great actor is more powerful from the back, because the cinema is all about frustration, all that one would like to see, can't see, and thinks one has seen.

You mentioned autobiographical elements in *36 fillette*.
I don't think it's possible to tell this kind of story without personal details, and this film draws on an experience in my life. As a young girl, I found myself in a hotel with a man whom I was madly chasing, but who horrified me at the same time. More or less the same thing that happens in the film. I think that at the age of fourteen/fifteen you can be attracted to someone but at the same time disgusted. So your behaviour is completely illogical. I wanted to call the book and the film 'Catch! or How Young Girls Ask to be Killed'. There is always a moment afterwards where you wish you hadn't slept with that person. It's about pride. The man has to take responsibility for the desire, even though it is mutual.

There's something schizophrenic about the young girl. When I was young, I was always coming across exhibitionists. I don't any longer. This isn't because they only like young girls, it's about supply and demand. The end of that story is the murder of the young girl. It's about young girls who don't know what they want, but who can't be accused of being sluttish, because they don't know of any other way to behave.

16

Jean-Pierre Jeunet on *Delicatessen*

*interviewed by Gilles Ciment, Philippe Rouyer
and Paul-Louis Thirard*

Jean-Pierre Jeunet, directing Dominique Pinon
on *Alien IV: Resurrection*

Jean-Pierre Jeunet is one of the very few French film-makers to have made it
in Hollywood in modern times, directing *Alien IV: Resurrection* (1997). Originally, a maker of animated films, his career as a feature film director has
almost all been in partnership with his friend, Marc Caro, with whom he co-
directed the hugely successful *Delicatessen* (1990), and *La Cité des enfants
perdus* (1995), one of the most resounding flops in all French film history.

It is hard to imagine, in the English-speaking world, just how important a
part of the counter-culture strip cartoons have been in France since the sev-
enties. They are published in a series of magazines, then collected into
widely read 'albums'. As in Italy, a whole generation of artists, writers, aca-
demics and other thinkers grew up under the influence of the cartoons'
combination of semi-pornographic humour and political insolence – the
spirit of which spread into newspapers, thriller-writing and music. That
spirit was slow, however, to move into film. *Delicatessen* was one of the first
major successes to be identified by French audiences as stemming, partly,
from this world of strip cartoons, even though the film's political undercur-
rents are a far cry from the left-wing provocation of the cartoons. The fact
that the film was released abroad testifies to Caro and Jeunet's ability to
transform their cult humour into a widely accessible style of their own.

Delicatessen

In a dystopian future society, 'The Butcher' makes his profit by trading meat for grain – the standard currency. His meats also fill the bellies of his hungry tenants – such as his mistress Madamoiselle Plus, the toy-making Kube brothers, and the Tapioca and Interligator families. What they don't know is that this meat is in fact the flesh of The Butcher's many hapless handymen, whom he murders in succession. Circus clown Louison arrives to fill the handyman role, and romances The Butcher's daughter Julie, unaware of his likely fate. But with Julie's help (plus that of underground vegetarian resistance movement, the Troglodists), love prevails.

Before your directing career, you were a contributor to several magazines?
Yes, at one time I wrote about animation in *Charlie mensuel*, and occasionally in *Fluide glaciale* and *Métal hurlant* too. Caro was a cartoonist. Then he started working as an illustrator and now he is a video graphics specialist.

When did you meet?
About fifteen years ago. At the Annecy Animated Film Festival. Caro had started a publication called *Fantasmagorie*, and I became a contributor. We decided we wanted to work together and then a few months later I shot *L'Evasion* (1978), and *Le Manège* (1980), which were animated puppet shorts. The heads were designed by Caro.

Because *Le Manège* won a César,[*] we were able to shoot a proper film, a genuine joint-venture, with both of us directing. We did everything together: screenplay, costumes, props, even the photography. That was a bit reckless, but it did teach us a lot. No one can catch us out on technical details now.

Despite the success of *Le Bunker de la dernière rafale*, you were not able to go on to make a feature film.
We were naïve. We'd written several screenplays, but didn't have the sense to come up with a cheap project like *Le Dernier Combat*.[†] We went mad, thinking up huge fantasy projects involving enormous amounts of construction, *à la* Spielberg and Mulcahy. Of course, the producers we met just laughed.

As we were unable to get going on a feature, we carried on making shorts and videos. Then the promo people started taking an interest in what we were doing. But it is very important to us that our roots are in shorts. We only got into commercials and promos by accident. We made a living that way, and kept working. And we learnt a lot. How to sell ourselves, for instance, how to tell a producer the film is going to be brilliant. I also learnt how to manage large budgets, how to

[*] The main French film award.
[†] The first feature by Luc Bresson. It was shot in black and white and was without dialogue.

Delicatessen: the unkindest cut for Louison (Dominique Pinon)

direct crews. At the same time, I wrote a comedy, without Caro, for which I got help from the Avance sur Recettes. I would have made that, if *Delicatessen* hadn't happened.

Where did the idea for *Delicatessen* come from?
Caro and I decided to go for something cheaper, which meant fewer characters in a single location. The starting-point of the synopsis was simply that, at the time, I lived above a sausage-maker's and every morning I heard chopping. One day, my girlfriend said, 'They're chopping up the tenants, it will be your turn soon.' I told Caro about this, and he thought it was a good starting-point. There was a title, *Delicatessen*, and so we started constructing a whole world around that one idea, including the characters and lots of things we'd been thinking about for ages. I sent the project to a producer, Claudie Hossard, who I'd met in the meantime, and she said yes straight away.

You wrote the screenplay with Gilles Adrien.
We've known Gilles a very long time. We wrote *Le Bunker de la dernière rafale* with him. This is how we work: I write the synopsis with Caro, then Gilles joins us to develop it; I write the visual scenes and he writes the dialogue.

What about the storyboard?
When the screenplay is all but finished, Caro and I lock ourselves away like two monks, in a house in the country. I don't know how to draw, so I scrawl out an

146

idea for each shot and Caro makes up the actual frame. Once we've got a storyboard, we don't play with it much. If an actor comes up with an interesting idea, we might work it in, but the storyboard is our guide. Time costs money on set. Better waste time on designing shots and working out continuity at the storyboard stage, and not start shooting till you're really ready.

You use a lot actors that come from commercials or shorts.
The idea is to choose the right actors for the part, regardless of whether they're famous or not. We've nothing against stars, but often they come with this baggage, even if, like Michel Piccoli or Jeanne Moreau, they cope with it well. Anyway, for that story, it made more sense to use unknowns. We found Sylvie Laguna (Mme Interligator) in a commercial where she just made a face, but Ticky Holgado and Jean-Claude Dreyfus are theatre actors. And we'd been wanting to shoot with Dominique Pinon for ten years.

You'd already directed him in *Foutaises*.
Yes, but that was a short which I made while *Delicatessen* was in pre-production, when we already had the cast. So the actors I chose for *Foutaises* were ones I'd already chosen for *Delicatessen*. It was a good way of rehearsing, even if the acting is fairly limited.

Why did you need a sixteen-week shoot?
We didn't do all that many takes, but there were a huge number of shots: 610, many of them with special effects, like the taps that go wrong.

What about the famous boomerang knife?
For the first time ever, we used video. The knife and the background were shot on 35mm, then we transferred the lot down to digital tape and went to Durand (who are the best in their field) to do a video mix and transfer back to 35mm. It had already been done in commercials, but the mix was noticeable, whereas I reckon we got a near perfect image.

Did you use this process for any other effects?
Apart from the three shots with the knife, we used it for the building exploding in the distance, Potin's mosquito, and a few things like the spark that makes the gas go off. If the process is to be ultimately invisible, the shot has to be fairly short and high-contrast. But this new process does enable one to do instant effects; the outcome can be monitored as you are working, without going through weeks of lab processing which may or may not come out right. Even in the last *Indiana Jones*, the process is visible in the balloon shots. Now, all directors are going to use these sorts of effects. Our control over lighting was also seriously affected by a special development process called 'without fastener', which increases contrast without destroying colour. It is a meticulous business, and we ran into some problems with the fog. No one will ever use this process

again. The labs have to treat every print individually and they won't have it. And no two prints are identical.

What were the sources of inspiration for the look of the film?
For colour, old Edward Hopper was a real help, and for the exteriors, in the fog – apart from *Quai des brumes* – we used a picture by Sabine Weiss, which is on the cover of one of her books. As far as costumes, sets and characters were concerned, Robert Doisneau was our official inspiration.

Some of the themes, like cannibalism and mutilation, had already appeared in some of Caro's strip cartoons.
At one stage, Caro was into hardcore. But I think *Delicatessen* is a different kettle of fish. It is certainly damaged and neo-punk, like *Le Bunker de la dernière rafale*. But we've been saying for ages, at least since the first feature script we wrote, that we want to be constructive. Crapping on everything is facile. Much better to be constructive, to give the audience some sort of pleasure. Not that we regret *Le Bunker de la dernière rafale*.

Were strip cartoons in general – other than Caro's – an inspiration while you were devising *Delicatessen*?
I don't really read strip cartoons. Goossens and Villemin, for a laugh, but they weren't really an influence. There is Tardi of course, but his work refers back to pre-war cinema. Otherwise, there's Bicot and Suzy. Or Rube Goldberg's drawings. Certainly the influence is clear with respect to all Madame Interligator's suicide devices. But I came to Goldberg quite late, and I was already thinking about something of the sort.

There's Charlie Bowers and *Pim, Pam, Poum* too.
True. But it's hard to know what really constitutes an influence. Influences are things that we like, that resurface. But the question of references is a game you play after the fact – except where Doisneau and Carné's films are concerned. We used them as examples when discussing our project with the crew.

What about *Brazil*?
The pipes and the troglo costumes bear an obvious similarity to the plumber's in *Brazil*, but when we noticed the connection, we were somewhat put out. Having said that, the pipes appeared in Caro's early drawings. Gilliam's background is in animation, as is ours. His references are not purely cinematic. In any case, *Brazil* is social satire, whereas our film is really about feelings. In our previous screenplays, we always set out to recreate a world, but we didn't have the budget. We remained fairly naturalistic, even if there is a certain overflow into fantasy. Our story is not set in any particular period.

The film seems post-atomic, though the style is 1940s and 1960s as far as the references to television are concerned.

It's a film of parallel universes, as if there had been some kind of time slippage. We are happy with this effect because initially the people who read our script didn't like its timelessness. As a response to this, we dated it 'Aubervilliers, 2015'. But we didn't use this label in the film. We were keen to make sure it wasn't seen as a period piece. If we'd set the action under the German occupation, people would have said we were trying to say something about war. *Delicatessen* is not *Uranus*. We were free to bring *troglodistes* into it and to use TV images.

The rotating selection of cheeses in the middle of the test-card is a nice touch.
We found that in some old commercials. It seemed an appropriate image for an interlude, that's why we included it. It's like another time slippage. It's easy to imagine that in a society deprived of food, TV would show endless pictures of food – either to give people something to fantasize about or to irritate them, who knows? What was crucial was the overall coherence of detail, otherwise all these references would have seemed gratuitous.

At first, when the threatening butcher appears, one might be forgiven for thinking, 'Oh, this is an effect', but later we discover that there is a good reason for his expression. Similarly, we don't know until later what the tracking shots in the tubes add up to.

Some directors use this technique masterfully. Sergio Leone, king of cunning. His aesthetic effects always serve the plot. Scorsese too. He always goes over the top, but no one ever notices.

Delicatessen: The pipes and troglo costume

You use humour all the time, even in the credits. Does this reflect a need to reassure your audience?

A need not to take oneself too seriously. As soon as we get too heavy, we undermine ourselves.

Is that why the only bloody scene is a dream sequence?

It had to come as near the start as possible. We wanted to give the audience a good fright, at least once. If the butcher seemed too farcical, he wouldn't have come across as truly dangerous.

There's an ogre and a ball of wool. *Delicatessen* is full of references to fairy-tales.

Indeed. The butcher is an ogre, as in the story of St Nicholas, and the ball of wool refers both to Ariadne and to Tom Thumb's pebbles. Both Caro and I love fairy-tales. The first screenplay we ever wrote, *La Cité des enfants perdus* was quite close to Perrault's *Tales*, as illustrated by Gustave Doré.

At what stage did you work on the soundtrack?

Mainly in post-production. Caro did all the extra sound effects by synthesizing pre-recorded effects. The whole of the last scene, for instance, is composed of sounds made up by Caro, then edited in by me. When we're imagining scenes, we put in the sound effects as we go along like kids. Then we have to find a way of putting those sounds on to film.

People talk of your work together as a 'cottage industry'.

We're proud of that. Our method is not intellectual. Our concerns are craft concerns, in the best sense of the term. We like working away at something to get it as near perfect as possible. If we were shoemakers or cabinet-makers, it wouldn't be all that different. What matters is that we should be completely satisfied with the result. Caro says we are manic depressives. If we get something wrong, we get physically ill. Before principal photography, we did 35mm screen tests with each of the actors; we tested the costumes, the hairstyles, the make-up, trying out a whole range of lenses on the actresses to find out how far we could go in deforming them. We shot all the different sets to try out the colours in 35mm. No one does that any more. But the final result is exactly what was intended. We designed the poster, the press pack, the trailer.

The trailer is a scene from the film. It lends some weight to the objection that you have produced a series of shorts dressed up as a feature film.

Just because our background is in shorts doesn't mean this film is a series of shorts. The objection may stand for the first two thirds of the film, but thereafter I feel that the stories combine and run in parallel. It's a different kind of writing. In any case, the story is set in an apartment block – in other words, in a series of different boxes representing the different apartments. And the action relates to what is going on in each one of those apartments, at the same time and in parallel.

This 'series of boxes' is not unlike the design of a page from a strip cartoon in book form.

Not at all. Cinema does not draw on strip cartoons. On the contrary. There are no examples of strip cartoons being adapted to cinema, whereas many cartoonists have drawn on Sergio Leone or other film-makers.

Was the set built in the studio?

Yes. Initially, we thought we'd find an apartment block due to be knocked down in or near Paris. But that wasn't practical. We built everything. It was a bit more expensive, but it meant we could control everything.

How did you work as co-directors?

The first day, we appeared on set with no preconceptions. As with *Le Bunker de la dernière rafale*, we both did everything and discussed every decision. But a technical crew needs to look to one person. So each of us naturally took responsibility for what he knew best. Caro was in charge of production design and costumes. I took responsibility for directing the actors and choosing the angles. Which is not to say that from time to time he didn't comment on the acting, nor that I didn't have something to say about a particular choice of colour. But neither of us would insist if the other seemed sure of what he was doing. Our system is founded on mutual respect. There was no need to discuss the atmosphere of the film. We'd glance at each other and know. We're a two-headed beast. We're so close that we never disagree, except on irrelevant points.

So you're keen to go on working together.

Yes. Though not necessarily for ever. If I never have anything to do with costume, and Caro never gets involved in photography, both of us will end up frustrated. From time to time, we'll work separately. In any case, we don't have quite the same taste. Caro's videos show a certain mathematical aesthetic which looks cold to me. I'm inclined towards the more personal style of *Foutaises*. When we collaborate, we meet on common ground.

Is there an element of self-censorship?

No. The common ground is genuine. When Caro pushes me towards a certain black humour, when I drive him towards a more personal approach, there's no compulsion involved. We both want that.

Interviewed in Paris, 24 April 1991.

17   Robert Guédiguian on *Marius et Jeannette*

interviewed by Eric Derobert and Stéphane Goudet

Robert Guédiguian

Robert Guédiguian was born in an old-fashioned working-class suburb of
Marseilles called L'Estaque. He is a former communist, and his political
views form a significant part of his inspiration. He has made nine other
films, all set in L'Estaque, starring his wife Ariane Ascarides and his best
friend Gerard Meylan. *Marius et Jeannette* was screened at Cannes, and was
one of the most successful films at the French box office in 1997.

Guédiguian has been working away for years developing a style of his own,
making each of his films in more or less the same locations, employing more
or less the same family of actors, without ever attracting much critical or
box-office attention. The sudden eruption of *Marius et Jeannette* on the
wider scene reflects an impatience with what many in France regard as the
narcissistic, boxed-in tendencies of art-house films, with their samey stories
of romantic attachments, their predictably young, middle-class characters
and their unendingly psychoanalytical dissection of emotional turmoil. It is
worth noting that before Guédiguian such English film-makers as Ken
Loach and Stephen Frears had acquired a tremendous following among
French audiences, outstripping even their domestic audiences, because they
were seen to offer a return to content, to humour and populist settings.

Marius et Jeannette

Jeannette (Adriane Ascaride) is a single mother, working on a supermarket check-out in run-down Marseilles; Marius (Gerard Meylan) is a security guard at a dilapidated cement works. They meet when he apprehends her in the act of stealing pots of paint from the site, but he gallantly offers to decorate her flat for her. A romance gradually develops – troubled only by Marius's drinking, which masks a guilty secret concerning the tragic fate of his own two children.

Where do you come from? What is your social background?

I was born in December 1953 at L'Estaque, a working-class district in the northern suburbs of Marseilles, where my films are set and where I shoot at regular intervals. My mother is German, my father was born in Marseilles, but my father's father was Armenian. I grew up in L'Estaque. I studied economics and sociology at the University of Aix-en-Provence. Then I went up to Paris, to be with my companion Ariane, who had won a place at the Conservatoire. I continued with my studies in Paris, partly at the Ecoles des Hautes Etudes, where I started a history thesis. At the same time, in 1978, I met René Féret, through Ariane who had had a part in *La Communion solennelle*. Over a drunken meal, he asked me, though I was just a boy really, to write a screenplay with him. So we wrote *Fernand*, which, originally, was supposed to be an adaptation of *Berlin Alexanderplatz.*[*] That got me going. Right away I wrote *Dernier Eté* in a fit of youthful enthusiasm, with Franck Le Wita who co-directed the film with me. Apart from the pleasure of writing, the thing that really mattered was the unsettling effect of stopping active political militancy when the Communist Party signed a joint manifesto with the Socialist Party. I had been politically active for twelve years, from 1968 to 1980. My films are an expression of that unsettling effect.

You are politically active by other means, but the Communist Party, of which you were a member, is not really a presence in your films.

True. I prefer telling simple stories that may, on close reading, have some kind of metaphorical impact. I would have trouble staging a Communist Party meeting. I don't know how to film institutions, hospitals, police stations. But I think that's to do with my manner – which is sensual and immediate. Nine times out of ten, hospitals are ugly. I don't see why I would put my camera in one. My patients, my terminally ill characters, are seen on the balconies of their council flats. I am not going to show them in a place where I have no desire to go. Sometimes this all gets very convoluted. If I could, I'd shoot only places and people and actors I like. Factories, waterside restaurants in the middle of an industrial zone, voluptuous

* German novel by Alfred Doblin which was made into a multi-part TV mini-series by Rainer Werner Fassbinder.

places, that's what I like. It's not just a matter of film-making; I'd love to spend my life there too. Just as I could spend my life with 99 per cent of my characters. There aren't many bastards in my films. What I don't like doesn't inspire me.

Your take on abandoned industrial locations seems libertarian rather than Communist.
Definitely. It's a gut feeling, I think. In L'Estaque, on the docks, people's Communism is rooted in anarcho-syndicalism, it's a big-mouth culture. We'd never put up a poster we didn't approve of just because the national executive told us to. No 'French is best' for us! We did as we pleased, no one could tell us what to do, it was quite libertarian. My characters, like Jeannette, tend to say, 'I'll do as I please, fuck you!'

From *Dernier Eté* on, you have always incorporated very famous bits of classical music into your soundtracks. In *Marius et Jeannette*, you use Vivaldi. Why?
I was about ten when I discovered how Pasolini used Vivaldi in *Mama Roma* and Bach in *Accattone*. I practically fainted, it was so glorious. Then I read his theoretical work on the notion of stylistic contamination, on the place of the sacred, and I liked the idea of borrowing that music for incorporation into my world, the world I am a part of. I feel that I too have a right to use Bach, my characters have that right. More seriously, I realized that this music suited me because I could work with it myself, in the cutting-room, even though I am not musical at all. When you choose to use existing scores for your soundtrack, you inevitably tamper with them, you use them for your own ends. In *Marius et Jeannette* we used digital technology to sample the intro to *O Sole Mio* and used it eight times. In *A la vie, à la mort!* we speeded up Strauss waltzes. I alter music, knead it, it's lovely. I can behave as though I'd written it myself. Which brings Brecht's notion of alienation to mind, as in Pasolini's use of Bach to accompany a fight in *Accattone*. As a result, the fight in question acquires a universal, allegorical dimension, detaching the audience sufficiently that they can think about what they are seeing without being too remote. I choose famous tunes partly out of provocation, to make the point that just because something is well-known doesn't mean it's bad. There is a self-righteousness about culture and taste which I find superficial and irritating. I don't see why I shouldn't remind people that Vivaldi is a genius, and it's too bad if they don't like that. I find *The Four Seasons* remarkable. Just because you hear it on answering-machines, in supermarkets and lifts doesn't mean it's somehow become bad music. It can be given new life by association with new images and meanings. However, things are not quite that simple; when I used Strauss in my last two films, it was in reference to supermarket culture and teenage fantasies.

Rouge Midi, your second film, is a history of the twentieth century seen through the eyes of one working-class family.
The initial idea was to trace the background of the characters in *Dernier Eté*. Who are

these people? Who were their parents? It is not exactly autobiographical. The characters are Italian, not Armenian. All the same, I was retracing my own past, using an unfashionable format and exploring a kind of secret history. I wanted to produce a cultural autobiography, which would concentrate on private life. I wanted to be able to comment on History with a capital H – the two world wars, emigration, generation gaps and so on – all within a family universe and within the world of work. I was keen on making an inventory, a picture book that would generate a succession of tableaux. But I feel I was too young to work on a project of that sort. I don't regret it though, it's my film. I've never worked to commission.

Why use the same actor to play grandfather and grandson, hardly differentiating the parts by make-up?
I wanted to comment on permanence. I didn't want one universe to give way to another. Which is what the character says at the beginning. You can't get rid of the past. I didn't want to use make-up because I wanted to avoid the usual tricks employed in family sagas. The effect of age is that it generates emotion and I wanted to avoid that, it's too artificial. Perhaps I took things too far.

The three protagonists of *Ki lo sa?* reject the notion of time passing, and it ends unhappily.
They are regressive. There is an imbalance between their upbringing and the world in which they function. *Ki lo sa?* is about becoming an adult, about learning to love in a world gone awry. I investigate the operation of history, of transcendence and reproduction at a critical juncture, when everything we believed in collapsed – including Communism, which for fifty years determined how many people thought. I was obsessed with the problem of not having anything to believe in. It seemed terrifying, like death. I was thirty years old at the time. I no longer believed in what had made me and I was clinging on by the tips of my fingers. It would have been nice not to lose faith. The children in that film have a dual purpose. They remind us of what the four main characters used to be and can now no longer be, but they are also exterminating angels come to warn of approaching death or ultimate sleep.

The bridge in *Dieu vomit les tièdes*, which appears in Renoir's *Toni*, seems to have special significance in your work.
It is the bridge upon which Toni dies. I don't quote it as a reference, even though I love *Toni*. I happen to find it very beautiful; it was built by Eiffel – like the cement works in *Marius et Jeannette*, which ought to be listed on the UNESCO list of World Heritage Sites. I see in these exceptional buildings a history of industry, of labour accomplished, of effort and noise and sweat. That's what counts, the world of work. The bridge is also designed to let ships through, it opens and closes, joins the two shores, it is a connection, a link with the Mediterranean, a circle, a secret childhood world, a place of vows betrayed, whatever . . .

A la vie, à la mort!

Why do you use the old-fashioned device of an in-camera fade-to-black?
To be honest, it's a piece of self-indulgence. It has no special meaning, I just happen to like it. It reminds me of silent films, of Charlie Chaplin disappearing at the end of the road. It is gentler than a straight cut and evokes memory and vanishing. I like its down-to-earth, archaic quality. A mechanical fade-out is part of the process of shooting. I like the object, the way it sits in front of the camera and closes like an aperture.

You once said, 'I'll never understand how film-makers can use a crane on a council estate.' What is so shocking about that?
The contrast between the means required and the subject-matter. It is a question of flaunting wealth in the midst of poverty. I even refuse to put down tracks in a council estate (though tracks aren't all that expensive). There is something very violent about bringing in all this sophisticated technology, using a tool that at today's prices costs $5,000 per day in a place where people are on the breadline.

Which is to say that you attach as much importance to the finished product as to the shooting conditions.
Yes.

You often insist on the simplicity of your style.
In an age of continuous cable and satellite images, the picture I'm interested in is the Lumière brothers. We need to see a branch swaying, a bird traversing the sky, a pedestrian sitting down to his newspaper, or just waiting. We need to remember

156

how we used to say, 'Oh, look, that's about reality', instead of chopping everything up as fast as we can. There was one shot I really liked in Abbas Kiarostami's *Close-Up*, when one of the characters kicks a can of insecticide, and he just holds the image. That shot is not taking me for a fool. Audiences should be left to their own devices. Cinema needs to get back to reality. I cannot stand television lighting, it is almost pornographic. I mean lighting that has no room for shadow, all gleaming, where everything seems very sharp, nothing has any texture, no weight or feature, no eyes. Rural simplicity would do us a lot of good.

Two features of *Marius et Jeannette* seem to contradict your praise of Kiarostami's style. The first is the shot of the group laughing. This works, it makes us euphoric, but it is fairly insistent. Is that not a way of depriving the audience of its freedom?

Every film-maker plays a game of cat-and-mouse with his audience. I enjoyed seeing those people laughing because I like them, they are together, they are friends. We were laughing for five weeks. We shot two hours a day. We hardly did any work. We laughed all day. That's what the film conveys. We cut it super-fast. It's the most spontaneous, the fastest film I've ever made. We wrote it in three weeks in March and by 15 September we'd finished the edit.

The other thing in *Marius et Jeannette* which seems to contradict what you say about letting the audience just sit back and watch a shot is your use of a recurring head-and-shoulders shot when characters speak, often in monologues.

There is nothing wrong with that, including where Marius speaks after the farcical fight scene. I wanted to go as deep into the character as I could. He doesn't speak much. Suddenly, there, he tells us his life story. Having said which, the scene is a big risk. Friends, close friends, warned me; they said the scene is a long one, and what Marius says is terrifying.

But why introduce such soliloquies with an apology for their lengths – in this instance the fact that alcohol makes people loquacious? Are you not apologizing for what we are about to endure?

In a way. I'm saying, 'This will be a bit long, but he's drunk.'

Why the surprising zoom shot on Marius as he goes up to the crane clutching a gun?

So that the question is asked, so that people discuss it as they leave. As I said, I like the odd clumsiness. I like to show film-making as a process. In Buñuel's *Los Olvidados* there is a scene in the prison in which one of the boys chucks an egg at the camera. That says, 'This is cinema.' I like that.

Your career has followed the course of changes in French society and French consciousness over the last decades. In the 1980s, when enterprise culture was at its height, your characters fade away. Now that society is stirring once more, the characters in your films, under the aegis of the women among them, are

growing more pro-active. What is the relationship between French film-making in general and your own progress?

There is none. I am an outsider. When *Dernier Eté* came out, Beineix's *Diva* appeared. There is no connection.

Can you tell us about your gang?

There is Ariane Ascaride and Gérard Meylan. Ariane and I having been living together for years. Gérard, who is a nurse by profession, is a childhood friend. We've been inseparable since childhood. They call us 'the twins'. We were militants together and that is how people see us in the neighbourhood. Together, we led the Young Communists. So between the two of them, I have a feminine conscience and a masculine conscience. They constitute the body of my films. Needless to say, we are all the same age. As my method is spontaneous, and explicitly subjective, I always deal with personal problems and have them embodied by those two, whether we are twenty-five or forty years old. I believe in them more than anyone else. Long-term group friendships always focus on some shared activity and in that sense film-making has allowed me to keep the gang going. Before that, it was political activity. Initially, the connection between us was spontaneous and friendly, then came politics and now there is cinema. Ariane and the others have chosen to become actors in order to say things, to intervene in the world, not for narcissistic reasons.

The point about my gang is that unlike 99 per cent of film shoots, mine involve no competitiveness. People's relationships generate not just the character but also the cinematic style, the sets and so on. Jean-Pierre Darroussin does not have to prove to Ariane that he can act when they play a scene. Neither needs to prove to me that, as a director, I was right to cast them. And I am at liberty to say on set that I have absolutely no idea what we are doing, that we'll see, we need to think. Everyone just laughs. The fact of the gang also changes the nature of acting. I am never certain whether my actors are acting or not. Things happen, a look for instance, that I feel I am stealing. At times, I feel I am simply in tune with reality.

Do you ever feel like using other actors?
No.

Do you recognize the influence of Marcel Pagnol, who is often mentioned in connection with your films?

I have contradictory feelings about Pagnol. I like some of his very much and some I loathe, like the trilogy novels, *Marius, Fanny, César*. He's a pleasant but mediocre writer. As a film-maker, I agree with the general view that his dialogue is excellent and that he uses locations very well. Then, Pagnol was right wing. When I was younger, I was in denial. Today, I like to think I can undermine him.

Marius et Jeannette: Adriane Ascaride and Gerard Meylan

For instance, in *A la vie, à la mort!* the scene in which Patrick learns that Marie-Sol is pregnant is consciously shot in a Pagnol-esque way.

Can you define popular cinema?
No. But the subject-matter must be popular for a start, the film must be accessible. I have no interest in playing a pioneering part in film-making, in influencing the way films are made. I can see how that might be of interest to some, and they in turn may influence me in my work. But my motivation is a desire to intervene, to affect the world. That's what popular means. One must be read, heard, listened to, one must be politically effective. Having said which, I realize that is something I have never achieved. Perhaps I shall with *Marius et Jeannette*.

18   Arnaud Desplechin on *La Sentinelle*

interviewed by Olivier de Bruyn and Olivier Kohn

Arnaud Desplechin, directing Emmaneuel Salinger in *La Sentinelle*

Arnaud Desplechin is one of France's foremost young directors. His most recent feature, *Comment je me suis disputé (ou Ma vie sexuelle)*, was in competition at Cannes. He is currently in pre-production in London. Previous work includes *La vie des morts* (1991) and *La Sentinelle* (1992).

This interview relates to Desplechin's first films, which seemed at the time to come from left-field, and marked the emergence of a strongly individual voice, corresponding to a new family of actors specifically associated with the director. In retrospect, what may be seen to have counted most is Desplechin's background in camerawork – a relatively rare phenomenon in France – which gives his films a visual depth and freshness not often found among his contemporaries.

La Sentinelle
Returning from Eastern Europe where – as the son of Western diplomats – he grew up, a forensic scientist finds a shrunken head in his luggage. He sets about trying to find out whose head it is. His sister, a singer, is about to give a concert in Russia and some of her 'contacts' warn him off, implying that his inquiries could jeopardize a forthcoming spy swap.

How did you start working in films?

I wasn't a great cinema buff. I had seen films, but mostly on television because I lived in the provinces. But I'd known for a long time that I wanted to make films. I don't know what influenced me. Perhaps it was Walt Disney's films, or the explanation in *Tout l'Univers* of the special effects in *The Ten Commandments* – the parting of the sea – something like that. I went to Paris after my baccalaureat and applied to the IDHEC film school, failed to get in, and then got in the following year. We were all very young, eighteen or nineteen, but in the end the atmosphere was quite tense, and it was a struggle to finish my diploma films. Then I worked as a cameraman.

Were you already writing at that stage?

I spent a year writing a screenplay that was no good, before beginning another more complicated one which took a year and a half, and became *La Sentinelle*. After obtaining a grant for rewrites, I was worried that I wouldn't get the Avance sur Recettes, so I wrote another script to submit to the Avance as well, knowing that I could make it anyway with the money I had scraped together, but that its length would be dictated by finance. It worked out well – it's 52 minutes long, and called *La Vie des morts*.

It has a depth that is unusual for a short film, with fifteen characters, and very complex situations. Basically, it's more like a condensed feature film than an elaborate short film.

That's the side of me that likes a Rossini steak – steak, then foie gras, then bacon, then more foie gras. That shows in *La Sentinelle* as well – there are lots of different things in the film, almost too many. There aren't usually very many different elements in a first film – I wanted the opposite for *La Sentinelle*.

Why?

In *La Vie des morts*, the number of characters was decisive in deciding the sort of film it was to be. With only two or three characters, it would have been a light comedy, quite different from what it actually is. I wanted to recreate that abundance you find in a certain kind of Western, in which you see communities settling, with lots of characters of equal importance. I was thinking of a marvellous film by Ford, *Two Rode Together*, with the same story as *La Vie des morts*. A group of people, rejected because their children have been kidnapped by the Indians, ask two men to get the children back. Then, when the children are returned, they in turn are rejected by their own families – one child is even hung by his family. Eventually the community settles down, everyone is reconciled. It's almost as if the murder is necessary in order for the parents to sort themselves out. I was very struck by this idea.

Making films that are of a particular genre seems important to you: the Western in *La Vie des morts*, the spy thriller in *La Sentinelle*. Was the latter inspired by the fall of the Berlin Wall?

No. The lead character came first. The political intrigue came later for several reasons, but not specifically the Berlin Wall. The unhappiness generated by East–West conflict has been around for a long time. I read a book written in the early 1980s by Joyce Carol Oates with a similar storyline; you also find it in Nabokov's 'Le Guetteur', the story of a man living in the West and missing the East. The fall of the Wall was just another episode.

Why did you combine this character and the East–West conflict?
I love espionage novels, especially those of John Le Carré, the thrill of it. But as well as being an avid consumer of thrillers myself, I felt the need to anchor my storyline in some sort of reality. When you're devising a thriller, you cannot just show off and give the audience a story completely divorced from the real world. You cannot lie. I wanted a rationalization for the film. I didn't want it to seem like make-believe. I thought that if I couldn't give a character a line that I believed myself, then the script was bad, and could only function on a level of fantasy.

There is a close link between the story of the world and Mathias's story.
I had to admit that my experience of frontiers was non-existent. So I began by filming an apartment and people who found it difficult to live together. Then came the idea of the two together, the frontiers of the apartment, and those of different countries. I became less ambitious. For example, you say to yourself that you want to make a film about the Bible, but, as you know nothing about it, you make a film instead about your girlfriend, and decide eventually that you could write Moses into it, because he's an interesting character.

There is also a common thread between politics and medicine.
This struck me immediately. It's simple: a scar, a borderline, the wounds of the world, and the wounds of the individual. People's approach to the two is very different. When someone is wounded, they show sympathy, but, when faced with a frontier, they say 'The Russians are bastards!' They see a line on a map, but don't know why it is there. In the film, there is, on the one hand, a doctor who looks at wounds and explains what caused them, and on the other hand a man who looks at maps and knows what they're all about. There is also a younger boy who can only deal with one death at a time and says: 'This is a dead man, this is what happened to him.' On the other hand, if this notion of frontiers is to work, it has to apply to every aspect of the film – the apartments, the families, the love stories . . .

In the film you seem to be fascinated by the breaking up of entities, not only in the themes you explore, but also in the editing. For example, during the discussion with the priest, there are several close-ups of Mathias's feet.
I wasn't aware of a fascination. In the priest's scene, it's done to show that the two people disagree on a theological matter, because one is arguing the spirit of the law, the other the letter of the law. Mathias doesn't believe in God, he simply wants to know what the law says in order to live comfortably with the head, and

to remain on peaceful terms with his neighbours. The priest, on the other hand, only sees the spirit of the law. To Mathias, encumbered as he is by the physical fact of a head, this is unimportant. Sooner or later, he wants to kick it – either to get rid of it, or just to make a game of it. But the law forbids this, as he knows, and the close-ups show his temptation to kick the head, although he's embarrassed by this and so talks to the priest.

Mathias: Emmaneuel Salinger

But he's very fond of this body, the notion of being its protector.
Not initially. At first, it's a disaster that befalls him, and he tries to get rid of it. Then he decides not to get rid of it, and to sort everything out. He's a scholarly, logical boy, and he thinks that if he just leaves it hanging around, it will make him unhappy. This is a Freudian concept, and he has every right to have read Freud! So, he goes to the priest to find out how to relieve himself symbolically of the head. Then he moves into the world of politics, and on to espionage. But, for the first hour, his only concern is that he is very unhappy, and wants to find a solution to this unhappiness. His solution is that he must solve his problems.

We do get the impression, right from the beginning, that, almost subconsciously, he identifies himself with the head.
Not exactly. At the beginning, he really feels violated, then he moves beyond that, and emerges, not passive, but exposed, sensitive. Like some women feel after giving birth. A friend told me that, after giving birth, she would cry every time she saw a tree, feeling that it was somehow part of her. Mathias feels like this when he gets off the train, and, when he finds the head, he feels it's somehow part of him. The paradox of the film is that this state of mind makes him unhappy, but

gradually it teaches him to be happy. To open yourself to others is painful, but at the same time very positive. This is what Bleicher tells him.

Did you change the screenplay during the shoot or in the cutting-room?
It was very structured, but written with gaps in, so that it couldn't just be shot chronologically. It's essential to sustain the feeling of constant evolution. During filming, we made a few changes to some of the scenes, rewrote the odd piece of dialogue, but not much more than that. The real work takes place at the editing stage. François Gedigier edits without knowing either where the scene comes in the film, or which is the first shot. The aim is to shake things up, upset the obvious order of things, even if it's just a sentence. We tried all sorts of things to avoid ending up with a 'pre-planned' film: beginning with the train scene, beginning with the hotel scene . . . So in a way, the screenplay is written in the cutting-room.

Were the actors involved in the screenplay at all?
When Emmaneuel Salinger was working on the screenplay, he didn't know that he would be acting in it, his role was very much that of co-writer at that stage. Whenever I have let myself be influenced by an actor, I've regretted it, I don't think it's a good idea for an actor to write his own scenes and dialogue. He has more freedom when everything has been done for him.

You use some of the same actors in *La Vie des morts* and *La Sentinelle*. Do you want to create a sort of cinematic 'family'?
It's more of a theatrical concept than a family one. I use the same actors simply because they are good, I'd love to vary the experiences, but it hasn't worked out that way.

This theatrical concept reminds me of Rivette.
It's my attempt to do away with the mythology that surrounds the cinema, and which creates a barrier between the film and the spectator. To do this, you say to yourself that the only difference between a theatrical performance and a film is that the latter is recorded: the Lumière Brothers used to get the actors to perform for the camera during the afternoon exactly what they were going to be doing on stage in the evening. That's enough to make a film. When you start, you think you're going to do this and that, a tracking shot here. . . you think you are going to inspire the actors. Then you're disappointed to discover that you are much too young to know anything about film-making, you haven't a clue how to direct the actors, and the audience doesn't give a damn anyway. When you've understood that, you can get to work.

When an actor recites a piece of Shakespeare that has no direct relevance to the plot, doesn't that put an added obstacle between the film and the spectator?
I think it's the opposite. At first, you think that you're writing wonderfully meaningful dialogue, but it's pointless. The end of silent cinema was a great loss, because

sound itself is a loss, it's just sound, not meaning. If an actor reads out loud from the telephone book, we'll pay attention to his voice, his movements, other things that are far more interesting and direct than the words he is saying. As soon as there is sound, we move away from the actors and away from life, and so away from the screenplay. In silent films, the dialogue is essential, not because of what's said, but because of the relationship between the actors. Sometimes we just took out the words during editing, and replaced them with any old bit of music, and everything became clear – the scene either worked or it didn't. Sound makes a profound understanding of the film harder to achieve. By getting an actor to recite someone else's text, and thereby making the sense of it worthless, I feel as if I'm getting closer to silent cinema.

Given your mistrust of sound, how do you deal with it?
The whole film is recorded live. We tried to dub the odd word, the odd sentence here and there, but gave up. With the sound like this, we come back to the freedom of the silent movie, we're filming reality. As soon as you redo a sound, you upset the balance and bring in an artificial element. So each shot is absolutely honest. I was worried that it would be difficult to avoid an academic aspect to *La Sentinelle*, given the screenplay. So it was important that the filming was quite raw.

Did you take many shots?
Yes. This may sound contradictory after what I said about the raw quality of the filming, but I realized that making a film about a head was a bad idea. Imagine two men living together, one of whom is a drug addict. There is a scene in which one says to the other: 'This is impossible, you've stolen my credit card to buy junk.' It only takes three shots. Now imagine explaining to two actors: 'You work in the police, he's a spy, well, not really . . . It's because he found a head . . .' Inevitably, the first take will be absurd. To achieve something realistic, you have to remove the head, the Security Services, the Quai d'Orsay, and everything else, so that all that's left is the two men in the room. To get there, it needs thirty takes.

The film leaves an uneasy feeling to do with the fall of the Berlin Wall, as if the memories of an old world are threatened.
It's interesting to see a film that says what a pity it is that all those great Communist dictatorships are disappearing, when the world is saying the opposite. The paradox is exciting. It is a standard tactic of espionage novels – muddling all the issues, inverting good and bad, generally confusing the reader. That's what makes a good read.

The boys, Jean-Jacques and William, seem fairly immature, which is surprising given their responsibilities.
On the contrary, on one level Jean-Jacques and William are appallingly old. By

comparison, Churchill and de Gaulle were wonderfully childish. Imagine a general who takes a plane with three other people to south-west France, finds himself in an office, and says 'In fact, I am France!' It's a remarkably childish act! Like an orphan who has lost everything. It's a childishly violent and theatrical gesture, quite Shakespearean. The boys in the film are already old, finished, they think too much. Another part of them is very immature, probably because I'm immature, and they're obviously a bit like me.

There is a very clear distinction between the boys and the girls, who are more distant and sensitive to artistic matters.
That is the point of the film, pinpointing the difference. The truth is that I would like to film inside someone's head. Garrel knows how to do that.* I can't, so I forced myself to use a false head. At the heart of the film is the idea that you must beat yourself up in order to open your eyes to someone else. I wanted to intensify all the differences; men and women, rich and poor, old and young . . . It seems to me more important to focus on the differences between things than the similarities. It's a depressing approach because people don't understand each other, but it's also quite positive because at least it means that people will go on talking to each other.

As for the girls, I try to use them like the apartment, to help me to deal with the world of espionage at a more modest level. I have tried to show that it's the girls, the minority, who suffer the consequences of the actions of the boys – a parallel with two Western countries who expand at the expense of an African country. When two boys get on well together, there is always a girl who pays the price.

The girls do allow me to 'place' Mathias. If you analyse the characters, Mathias is sometimes wrong in his relationships with the boys. If he only listened to Jean-Jacques, for example, he could learn a lot about humour, and how to behave with girls. He could learn from William too – he isn't loaded, he believes that it is better to be rich than poor, but he knows it's not the end of the world to be poor. William could teach Mathias to have a healthier relationship with money. But the way that the film evolves proves Mathias is right, because he deals with his problems, and the others don't. To balance this, I wanted him to be proved wrong as well sometimes, and with the girls he is wrong three times. This inability to deal with things – the girls, among other things – is the other side of the coin. Mathias asks himself a lot of serious questions, which he obviously can't answer. But at least he asks.

* Philippe Garrel is a well-known French film-maker who has graduated from experimental film-making in the 1970s to his present, established, art-house status. His most recent films are J'entends plus la guitare, La Naissance de l'amour and Un Coeur fantôme.

19

Manuel Poirier on *Western*

interviewed by Stéphane Goudet and Claire Vassé

Manuel Poirier

Manuel Poirier's first major commercial success, a road movie set in rural
Brittany entitled *Western*, won the jury prize at the 1997 Cannes Film Festival. Previous films include *La Petite Amie d'Antonio* (1992), *A la campagne*
(1995) and *Marion* (1997).

The basic idea behind *Western* is a simple one: what happens if you make a
road movie without cars? The answer is that the central relationship
between the protagonists is quite different, slower and more strongly
infused with the light and tone of landscape. The film is shot in one remote
corner of Brittany and its main strength lies in the way two oddball, foreign
characters gradually succumb to their faintly hippyish fate. But Poirier's
films avoid the risk of seeming maudlin or fey by gently enforcing the view
that emotional relationships provide private redemption when the noise
and the haste of the world has nothing solid or sane to offer.

Western
A Catalan shoe salesman, Paco (Serge Lopez), beats up and hospitalizes a
Russian vagabond, Nino (Sacha Bourdo), for stealing his car. But this is just
the start of a promising friendship, and the duo embark upon a tour of
western France. They hitchhike round Brittany, and along the way gate-
crash a wedding, where they make persistent efforts to chat up women –
Paco being much the more successful of the two.

How did you come to make films?

Quite late. I didn't have much schooling. I stopped at the fifth form. I've done lots of different jobs, including being a cabinet-maker, which was something that meant a great deal to me. I also went through periods of doing nothing, of hanging about. However, I had been wanting to make films for a long time, without being entirely sure that I would be able to bring it off. One day, I was working in a cultural institute and I thought I ought to have a go. I did a little research and found out that there was something called the Groupe de Recherche et d'Essais Cinématographiques (GREC), which gave non-professionals grants to make short films. I managed to get one for my first film, *La Première Journée de Nicolas*; then I was incredibly lucky to get a state grant for my second short, *La Lettre à Dédé*. Then Canal Plus gave me carte blanche to make a third short, which was called *Appartement 62*. All of which led to my taking on short commissions from France 3. Very soon I found myself wanting to make a feature. I wrote a screenplay and tried to find a producer. After four years, I realized that no one was interested. The fact that I was unknown – as was my crew – that it wasn't a comedy and that the subject-matter was not exactly riveting counted against me.

Didn't the fact that you'd made shorts help?

It resulted in a few lukewarm meetings. No more than that. I thought it would count for a lot more, but in fact it just brought me a bit of corporate work and gave me a bit of a name. But it had no real impact on the way my first feature was produced.

How were you able to make your first feature, *La Petite Amie d'Antonio*?

I shot the first twenty minutes as a short, hoping that would generate the money to finish the film. I was never interested in showing that section as a short. It was always a feature. The trick was to get finance that was meant to go to shorts – for instance, from the Normandy Regional Film Fund, which later gave me money to finish the film. I also got some money from Canal Plus. With that money I was able to restart the shoot, after an interval of one year. The film was made with very little money.

Why did you want to make films?

I don't think it was seeing films particularly – although Bresson, Cavalier and Pialat have meant a lot to me. It was more to do with the fact that what I felt when I went to the movies was something shared between me and others, and that meant I was less alone. I felt that the magic of the movies lay in the fact that they make you feel less lonely.

Is that something inherent in the nature of the cinema?

I think so. This may come as a surprise, but I don't really feel that cinema is totally an art, unlike literature, painting or sculpture. Very few films are really works of art. I feel that the word 'artist' is somewhat debased these days. It doesn't mean much. TV presenters call themselves artists. You can be involved in something which has an artistic aspect, but the word 'art' should be reserved for something strong, ambitious, profound. When I make a film, I am deeply involved in each successive stage.

Which is your favourite stage?
That's hard to say. Each stage is utterly different. Each film has its own life. Sometimes, writing a screenplay can be intensely pleasurable, then what comes after is painful. Sometimes, it's the opposite.

How do you write?
It's a lonely process. On both *La Petite Amie d'Antonio* and *A la campagne*, I did the writing entirely by myself. The idea for *Marion* came out of a discussion I had with my wife, and we did collaborate a little, but very soon I found I had to make it all my own. It's a gut reaction. I am always deeply involved in the subject-matter, and I need to be in charge of the structural foundations of a screenplay. I don't know if that sounds like I'm hungry for power or self-centred, but I can't really envisage working with anyone else on a script.

Your style is often described in negative terms, the fact that you avoid dramatic tension, for instance.
That is no coincidence. I believe that my ability to say no comes from a kind of respect for the characters I have created, I want to see them free. I don't want a possessive relationship with my characters, I'm there to protect them, to give them all the space they need, both in terms of the writing and the way I shoot. By the time we get to the shoot, we're talking about real human beings. They embody characters, but they are autonomous, they control their own lives and belong as much to the audience as to me. I don't like things that are categorical. I'd rather leave a question hanging, suggest certain impressions.

Are you sensitive to criticism?
I know this sounds self-centred, but I ignore what people say about my screenplays. When someone makes a remark they may be right in the context of the moment, but not always in the context of the film as a whole. I may have doubts, but at least they are mine, I don't know how to use other people's doubts. It's like someone dropping by when you're in the middle of painting a picture and saying are you sure that's the right colour? When that person goes you're the one that stays behind with the doubts, and you don't know what to do about it.

Your films catapult us into your characters' lives. Is the lack of exposition important?
Yes. I have to go straight to the heart of the matter. I like to embark on a story as the characters do. I don't believe that there is such a thing as a beginning or an end, not in my stories. It's too easy, you don't just press 'start' and then shut the door at the end. I'd like to think that the characters live on without me.

Do your actors often find themselves in unexpected situations?
Indeed. I do as much as I can to provoke the unexpected during a shoot. I try and make sure the actors don't have too many reference points, which make things too safe, too predictable. I change their lines, bring in new characters. On *Western* I rewrote the screenplay as we were shooting. I cut some scenes, added and changed others. This method gives the actors more freedom, they produce something which genuinely belongs to them. I do all I can to produce impressions and emotions that correspond to my chosen path, never forgetting the underlying direction. I do try and provoke myself, though, such as by deliberately wasting time so that I then have to work fast. In this manner, I go straight to the point.

One of the characteristics of your work is the duration of some of the scenes. We never know at the beginning quite where they will lead. How much goes unplanned?
I leave some scenes in the script without dialogue, as though they were not really important. Those tend to be the scenes I care about most. The dialogue happens on set; I give the actors a general outline and let them improvise, within the boundaries of their character, the situation, the set. I feel very close to the actors and often go off and have a drink with them and talk about something quite unrelated to work before we go and shoot. I love shooting meals because they naturally suit working like this. For one of the scenes in Marion – when Marion's parents have a meal with the Parisians – I kept the actors waiting so they had a drink or two and developed their relationship. Then as they got tired and tense, I started shooting without telling them. In the other meal scene, I used the same destabilizing technique. Just as they had got their concentration up, I said, 'Cut!' It was getting dark. They were even more tired, they had had even more to drink and I didn't start shooting till a bit later. In this way, actors can express their talent, their own personality and what I want to obtain from them.

The scene with Marion's parents gives a great impression of freedom and blissful spontaneity, though the style of direction is actually impressively controlled in the way it focuses on the characters' misleading friendliness. How do you achieve this balance?
As far as I am concerned – and I am talking only about my own work – the director should be invisible, as should the editor. By choosing to place the camera behind the mother's chair and ensuring that she never turns round, I was making her a witness, slightly apart from the others, as she faces her husband who is stuck between the two Parisians. In this way her reaction is delayed. You can't tell what she is thinking until later, in the car. My feeling is that the style of directing is implicit in the screenplay, in the choice of subject-matter, in the characters' relationships and their development. It is also implicit in the casting and the schedule – in other words the order in which the scenes are shot. Either the film is to be

shot chronologically, or I need to have several strong scenes coming together, so that the intensity of one affects the next. The crew's attitude, the climate it induces, affects the style of the film too. All these things taken together mean that the style is determined before I start directing the actors, who find themselves conditioned without really knowing how.

A la campagne was shown at the Avoriaz Film Festival in a longer version and then cut to its present length. How do you decide on a final version?
In the cutting-room I try to determine what I was originally after and also what happened during the shoot. When these intentions and impressions fail to materialize, I want to know why. There is then another phase during which, without wanting to sound too artsy-fartsy, I need to listen to the film. When you create a character, you need to let that character develop of its own accord and listen to that process. When I see the film, when I see its pace, its plot, its atmosphere, I remember what it was I was trying to do and I find that some things need cutting. The difficult part is cutting favourite scenes that you don't want to lose. But the film says they are superfluous, they are not part of the whole, they unbalance it. The directing style is determined during the editing as well. Choosing to cut into an actor's work just as he is about to complete a gesture is a significant decision. Editing is about pace. I love to digress, but one digression can hamper the potential of other digressions and undermine the overall feel of the film. The same is true of music. Lots of different types of music heard in succession can harm each other and lessen the overall impact. Film-making is about choosing one's priorities. Not everything can stand at the same level. You can't give equal importance to actors, technical perfection, real time and plot . . . Editing is about finding the right priorities.

Your narrative technique relies not just on digression but jumps in time as well, as when the Parisian woman appears in _Marion_ for the second time, one week after her epileptic fit.
I love jumps in time and digressions. There are different ways of putting a story together in the cutting-room: one can follow a train of thought, one can create technical cuts that change or preserve unity, one can change the angle in such a way as to lead the audience inside one of the characters' minds in order to follow its progress. I love it when a jump in time takes place within a shot. The connection has been made and the audience cottons on to it after the fact. It is like when you see someone you do not immediately recognize and you only recognize them after a ten-second pause. That moment seems to me to be a moment of freedom. Sometimes, a straight line between two points is not the best way. Sometimes a detour gives us a better view of where we are going. Digressions enable one to wrong-foot the audience and prevent it from jumping to conclusions. My choice of the road movie format has a lot to do with this. It makes for deliberate, ubiquitous freedom, which, as far as I am concerned, has to be present right from the

Western: Elisabeth Vitali and Serge Lopez

start, when I write, and governs narrative, governs my rapport with a character and lies at the root of my method.

Would *Western* have been an utterly different film if it had been made in Normandy rather than Brittany?

Yes. Because I cannot catapult two characters on to the road and stay in the region where I live. It would have made no sense, not to my way of thinking. It would have been like saying, 'Off you go, on the road, and I'm staying here, at home.' I had to catapult myself with them, go elsewhere. I wanted to start with a port, a place open to the world, conduct the narrative through the hinterland, and return to the coast at the end. I liked Guilvinec a lot. I thought it was very beautiful, very real, like all the Finistère country around. So the location was decided right at the start. I could shoot my films anywhere in France – except Paris and the big cities.

Why do you so often oppose Paris and the countryside?

The countryside only exists in opposition to Paris and other big cities, even in demographic terms: namely, the number of people per square metre. How can one have any kind of meaningful relationship with someone in a crowd? Any intimacy, whether town or country, involves cutting oneself off from others. I don't mean this as an absolute truth. I am speaking for myself. Being in the country seems to amplify things, good things and bad things, happiness and unhappiness. Everything is enormous. Intimacy is more powerful by the sea. And this applies to friendships and to grudges one never forgets. In the city, you can look elsewhere, change your friends. Feeling low in the country is ten times more oppressive than in the town, but then the moments of elation are much stronger too. Social divisions are much more apparent in Paris than in the countryside. Cities remind one constantly of money and social status. I left Paris because I didn't want to live like that, not because I particularly wanted to live in the countryside. I felt bad. I found it hard to get on with people. I found the 'What are you up to?', the 'Who are you?' questions too complicated. Plus the cars, the aggression, the permanent stress which stops you thinking and remembering who you are. It seemed preferable to face the hardship of being alone with oneself. Sometimes that is the only way to get on with others. I feel closer to my characters because they don't belong to the Parisian whirl.

This distinguishes your work from many other contemporary film-makers, who are often accused of being too 'Parisian'.
True. French films tend to focus on the capital. Often when people say France they mean Paris and vice versa. Yet France is a collection of people and places. Perhaps one makes the most of a Parisian character by placing him out of context, in the countryside.

Do you feel that your work is political?
Definitely. All my films are political in their own way. I've been asked if the title sequence in *Western* is a political act. I come from Peru myself. I cast two foreigners as my main characters, and the characters they meet come from all sorts of different places. This diversity was reflected in the crew. Mixing colours, flags, was initially a poetic idea, not a political one, but now that we have the government's campaign against illegal immigrants it does remind audiences what France is made of.

It feels as if Nono, one of the characters in *Marion*, inspired the two main characters in *Western*. Indeed, some of the actors in the earlier film reappear in *Western*.
I am very fond of my characters and I try not to cheat them, as I have said, particularly regarding the extent to which they can enter a group or not. Every film is a new departure, yet the same characters and actors can recur. I first met Serge Lopez when I was casting *La Petite Amie d'Antonio*, in an acting class for foreign students. I didn't know who he was, but we got on well. I trusted my instincts. The shoot went well and we became friends. My films may give the impression that they are made with friends, but Serge is someone I cast as an actor before he became a pal. I wanted to go on working with him and so I said, 'I'd like you to be in all my films, since you were in the first.' Even if there is no part that is right, I give him a walk-on. Up till now, I've managed it – without writing for him in a formal sense. *Western* is a road movie that takes place over about ten kilometres with two characters, one tall, one short, both foreign, with heavy foreign accents.

In that case I knew Serge would play the part, but I tried to think about it as little as possible. Casting too soon places constraints on the writing. You end up writing for someone. You exclude situations which might not suit, even though in doing so you may damage the part. If I don't write for Serge, he may come up with something neither he nor I could have predicted. Surprises are nice.

20

Jacques Audiard on *Un Héros très discret*

interviewed by Noël Herpe

Jacques Audiard

Jacques Audiard is the son of a well-known screenwriter of the 1960s, Michel Audiard, who was responsible for the dialogue of Claude Miller's *Garde à vue*. Jacques Audiard is the author of two well-received feature films entitled *Regarde les hommes tomber* and *Un Héros très discret*, both starring Mathieu Kassowitz, who directed *La Haine*.

Un Héros très discret is another picture which deals with the moral ambiguities of French wartime behaviour. What most characterizes the film, however, is a professionalism quite unlike the naturalistic, post-Nouvelle Vague tone adopted by many young film-makers of Audiard's generation. The fact that his prime concerns are moral, rather than emotional, and that his style is deliberately sophisticated, has attracted audiences hungry for a return to a more elaborate storytelling.

Un Héros très discret
It is the 1930s, and a fatherless child called Albert Dehousse lives in an elaborate fantasy world. Later, unfit for service in the war, he instead marries and becomes a travelling salesman. Dehousse ends up in Paris, reinvents himself as a Resistance hero, and becomes a Lieutenant Colonel with responsibility for weeding out traitors. Though he enjoys a charmed life, his conscience is increasingly racked in his new role; but he learns that people would rather take him for what he is not than for what he is.

What prompted you to do an adaptation of Jean-François Deniau's novel?

Firstly, the period in which it's set interests me: I was born in 1952, so I was the direct product of all that trickery. I had read Modiano's *La Place de l'Etoile* in 1968, and even though I didn't completely understand it at the time, I was fascinated by Modiano's writing: the way in which he reconstituted the events, or – more to the point – didn't, and changed them. It's an iconoclastic approach to history, as if he were saying: 'Why not lie, because it's all a lie anyway?'

Then, later, I saw Deniau being interviewed on television about his book. He talked about impostors, and I found the theme fascinating. Individual imposture, and, taking it a step further, collective imposture, seemed to be a great potential subject for a film. I don't think that you can just become an impostor without some kind of learning process. And this intrigued me.

This story could have happened at a different moment in history.

No, I think that everyone between the ages of thirty-five and forty-five was a product of this lie which persists, despite all proof to the contrary. I focus on the generation which is owed an explanation. There aren't many films on that period.

Is your adaptation of the novel fairly faithful to the original?

Quite a few of the secondary characters – the captain, Yvette and her family – are taken from the book, but the subject-matter is treated differently. The story is not linear, it jumps backwards and forwards. I loved some aspects of the novel, but I didn't know how to deal with them: for example, Deniau gives factual information, and as I wanted to deal with truth and lies, I brought in the interviews as a contrast.

Were there lots of different versions of the screenplay?

Five or six. The first version was written just before I started preparation on *Regarde les hommes tomber*. We originally wrote it with Le Henry in mind as director. I had no intention of directing. But then the producer, whom we had sold it to, asked me to do it, so we had to rewrite in various different stages. The big changes all happened at this point.

What kind of changes?

We had written things that weren't integrated into the different versions. Elements that were present, but very peripheral, that could be brought in more, like, for example, Trintignant's appearances during the film. They were written in, and then – I can't remember why – we took them out. During filming, I wanted them in again, because I felt that they were helpful in giving the character certain important ideas and feelings. Sometimes you worry, at the writing stage, about how many different things you can bring into the story, and then, during filming, everything becomes more fluid, and you feel liberated, as if all the boundaries are down, and everything can be encompassed in the film. Then you have to be confident enough to convince the others involved. I think that you reach a point where the only real blockage is your own ability to stretch your imagination, and create the fiction.

As a director, I want to move beyond the script, it's too rigid; the words and sentences follow each other relentlessly, so I want to break them up. It was nice that I had things in reserve that I could slip in during filming.

Is this when Alain Le Henry came in?
Yes, and he participated all the way through. I asked him to be involved in the casting, on the set, when we were projecting the rushes; I wanted his opinion. We understood and could anticipate each other's thoughts, but also take each other by surprise. I needed Alain to remind me of what we had originally had in mind when we had such and such an idea, so that I didn't lose track during filming. During the shoot, it's easy to forget the screenplay.

You've often done book adaptations. Is this a necessary starting-point for you?
Not necessarily, but I enjoy immersing myself in someone else's imaginary world. It's fun, as is editing. It's like a game, shifting the pieces around, thinking about how long it should last.

Why do you fight against the screenplay?
Because it's boring! You have to fight to achieve real 'cinema', not just a sort of speaking postcard taken from the screenplay. The conflict between them is what makes the film work. When I arrive on set, I'm not thinking about the script, I'm thinking about a film, a film that I try to give form to by discussing the break-down with the cameraman. At this moment, I'm always frightened that, in doing this, the magical quality, the 'cinema', will disappear.

How did you prepare the film?
With this 'idea' of a film that I've just mentioned; there are lots of questions to be answered, some of them difficult: 'How am I going to enact the scenes? What will I do with the actors? Am I going to film the sets from two or three different angles? What light will I use?' Then I draw on my references: Truffaut, Guitry, *Le Chagrin et la pitié* . . .

Zelig . . .?
Very useful as an example of what not to do! Not in a pejorative sense, obviously – it's just that Woody Allen doesn't want the spectator to empathize with the character, whereas this is exactly what I wanted in *Un héros très discret*. I didn't see the point of fitting the character in with archive material, because we realized that, apart from a few news items necessary to place the film in a historical context – reminding younger viewers of the existence in 1943 of the 'Service du travail obligatoire' – we should avoid references, otherwise we would be caged in by them. We wanted to be totally creative, as I liked the idea of everything being false.

Mathieu Kassowitz in *Un Héros très discret*

What general decisions did you make about how to direct this film?
We decided to use colour, but to do the lighting as if we were using black-and-white, to get the contrast – the opposite of *Regarde les hommes tomber*, in which the film was flooded with indirect light, grey and shadowless. Here the lighting is clear and distinct. When you can see where a light is coming from, or in what direction it's going, this presupposes that there is something going on behind what you can see. In *Regarde . . .* , you hardly ever got the impression that something was coming from outside. At the same time, the character in *Un Héros très discret* is in a closed world, and I wanted Dehousse's universe reduced to almost nothing, an impression we tried to create through the set designs and the camera movements – surrounding the characters with tracking – and the focal distance.

Why did you use musical punctuation, with shots of the musicians?
I liked the idea of making a sort of mini-opera out of this story, in the same way that *Mahagonny* or *Nixon in China* by Sellars and Adams can be considered as mini-operas. An opera about day-to-day life. Originally, I wanted an African orchestra, with a *griot*,* who would sing a collection of epic poems centred on Albert Dehousse, a bit like in *Antonio das Mortes*. Then, I moved to a chamber orchestra. It was an intuitive decision; I just felt that, as a spectator, I would like to see history recounted to this gentle and pure music, coming and going in waves.

There is a contrast between the words of the witnesses, noisy, and argumentative, and Trintignant's voice, which is clear, and brings us out of confusion.
That's true. Trintignant is the voice from inside. In order not to be completely

---

* A *griot* is the word used in French-speaking West Africa to describe a certain kind of magician. Griots, as opposed to witch doctors (in French, *marabouts*), recite epic poems.

detached from the character, I needed a voice from inside, but not Mathieu Kassowitz's. There had to be a certain distance, an age difference, and I had to show that, despite the time that had gone by, Dehousse's wounds were still hurting, as if still open. I didn't want a character who would be reasonable, I wanted someone who would talk about it as if it was still alive, so that there would be at the same time both a distance – which we see on Trintignant's face – and an intimacy which enables him to express the emotions of a young man.

There is also an all-knowing narrator, for whom you use your own voice.
This gives an illusion of objectivity. I wanted the theme of the lie to be ever-present.

The film's point of view is ambiguous: on the one hand, we are inside the mind of Dehousse, who is rebuilding his life in an ideal world, and, on the other hand, we find ourselves denouncing historical propaganda. Where do you stand on this?
Both sides. Dehousse isn't a demiurge impostor endowed with superhuman powers, he's too shy. We see him in a job, learning about things and people. He's deliberately not a big-time fraud, to show, by comparison, the enormity of the global dishonesty that exists. This was an interesting aspect of the novel – the era wants and is sympathetic to the lies.

Aren't you worried that people will accuse you of taking a 'relative' approach to history, which somehow puts everything on the same plane?
Everything isn't on the same plane! If I was dealing with Brossolette's destiny, I wouldn't have filmed the same way.* I don't doubt for one moment that someone crossed the Channel to announce that the war was continuing, but I focused on a different moment, the moment when everything had calmed down, and the goodies were going to be shared out. So the only people involved are those who want the goodies, those who feel guilty, who've been dealing in the black market, or small-time fraudsters like Dehousse, who jump on the bandwagon

Aren't you attributing him with too much intelligence?
On the contrary, the captain shows him everything. In my opinion, the captain is a real hero. He is cynical and amoral, a little heavy-handed; but he really did something. If he hadn't shown Dehousse the train, Dehousse would never have noticed it. At that stage, he had no experience, knew nothing about anything. As soon as he's shown it, he sees. He's an empiricist.

Does he feel guilty when he leaves his mother's house?
He feels bad about his mother, but he's fairly pathetic about it. He doesn't do anything, just leaves it up to his wife to sort out. Beforehand, Dehousse has no conscience. The events teach him everything. This is the subject of the film. If you pay attention to the events around you, you can learn certain things from them that will

* Pierre Brossolette was one of the best-known French Resistance heroes of the Second World War.

help you move up the social ladder. Dehousse's morality stops and starts here.

He's another in the string of literary characters who dream their lives away: Madame Bovary, Lord Jim . . .
His relationship with books is a deliberate cliché, but what follows is the realization that without the war, and the Nazis, Dehousse would have remained in the countryside, a good-for-nothing rather than a hero. That's a dreadful thought.

Over and above the individual, the way you deal with the whole subject, using, for example, the fake interviews, goes beyond a study of that era, and brings into question the media as a whole.
I'm interested in this, because it's scandalous. We live in a country of blind people, of shortsighted people, and journalists don't do their job properly! I am amazed that Le Pen's book is a success. It's title is admirably objective: *Une jeunesse française*; but the contents show complete ignorance of the ways ideas have changed in France since the Dreyfus affair! To be surprised that a man can go from being a xenophobic right-wing extremist to being left-wing is a sign of ignorance. That's the painful contradiction of our country, which has led to ridiculous oversimplification in our judgements and justifications. I am of a generation for whom everything seemed very simple, until we had to make sense of the fact that France was defeated in 1940, and was then a conqueror in 1945. The gulf is too wide to cross.

Kassowitz with Jean-Louis Trintignant in *Regarde les hommes tomber*

Mathieu Kassowitz seems an obvious choice for the role.
Actually, not immediately. On the set of *Regarde . . .* , Mathieu kept telling me that he wasn't an actor, that he didn't want to be an actor, and I was busy saying that I didn't want to be a director, and finally we believed each other! So I looked

around for actors, before realizing that, almost subconsciously (I don't believe that anything that takes five or six months' work is subconscious), we were writing the part for Mathieu. So all was clear. Dehousse was a continuation of the character in *Regarde* . . . Both characters are naïve and youthful, but roguish at the same time.

How did you work together?
We got together in the preparatory stages of the film, but we didn't have an awful lot to work on. There are lots of scenes in which he's alone, ruminating, so we discussed everything for hours, and decided not to rehearse too much. Mathieu is always frightened that rehearsing will wear him down. On set, I probably spoke less to him than to any of the other actors, because we had clarified everything at the start.

The female characters are slightly in the background, despite the important roles they play, until they meet at the end of the film.
They are going to live together, which doesn't worry him because he likes them both a lot. Even if it seems slightly immoral, Dehousse uses these women in the same way that he uses everyone else, even if he gets hurt when they humiliate him; he just takes what he can, that's his character. I think that a girl like Servane realizes intuitively that he's not honest, but is sufficiently adventurous to appreciate his act. She credits him with fantastical qualities as a man and lover. It's as if she says to him: 'Continue! At least that's amusing. When you stop, you're boring . . .'

It's she who makes him finally confess.
But he does give himself up. At the end of the day, he realizes that, exposed, his imposture doesn't provoke anything very revolutionary. Face to face with his own dishonesty, his life doesn't change. I can imagine that a fraud would wish, at some point, to be caught out, but then, when he admits all to Servane, she tells him not to change. Society tells him the same thing. So the last step he has to take is a personal one, he has to grow up and face his feelings. This means getting people shot.

By giving the orders to shoot, he's contributing to the collective dishonesty.
Exactly. But the others see this as a heroic act. I can't imagine what goes on inside a soldier's head, but I suppose that anyone who shoots traitors gets Brownie points, and would be seen as someone who didn't have complete confidence in the Republican law courts. All this paints the picture of someone heroic, who makes decisions, even if he himself doesn't see it like this.

Confessing to the lies gets him nowhere.
In his case, there's nothing behind the lies, that's all he's got. The hardest thing for me was to find a way to make this character likeable, since he's ambiguous,

weak, opportunistic, and not very bright. I tried to create and portray a world in decline that inspired pain, the carrier of which was a character the spectator grew to like.

Dehousse is fascinated by the dictionary, by words in their simplest form, out of any context.

This brings him back to what he really is: a fairly talentless actor who just repeats words that he doesn't understand. Gradually, he learns to put them together on his own. When I film him saying, 'I only smoke English cigarettes, the taste is divine', the situation is totally theatrical – he appears and disappears through the half-open door of a dressing-room. The acquisition of knowledge has a comic element that I like a lot. It's an important moment in the film, like when a child is learning to talk, and uses a word . . . and then waits to see if he has used it right. In comic terms, I believe that if you watch someone trying to learn something, and that makes you smile, then you are on his side, and you can throw in a joke at his expense. The more detailed it becomes, the funnier it gets.

Are the liberties you take in the narrative a way of bringing into the cinema elements that are usually attributed to literature?

Possibly. I did want to have the same freedom in filming as I have in writing. The way you tell a story is so important, the waiting game, the joy when things are unravelled. But all these elements must have a reason for being there, otherwise things become stylized. A director like Resnais has both the generosity and the discipline to achieve this. I'm very impressed by both his control, and his ability to find new ideas. When you see a Resnais film, you never know what to expect. Each time, he has created a world from nothing, that is unique, if not completely different. His aim is to create emotion, he doesn't just assume that it is there.

In *Regarde* . . . there is a moral angle; there isn't one in *Un Héros très discret*.

That's because ambiguity is essential in *Un Héros* . . . I can't find a definitive moral take on Dehousse's dishonesty. Is he a bastard, as Sartre would see it? I don't know. The subject is ambiguous, as is the whole era. That's what the film is all about, the fact that people can tell one truth, and then another, about a particular moment in time. Nothing is absolute. I have a fundamentally moral outlook, but our morals are shaky as regards that particular era. Why? Because there was a lie. A story was invented that became History. It lasts, and continues to provoke emotions. I was moved by Mitterand's departure from the Elysée, because I felt that something was drawing to a close, the last witnesses were leaving, the last to be able to say: 'That's true; that's false.' They didn't say it, they lied . . .

Interviewed in Paris, 30 March 1996

interviewed by Thomas Bourguignon and Yann Tobin

Mathieu Kassowitz

Mathieu Kassowitz has directed three feature films, _Métisse_, _La Haine_ (1996, César for Best Film) and _Assassins_. He is also an actor and screenwriter.

The peculiar thing about Kassowitz's _La Haine_ was that it was seen by many, both in France and abroad, as one of the first films to tackle the brutal reality of the Paris suburbs, with their endemic violence, their urban decay, their cops and their robbers. And it is true that the film marked a break with the somewhat prettified image of Paris that French cinema has exported around the world. The director's spectacular camera style – a style more often seen in commercials – helped. It was intended as an inducement to young film-goers who, in the 1980s, seemed to be abandoning French films for more raucously violent American pictures. It could be argued, however, that in script terms, there is nothing realistic about _La Haine_, rather the story is a contemporary fairy-tale revolving around three unlikely buddies – of symbolic ethnic origins: one Arab, one black and one Jewish – who get caught up in a drugs saga.

La Haine
A Parisian housing estate (or 'banlieue') is rocked by rioting after teenage resident Abdel is seriously injured in police custody. Three friends – Saïd (an Arab), Vinz (a Jew) and Hubert (an African) – are caught up in the repercussions. Vinz discovers a pistol lost by a policeman in the riot, and tells his friends he'll avenge Abdel's death if necessary. They head for Paris

to meet a drug-dealer, Asterix, who owes them money. But there, loose cannon Vinz leads them into trouble with police, marauding skinheads, even traffic wardens. Inevitably, the presence of the gun serves to worsen rather than to alleviate their plight.

How did you come to make films?
My parents were in film. If they'd been bakers, I would've become a baker, but they were film-makers, so I became a film-maker. When we went to the movies, there was a different way of watching a film. Camera movement mattered, nothing was there by chance, everything had been thought out. That taught me to try and see things differently when I went to see a film.

Did you shoot an enormous amount when you were making *La Haine*?
Not an enormous amount, no more than four takes. We had maybe ten usable hours of rushes. We edited digitally: during the shoot, all the rushes were digitalized into the computer. The shoot ended on a Friday and on the Monday I was in the cutting-room. Ten days later, we had our first assembly, which was in essence the film as it is now. We never had a 140-minute cut that needed reducing to ninety minutes. The rough cut was 110 minutes. We cut out two scenes and tightened the whole thing up. All the housing-estate scenes were in a single section and that worked well, but once the story moves to Paris structural problems arise. Should the interrogation scene come before or after Vinz? There is no real continuity, so we could do anything we liked. But I don't really like to discover this during the edit because there are always stylistic considerations that govern the passage from one scene to the next. For instance, when they arrive at the police station, on the estate, Vinz is in the back seat. He turns and that cuts in with him turning round inside the police station. Those kinds of things are fun to identify, but if you don't know the order in which you are going to cut those scenes together, you can't use them.

When writing, is it character or action which is paramount?
My first film, *Fierrot le Pou*, was short, we had very little money. The next was adapted from a comic strip called *Cauchemar blanc*, it was less personal. With my first feature film, the title came first (*Metisse*), and then an atmosphere. The atmosphere is what I am interested in describing, even before I know the story. This is the 'message'. Atmosphere and title are what come first. With *Métisse* and with *La Haine*, I knew the ending before I knew the storyline. Everything is about the end, the last five seconds.

The two endings are similar.
Yes. In *Métisse*, you don't see the baby, you don't know who the father is. In *La Haine*, you don't see the shot, you don't know who kills who.

Mathieu Kassowitz on the set of *Métisse*

Your feature films are like a countdown.

Endings matter because they throw a whole new light on the rest of the story. Stories gradually unfold, but the last few images reveal another aspect. For instance, in Scorsese's *Mean Streets*, which is my favourite film, the redemption comes at the end. It is a constant subject of discussion, but it only becomes visible at the last minute. *Brazil* has a very good ending, which influenced me a great deal. William Friedkin's *To Live and Die in LA* also. The last ten minutes are unbelievable. It's the first time I've seen a film in which you follow one character for one and a half hours then forget him, just like that! He's a cop who's after someone and suddenly he's shot. When he dies, his number two takes over and makes the arrest in ten minutes. The end. It's very peculiar. I've always enjoyed that. I'm currently writing my third film, I've got a title, I've got the atmosphere, I've got the ending, I have the first twenty minutes. It's hard to describe, I don't know where I am going to take things from here.

You had the ending, you had the set-up, but where did you find your characters?

When Makome was killed in a police station in the 18th arrondissement, I went to the demonstrations that ended up as riots. I thought, this is unbelievable, a man wakes one morning and that night he gets killed. That was my story. So I thought, how do I develop this further? Do I follow him? Are there two of them? Or three?

La Haine: Vinz (Vincent Kassel) and Hubert (Hubert Kounde)

La Haine: 'I wanted Paris to seem violent.'

whole gang? Then I thought of my friends. I met Hubert Koundé when I was shooting *Métisse*, I knew he had the potential to do something diffferent. I've known Vincent Kassel a very long time. There was something about him I'd noticed in private which he had never used professionally. And Saïd was a mate of Vincent's who I met about the time I was planning *La Haine*.

He's a kind of in-between character. There's one very striking thing about *La Haine* and that is the importance attached to the question of through whose eyes one is seeing a scene and how they see it.
I was trying something which didn't really come off. I wanted the film to be seen through the eyes of the character least involved in the action. I wanted Hubert to be our eyes. Very often the audience follows the action through the way in which he sees things. When he is having a joint, for example, the audience sees things differently. You couldn't make a film called *La Haine* with three characters and then have Vinz as the protagonist, that would not have been possible, it would shut off too many avenues. We needed an outside eye and the furthest removed character was Hubert.

And yet you maintain your own point of view, and you include characters who are apart from these three.
Yes. Vincent Lindon, the little old guy in the toilets, Asterix, Darty . . .

Not to mention the third cop, the one who watches.
Yes, that is fantastically important. There's no point telling the audience, 'Look at this', and then showing some bit of violence. What matters is to show what some-one else is seeing and through his point of view discover what is going on in his head. That policeman watches his colleagues torturing Hubert and Saïd, and maybe he's ashamed to be a policeman. He is our counterpoint. If he hadn't been there, it would just have said, 'Policemen are bastards.' But the young policeman is going to end up like the others because they are trained to do so. He knows this and feels ashamed of it. But there's nothing he can do.

This business about point of view recurs in the scene with the little old man. And in this case, we are actually looking in a mirror!
Yes, the whole scene is about mirrors. It's a good shot, it's well-executed, but only because the design of the room allows it, it's not something we did on purpose. There are a lot of mirror scenes – for instance the homage to *Taxi Driver*, when Saïd looks at the camera, though in fact he's looking in the mirror . . . Mirrors are essential to film-making.

Somehow it looks as though you've added a kind of madness to your Paris scenes, to show that people in the suburbs have adapted to one kind of violence whereas in Paris there are other rules at stake.
We spent two months on that estate, one month in pre-production and one month

for the shoot. I'd come home to Paris every other weekend and I couldn't believe it! Paris is like another world, with all those lights, everything seems to move, there are cars! I wanted Paris to seem violent. Originally, we were going to have black-and-white on the estate, so that everything looked the same, and then colour in Paris, or shoot the estate in 35mm and Paris in 16mm. But that was too dogmatic. So we ended up with day and night. On the estate we had the full works, tracking shots and everything, whereas in Paris we had a small crew. I wanted nothing but a tripod and handheld shots. There are no tracking shots in Paris except for the stunt, when Vinz takes a shot at a cop, but that's a dream sequence. We also heightened the sound contrast. The estate is done in stereo, with broad sound, whereas Paris is all in mono. Unfortunately, that doesn't really come across. The sound in Paris ought to have been less clean.

The first Paris shot makes it seem like they are literally entering another dimension.

Yes, it's a travelling shot and a zoom. The idea – though it's hard to bring off – was that on the estate we should use short lenses, to fix people against the back-ground, and then much longer lenses in Paris, to detach them and really have them stand out. But this is very difficult to pull off, you need to be very strict. It's like stereo slipping into mono, it works unconsciously but the effect is not really perceptible.

On the estate, there is one camera movement which is extraordinary, when they are listening to the music.

That's something the Belgians do with a small, remote-controlled helicopter, but it's not what I wanted. The idea was to go above people's heads, have everyone look up to see where the music was coming from; go above the riot police, between the tower blocks, not above them; then come on to the square where Vinz and Saïd are looking up at the sky, cut and find them in the next shot look-ing down again. That was the idea, but we cut earlier because the pilot did not make it all the way through.

Did you always want it to be partly in the suburbs and partly in Paris?

Yes. I didn't want to make a film just about a housing-estate. I don't come from that world, so there's no way I can make a film exclusively set there. Anyway, it seems reasonable to show that there are problems in Paris too. In the suburbs, rela-tionships between policemen and young people are incredible, they know each other by name and the kids insult them personally. Paris is different, less personal.

When did you decide to structure the film as a series of one-hour chapters?

Later. During the shoot and then mainly during the edit. To emphasize that this is diary. Like in *24 Hours* on Canal Plus. It's always nice to know exactly when something takes place. And it enables the audience to understand that they are not following a linear plot, they are being presented with an event at a specific

188

Mathieu Kassowitz in *Assassins*

time: the hours go by and then something is going to happen at one precise moment. That's why the audience don't mind there being no plot, it's like a diary or a news report.

You play only a small part in this film, whereas in *Métisse* and in two of your shorts, you have a big part.
It's a matter of chance. With *Fierrot le Pou* it was just the easy way out and it was fun to do. I wasn't in my next film because I've never wanted to act, so I cast the film normally. I made *Assassins* as I was in pre-production on *Métisse*. Christophe Rossignon, the producer, and I decided it would be fun to see if I could act and direct at the same time. It was quite a challenge!

Why did you cast yourself in a small part as a skinhead?
Take an actor, he really wants to act and you say, 'Look, there's nothing to it, you just get smashed in the face, you're seen from behind, your face is hidden, and you scream because someone is going to shoot at you.' It's not very gratifying. And I was happy to do something unexpected.

Could you have played Vinz?
Everyone says that. I acted in *Métisse* and in Audiard's film – but no, I don't think so. The film was quite difficult enough to direct. I'm not superman. I don't know how I could have managed. I would have had to ask someone to come in and direct the actors.

Introducing each character by having his name come up in letters, like in a strip cartoon, is a nice idea.

Scorsese did it with *Taxi Driver*. Tarantino copied him. I found it annoying in *Reservoir Dogs* that he should copy Scorsese. So I tried to do something different, it's a little joke. It's also a way of showing that the protagonists are those three and no one else. In fact, it reminds us this is a movie and not some news report. It's both fortunate and unfortunate that cinema needs to embellish reality, we need a bit of romance. Even when we're trying to be as realistic as possible, we caricature things a little bit to keep the interest up. And we have to have a story, even if it's not really plausible. Initially, the idea with *La Haine* was that nothing should happen. But if we had stuck to that, everyone would have got bored. Supposedly, in Jarmusch's movies nothing happens, but you still get people escaping (*Down by Law*)! That's why we do so much work on characters, what they look like, their way of walking, their hairstyles . . . Everything has to seem real and yet be graphically interesting. Vinz is a little shit. Vincent didn't want his head shaved, he said, 'I'll look awful.' I said, 'So what?' I think he's learnt a lot since making the movie. He's less interested in his appearance, more interested in what is going on inside. But getting him to shave his head was a battle, he knows his ears stick out. He kept trying to find poetic streaks in his character. I told him to forget it, and that if he believed in himself, the character would work. Kids are like that. There's nothing explicitly poetic about an estate. No one says, 'I want to see the sea, I want to hear the seagulls flying overhead.' They have no possessions and what they say is, 'I want some cash, I want to get a BMW.' It's quite poetic enough. There's nothing else to say.

You treated the estate as you treated the characters.

Yes. The aim was to make the estate seem beautiful, supple, fluid. I had the money I needed. It seemed too much at times, a bit of a come-on, like a pop promo when the director's ideas are bad. That's the danger – when you can afford to you're tempted to use every trick you can think of. That's the way I am. If I know I've got tracks in the truck, I can't just leave them there. During the chase scene, when you see 'Arash ta mère' on a door, we didn't have much time, we had to do a fixed shot. So as they were getting set up, I said to the grip, 'Get me some track, one yard, I don't need more.' And that movement is what's needed to finish the scene. Spielberg specializes in that kind of thing. But he makes it more obvious. Also, there are lots of different references in the film. *Scarface* by Hawks, with the poster which says, 'The world is yours.' I put that in because everyone on those estates knows De Palma's *Scarface*. As soon as you mention the movies, they say, 'Oh yeah, just like in *Scarface*.' Naturally, they don't know the original.

Did you rehearse the actors?

They had six months' warning I was writing for them. That's very exciting for an actor, if you know your mate is bound to get the money to make his film and he wants you in it. I used their first names and I asked them to work on the writing, so they would feel committed and could have their say. Then we did what we had to do, we went off for a week, we had some readings. We thought the shoot was going to be very tough, spending a month on a rough estate, living with those guys. We could easily have had stones chucked at us within two days and that would have been that. We go into their world, we step into their shoes and then we leave. It's an odd thing to do. You have to respect them. So we thought it was going to be tough, we thought we'd have fights, so we might as well have our fights before we start shooting so that all the problems could be solved in advance. But then we had more fights afterwards.

What about your relationship with your crew?

Brilliant. A powerful shoot. When I say that, I feel like I'm Schwarzenegger who always says crews all love each other. But in this case, we still hang out, we call each other up. Lots of people had worked on *Métisse* and even my shorts. You have to know how to handle an estate, it only takes someone on the crew to hit a child because he's sick of being insulted and that's the end of the shoot. We all knew that. We were very tense, but it was good tension. We knew we were making a film which was 'different'. We tried things out. As a director, I refused to play safe and get lots of cover. I took risks. That was exciting. The cast and crew did too. I had to talk them through everything. That's great. Occasionally, it went wrong. The skinhead fight is no good, I should have done more angles. And the character who slows things down is the one I play! In the cutting-room, I saw I should have added another angle.

How did you work with Pierre Aïm, your director of photography?

He's someone who needs plenty of time ahead of a shoot, he needs time to take things in. With *Métisse*, Pierre finally agreed to produce a quality of picture that was not slick, in 16mm. If you've gone for a particular style, you have to go all the way, like Kusturica, like Welles. We didn't have much money and we decided not to pretty things up. Which lost him some work. People saw *Métisse*, then wouldn't hire him. Usually, his work is amazing and very elaborate like in *Assassins*. With *La Haine*, I had to talk him through everything, I had to insist, for instance, that the Paris shots should be more grainy.

The camera operator is almost your alter ego.

Georges Diane. He's my neighbour. He's brilliant. I'm obsessive about framing, even though I'm really bad at it myself.

You know what you want.

I know what I don't want. I don't want a Russell Mulcahy thing. You can't have tracking shots for the sake of it. There is a kind of ethic. If you use a crane or a

Steadicam there has to be a reason. The director who knows that best today is Spielberg: he combines a sense of the audience's enjoyment, intelligence and thinking about style. Everything he shows you in a shot is there for a reason, nothing is left to chance. You can see that in *Schindler's List*, though he had lost his touch for a bit before that. To me, this business about cinematic ethics is more a question of how you frame a shot than how you light it; which is why I like the camera operator and director of photography to be different people; the job is not the same. Framing shots is a kind of choreography, it builds rhythm. To me, pace is of the essence. The same is true with acting, it's like interpreting music – even if you've got a metronome going all the time, if you're out of time, the audience can sense it. I didn't want a score. There isn't any film music in *Métisse* either. There's only the music which is played, radio and records and a musical scene. Sometimes, it's hard to stick to the no-music rule. The editor would try to lay on great layers, which always seemed to work. He tried the music from *Léon* at the end. It's incredible, you can't help crying. I don't like that. Getting rid of the music means you work harder at editing sound properly. We used city sounds which became a music of our own – a growl, a layer of sound but a *natural* layer. The sounds you hear on an estate like that come at you from all sides. The stereo effect is amazing, I wanted to get that feel during the sound-mix. I love it when sound works on several layers at once that are out of kilter with the picture. On my next film, I want a Nagra 4D to have live sound on four different tracks, and then mix it like music. So I can say, 'The one I want to hear is not the one in the foreground, it's the one whispering at the back.' That's how you get a point of view across.

On the estate, it seems like there's urban warfare going on, the police station is Fort Alamo.
That's nice! I was worried, after the real riots scene in the title sequence, about our paltry thirty riot police extras, who are meant to represent two hundred. But we wanted to keep strictly to what we had seen on that estate or others like it. When the cops pass through, the tension certainly mounts. Though that doesn't stop the kids from having a laugh or smoking a joint. The cops are right there and there's nothing they can do. That's what I wanted to show and that's why I didn't show the action before the riot. Vinz's death doesn't cause the riot, it's the riot which causes Vinz's death. Anyway, filming a real riot would have cost too much.

There is one extraordinary shot when the boy describes the TV programme. Was the dialogue written?
That's my favourite shot. It was entirely written and rehearsed, but the boy brought it to life. He was incredible. There he is on the estate with three stars and a two-page soliloquy to be done in a single take and the director shouting, 'Off you go!' Not to mention the fact that I'd told Saïd to chuck stones at him. And I'd

told the kid, 'When he appears, don't stop, use whatever happens.' He was superb. The second take is the one we used. Which gives one faith in the notion that if everything is as it should be, you just step up the camera and roll.

You've certainly got the jargon right.
Among my friends, we all talk like that!

Interviewed in Paris, 18 April 1995

EDUCATION

PROJECTING FRENCH CINEMA TO SCHOOLS
WITH FILM EDUCATION

Film has become increasingly popular on A level French syllabuses both as a discrete element of exam and coursework and as a possible choice of topic for oral and project work. The study of film also enhances the teaching and learning of French history and culture and exposes students to a range of authentic voices and registers as well as new vocabulary.

Film Education currently offers a number of film workshops for French A level teachers and students.

INSET: Using French Film in the Classroom

Using extracts from classic texts such as 'Jules et Jim' alongside Jacques Audiard's recent and critically acclaimed 'Un Héros Très Discret' and Luc Besson's ' Nikita', this teachers' day introduces a range of strategies for analysing and exploiting film in the classroom.

INSET: The Occupation

This teachers' workshop focuses on a selection of films which represent the Occupation in different ways. Texts examined include documentary such as 'Le Chagrin et la Pitié', contemporary newsreels and feature films such as 'Lucie Aubrac', 'Au Revoir Les Enfants', 'Pétain' and 'Section Spéciale'.

Student Workshop: An Introduction

The students' day is conducted in French, and comprises a full length screening preceded by a brief introduction to the film's context. This is then followed up by small group discussions on topics arising from the film.

If you are a teacher and would like further details on these and other workshops and resources available from Film Education, please write on school headed paper with your request to the following address:

Film Education (Projections)
Alhambra House
27-31 Charing Cross Road
London WC2H 0AU

or e-mail projections@film-ed.u-net.com

POSITIF

REVUE MENSUELLE DE CINÉMA

John Boorman
Shohei Imamura
Cédric Kahn

Dossier
Raoul
Walsh

jean *michel* place

'By a clear margin, this is Europe's best film magazine.'
Variety International Film Guide 1999, edited by Peter Cowie